add

200 A282

APR 15 2009
050809

The Red Carpet

10,000 MILES THROUGH RUSSIA

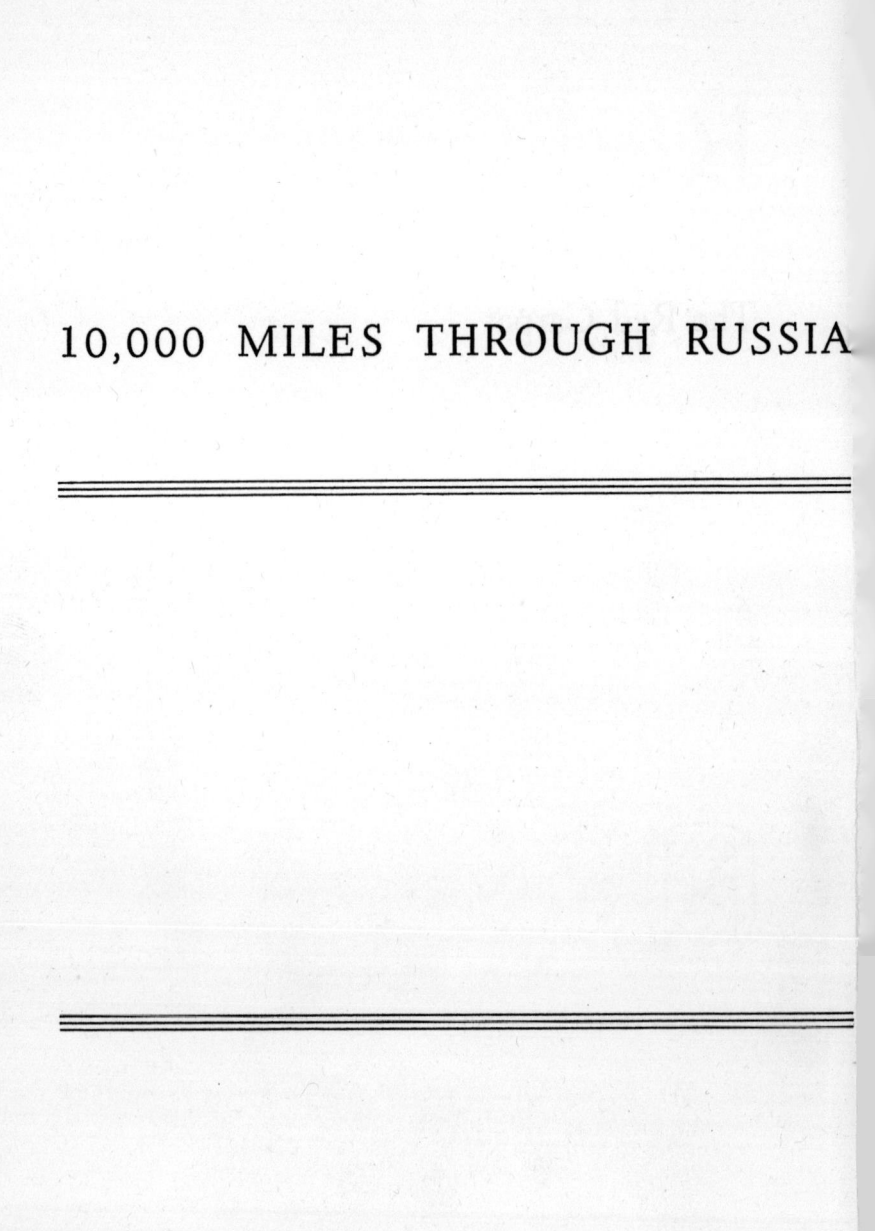

THE
Red Carpet

ON A VISA FROM KHRUSHCHEV

By MARSHALL MacDUFFIE

W · W · NORTON & COMPANY · INC · *New York*

COPYRIGHT 1955 BY MARSHALL MACDUFFIE

FIRST EDITION

PRINTED IN THE UNITED STATES OF AMERICA
FOR THE PUBLISHERS BY THE VAIL-BALLOU PRESS

TO MY WIFE

Contents

	Preface	xiii
1.	Return to Russia	3
2.	Journey into Moscow	12
3.	On the Intourist Chainbelt	22
4.	Russian Justice	38
5.	A Case of Socialized Medicine	53
6.	It Pays to Advertise	62
7.	The Road to Minsk	74
8.	Factory-Farming	85
9.	The Play's Not the Thing	94
10.	Minsk Automobile Plant	108
11.	Kiev Seven Years Later	117
12.	Reunion	135
13.	The Pittsburgh of the Ukraine	154
14.	The MVD and I	166
15.	Town and Country	179
16.	Interview with "Mister Communist"	197
17.	Ceremony in Red Square	215
18.	Over the Urals and Far Away	224

19.	Scratch a Tatar and You'll Find a Russian	235
20.	Home of the Uzbeks	248
21.	*Silver Dust* and Golden Samarkand	261
22.	Oil City	271
23.	Inside Russian Homes	288
24.	Mustaches and Toasts	298
25.	Homeward Bound	308
26.	"I Said I Wouldn't Generalize, but . . ."	313
	Index	321

Illustrations

(*Between pages 162 and 163*)

Nikita Sergeyevich Khrushchev
The author at the start of his tour
Moscow University
View from the author's rooms in National Hotel, Moscow
The heart of Moscow
Krimsky Bridge, Moscow
Yard of a Moscow Nursery
A class of eight-year-old girls
The third grade
Moscow Middle School
A typical street in Moscow
The broadest street in Moscow
Lubyanka Prison and MVD headquarters
Urban housing
Student's room at Moscow University
Moscow District Court
Moscow's only synagogue
Wine counter in a food store
Fashion show
Two MVD men
Train passengers cadge breakfast
Twenty-five-ton truck
Minsk's leading department store
Bolshoi Theater

A typical broad street in Minsk
New workers' flats in Minsk
Mr. Goodbye
Doorman and elevator operator
Hotel band in Kiev
Photo for which the author was arrested
Kharkov police station
Cops who arrested the author
Clothing factory in Kiev
Reunion dinner with Ukrainian officials
Postwar buildings on Kiev's most famed street
Minsk city hall
Women laborers
Zaporozhe market
Main road between Kharkov and Kiev
Market in Poltava
Co-operative knicknack booth
Tipsy-windowed house in Poltava
Parade toward Red Square
Penza airport terminal
Kazaks playing dominoes
Alma-Ata free market
Alma-Ata collective farm
Empty street in Alma-Ata
Two secretaries, Tashkent
Children at Tashkent Collective Farm School
Tashkent girl
Uzbek interpreter and friend
Tashkent toy store
Three gentlemen of Samarkand
Road to an ancient king's tomb, Samarkand
Tanktown, just north of Iran
Two Georgians
Arcade in a Baku department store
Baku court
Choreographer for the Baku ballet
Doctor from Tashkent
Azerbaijan educator, Gadjiev, with family
Typical oil worker's flat, Baku

Illustrations

Neighbor's family and apartment
Peasant in front of farm home near Kiev
Interior of the same home
Church in Zaporozhe
Hotel room in Tiflis
The inevitable chess game
Club house on a Georgian Farm
Typical home of a Georgian peasant
Interior of the same home
Stalin's birthplace
Grave of Stalin's mother
A street in Gori
Peasant hospitality
Main square in a Caucasus mountain village
Map of the author's journey

Preface

TWICE since the war I have had the opportunity to travel through large areas of the Soviet Union. In the first half of 1946 I was in Byelorussia and the Ukraine as chief of an UNRRA mission. I met government officials and various administrators in Kiev (where I resided), Minsk, Odessa, Kharkov, Zaporozhe, Dniepropetrovsk, Poltava, Kremenchug, Zhitomir, and Lvov, and I went to Moscow several times—seeing it under the snows of winter and in the heat of summer.

In the fall of 1953, for sixty-five days, from mid-October to late December, I journeyed some ten thousand miles through the U.S.S.R. In addition to visiting places I had seen before, such as Moscow, Minsk, Kiev, Zaporozhe, Kharkov, and Poltava, I also went deep into Central Asia to Aktyubinsk, Alma-Ata, Tashkent, and Samarkand, and I returned to Moscow by way of Baku, Tiflis, and Stalingrad. This trip took me through the eight republics which have over 90 per cent of the Soviet Union's population: the Russian Republic, the Ukraine, Byelorussia, Kazakstan, Uzbekistan, Turkmenistan, Azerbaijan, and Georgia.

In Russia I scribbled over nine hundred pages of notes, writing them either during conversations and explorations of factories and farms, or as soon as possible afterwards. Immediately upon my return to the United States, *Collier's,* for which I wrote several articles, arranged to have the elaboration of those notes typed (filling over 2,100 pages) and permitted me to turn over full sets to the Government and certain universities specializing in the study of Russia. From those notes I have written this shorter account so that I could share my experience with as many people as possible. I hope I have given an accurate and fair picture of what I saw and heard and did.

There were, inevitably, aspects of Soviet life that one in my position in such a period of time could not get at adequately: the extent of concentration camps and conditions within them; the inner mechanics of governmental control; the substance of their teaching and their literature; and the intimacies of Russian family life. I tried, however, to absorb the maximum available to a stranger, and here is the result.

There is a deliberate attempt in this book not to draw many conclusions. Too many "two-week experts" have contributed to confusion. As to my personal attitude—I like to quote Dmitri Manuilsky, Ukrainian Foreign Minister at the time he made the remark (1946) and former director of the world-wide Comintern (Communist International), who said, after a heated argument, "Mr. MacDuffie, with respect to the United States, you are a great idealist; with respect to the Soviet Union, you are a rough materialist."

Why did they let me in and give me so much freedom? My guess is that it was an experiment. The new regime was temporarily willing to see what a non-Communist, non–fellow-traveling American would do and say. To begin the experiment, they chose one with whom they had dealt at arm's length and who had seen the Soviet Union when it was still gasping from the devastation of the war. I was bound to see vast improvement.

I came out as before—impressed by Soviet ability and drive, troubled by Soviet methods and aims, abhorring Communism more than ever, and quite fond of the Russian people.

The Red Carpet

CHAPTER 1

Return to Russia

THE PHONE rang in my New York apartment late one night in September, 1953, and when I answered it, a mysterious foreign-sounding voice asked, "Mr. MacDuffie, do you want to go to the Soviet Union?" That terse, unexpected question set off a remarkable series of events. Six weeks later I was in Moscow. Four weeks after that, I had a four-hour personal interview with Nikita S. Khrushchev, then Russia's No. 2 man and holder of Stalin's old job as boss of the Soviet Union's Communist Party.

How did it all happen?

It began when I read the description of Stalin's funeral:

"Comrade N. S. Khrushchev, Chairman of the Funeral Arrangements Committee, invited Comrade Georgi Maximilianovich Malenkov to speak." Next Beria spoke, and then Molotov was the final orator at Stalin's bier.

The attention of the world was riveted on those three speakers. The power struggle was on. Who was the most important? Who would win? Who might lose his position and his life? Which of the three, Malenkov, Beria, or Molotov, carried the most weight? So ran the speculation in every land. But my eyes were on the fourth man at that ceremonial, Nikita Sergeyevich Khrushchev, because I knew him personally.

A few days later Malenkov, the new Premier, spoke to the Supreme Soviet upon the ratification of the new government. Pictures of that occasion in the Kremlin showed a number of Russian dignitaries on the platform behind the speaker. Set apart from the rest in a position of special honor were four men: Molotov, the Foreign Minister, Beria of the secret police, Bulganin, marshal of the Army—and Khrushchev.

At first Malenkov held two titles in the new administration, Chairman of the Council of Ministers and Secretary of the Central Committee of the Communist Party. Then he gave up the latter title. He was replaced as boss of the Communist Party of the Soviet Union by Khrushchev. The importance of the position is obvious, for it was Stalin's main source of power for many years. When Stalin relinquished it in his later years, the job went to Malenkov, and from there Malenkov stepped into the number one governmental spot.

I first met Khrushchev in 1946 in Kiev when he was Prime Minister of the Ukraine and I was chief of the United Nations Relief and Rehabilitation (UNRRA) Mission to the Ukraine. My staff and I met with him a number of times, both on official business and socially, and I was in almost daily communication with him through a former partisan colonel, Vassily V. Khomyak, the Ukrainian official appointed as chief of the local UNRRA.

The UNRRA Mission was in charge of bringing some $180,-000,000 of relief supplies to the war-devastated and drought-stricken Ukraine. There was no question that the Ukraine needed assistance at that time. About one hundred and twelve million dollars of the program was in food, for, aside from some bread, there was almost nothing available, the Germans having done a thorough job of destruction of crops and cattle and swine. Those of us who sought to help the Russians at the end of the war did so in good conscience. They had been allies in defeating the Hitler peril; they had suffered grievously; and they had made a formal request for aid from the organization which represented the first attempt at forming a

Return to Russia

United Nations operation. We held out the hand of charity and good faith. To have assumed automatically and immediately that our allies were no longer our friends, without first giving them a full opportunity to co-operate, would have been completely contrary to the American character and our Christian civilization. Any other course at that time would have left us always with the troubled thought that things might have been different if we had only tried to co-operate. There would have been a burden of guilt upon our consciences and a doubt in our minds and hearts which we do not now have. Now we know we tried to help them. It is not our fault the Russians went their separate way.

Our United Nations Mission, like Herbert Hoover's American Relief Mission many years before, had a unique opportunity to deal amicably with the Russians. We were there only to help them. And we stuck to our business. We were blunt and critical when we had justification, but we were always trying to make the relief program a success. Inevitably, if there were any personal feelings among the Russians, those of us on the mission—most of whom were Americans—should have had a small bank account of Russian good will.

I chose to draw upon it.

There were three reasons for my believing I might be able to get back into the Soviet Union. First, I guessed that with the death of Stalin there would be some minor changes in operations and policy, but not in strategic objectives. Free of the rigidity of "the old man," the new rulers might be disposed to experiment a bit. Second, I reasoned that they probably had made enough improvements to show their face once more to critical outsiders and that, since I had dealt honestly with them before, they might be willing to try the venture with me if I put the idea in their heads. Most important of all was my knowing Khrushchev, who had growing power.

I had heard of reporters who occasionally obtained interviews from Stalin—when it suited him, no doubt—by a direct cable. I found out that cables to Moscow were permissible, got a friend to translate my words into Russian, and then simply addressed the following night letter:

NIKITA S. KHRUSHCHEV, THE KREMLIN, MOSCOW: I WOULD LIKE OPPORTUNITY TO REVISIT THE UKRAINE AND BYELORUSSIA WHICH I VISITED AS CHIEF OF UNRRA MISSION IN 1946. AM INTERESTED IN OBSERVING CHANGES THAT HAVE TAKEN PLACE SINCE 1946 AND ALSO WOULD LIKE TO VISIT ELSEWHERE. REQUEST PERMISSION TO BRING MY OWN INTERPRETER.

I sent the cablegram in the late spring, hoping to spend the summer there. Weeks went by without a reply. Finally I forgot about it. By the time September arrived, it was completely out of my mind. In fact, I began to think I had been too impulsive and therefore refrained from telling friends about my shooting an arrow into the Moscow skies.

Then that night in September the phone rang in my New York apartment, and the voice with the foreign accent asked: "Mr. MacDuffie, do you want to go to the Soviet Union?"

"What? Oh—er, yes."

For a moment I did not know what the man was talking about; then I remembered my cable, and simultaneously realized that only a Russian could be putting this question. This was no prank. The man said his name was Petrov and asked for an appointment. I suggested ten o'clock the next morning at my apartment, wondering a little what the FBI would think of this, but determined now to go ahead with it.

Promptly at ten my doorbell rang. There stood two men who by appearance and clothing were to me obviously Russian. Mr. Petrov introduced himself and his associate, a Mr. Olifirenko, whom he said he had "just happened to bump into in the streets of New York."

I invited them to sit down, and since it was a very hot day, we all took off our coats. Mr. Olifirenko, who had been "just bumped into," did most of the talking. They stated that they were both second secretaries of the Soviet Embassy in Washington. At this point I felt like a man who had intercepted a

Return to Russia

forward pass. The ball was in my hands, and I knew I was going to run hard with it. As soon as the first phone call terminated, I had realized that a visa was within grasp. This journey all the way to New York by two Soviet diplomatic officials was extraordinary. The cable must have worked!

The conversation circled aimlessly for a few minutes . . . the weather . . . the view from my penthouse . . . we understand you have been in Moscow . . . when was that . . . Then out it popped. They had been instructed to inform me that they had a visa for me and my wife. (As I was not married at the time, it immediately occurred to me that I ought to put an ad in the papers.) I did not get up and cheer, but treated the information as though they had said, "Please pass the coffee."

"Thank you very much," I replied, and nodded in acknowledgment. "But of course I have a number of questions. Can I bring an interpreter? Where will I be allowed to go? What sort of an exchange rate will I get? I need a good deal of additional information. How long can I stay? What restrictions or limitations are involved?" So the conversation started.

I said I was not interested in going unless I could have access to ordinary people and could take notes, that I had heard their Official Secrets Act made unnecessary communication with foreigners a crime, and that I didn't want any Oatis business arising; that we must be clear as to my right to take notes and bring them out with me. They said they thought I could take notes, but that on the other questions they would have to cable for instructions. I went further: "I also want to take a camera and a moving picture camera." The Russians said they would ask Moscow.

Now came their turn. What did I have in mind doing? Why had I wanted to go? Did I intend to write about it? I answered that I was just curious; I hoped I might obtain enough material to write and speak about, though this was not my profession. When they asked me what had been my most recent activity, I replied, "I am a lawyer; most recently I have been in France assisting a French company in its contracts to manufacture shells and rockets." I can't imagine anything more anti-Russian and anti-Communist than helping a Western ally develop its defense program, but I figured they might as well have it directly.

They took this information in their stride, but then their curiosity could not be restrained. It had become clear that an iron instruction had sent them running to me and that they apparently didn't know what had been the origin of their instructions. One finally asked, "Mr. MacDuffie, how did you happen to request this visa?"

"Oh," I replied casually, "I sent a cable to Khrushchev in the Kremlin."

One of the Russians seemed to bounce three feet out of his chair as he bellowed, "*Khrushchev?*"

Despite the legend that the MVD knows the exact location of every Western official and former official who has ever seen any part of the U.S.S.R., the Russians revealed that they had been looking for me, for some strange reason, in Ossining (the home of Sing Sing prison). When I remarked that my name and address had always been in the New York telephone book, one of the Russians answered in a small voice, "But Mr. MacDuffie, we don't have a New York telephone book in our Washington embassy."

On September 18 I went to Washington to pick up my visa. This time I talked to Mr. Petrov, and again a second Russian was present—the consul general. I learned that I could not get a special ruble rate (later in Moscow I was able to obtain the standard Intourist booklet giving the foreign traveler room, board, and daily use of a touring car for four hours at a total cost of nineteen dollars per day; the two Russian diplomats seemed never to have heard of this arrangement). They told me I could not bring my own interpreter but that "good ones would be available" (they were good). Permission had been granted for me to take an ordinary camera, but no instructions had been received with regard to my bringing a motion-picture camera. This I took to be the usual Soviet "no," and, since I had never taken still pictures, let alone movies, I decided not to press it further. The Soviet diplomats said that a Russian plane flew from Helsinki to Moscow twice a week, and if I gave them ample notice, they would wire ahead for a reservation and for someone to meet me at the Moscow airport.

Then came an amusing incident at the State Department. My passport issued some time before bore the legend, "Not good for Rumania, Bulgaria, and Hungary," but its language for some reason did not bar passage to the Soviet Union. When the Russians inserted their visa, the passport on its face was valid for the trip. I had a suspicion, however, that the McCarran Act or some new regulation might cause me trouble. Besides, I clearly intended to have my government know what I was up to and give me some indirect approval. I went directly to the office of Mrs. Shipley, the legendary tyrant of the Passport Division and one who notoriously discourages anyone from going near a Russian.

I folded my passport around the Russian visa, handed it to a secretary, and said, "Please show this to Mrs. Shipley."

In less than thirty seconds the elderly Mrs. Shipley came whirling out of her office at a pace that would make Mel Patton, the world's fastest human, quiver. "Where did you get this? Where did you get this?" she cried in a flurry.

"At the Soviet Embassy, where else could I?"

This sequitur was a mistake. Paying no attention to me, she turned to the secretary and shouted, "Put that stamp on it; put that stamp on it," and quicker than you could say, "Soviet Union," her secretary had stamped my passport in large red letters: "VOID." Then Mrs. Shipley veered toward me. Until that moment her eyes had been only on the passport and the appropriate stamps. "Don't you know the regulations?" she said.

"Well, I thought there might be one . . . that's why I came here," I replied.

"Why," she retorted, "they're printed in the newspapers!" I let it go, but I felt like saying, "Every morning when I wake up, I call my friends and say first thing, 'What's the latest news in passport regulations?' "

My next encounter was not so trivial or comic. It was a discussion with one of the most important officials in the State Department. I reported how I obtained the visa, why I wanted to go, and requested adrenalin be administered to the lady holding the pass. He was a very tough and knowledgeable man, one of those unsung heroes of our government who make this country great—and protected. I asked him if he thought I was safe in venturing alone through the Soviet Union at that time. He replied in words which were to hang over me oppressively, to come back in the stillness of the Soviet night, to harass me every time a Russian policeman checked me. He said, "I think you're safe with that visa in the Soviet Union. But let's face it. They'll try to use you for their own purposes, and they can be very ruthless if it suits them. If they choose to frame you as a defector to Communism or label you an enemy agent, they will. Remember what the Czechs did with William Oatis."

This had a heavier deterring effect upon me than I realized when first I heard it. Several times in my lonely journey I wondered if I had gone too far in my snooping and questioning and snapping of photos. There would come a knock on the door, and I would rise with a start. Possibly now and then it caused me to check a line of questioning. Just that single instance—what happened to Oatis when an insignificant item of improper information hung upon him led to months of suffering in jail—made me reflect upon the Communist use of the punitive example. What check upon our Ambassador Bohlen's words or actions, possibly unconscious, was the sudden declaration that the previous American ambassador, Kennan, was *persona non grata* because of some honest thoughts too publicly uttered? What check upon the present-day Russian worker—where employers now deny that workers are severely punished for being late—is the public record a few years back of a sentence to prison for one too frequently tardy?

The diplomat and I also pondered the reasons why the Russians had given me my visa. After exploring various possibilities, he threw up his hands, as one often does in such speculations, and said, "Hell, Mac, maybe somebody just got drunk one night in the Kremlin and said, 'Oh, let him in.'"

In a few days the State Department sent me an approval: "Good for one round trip to the Soviet Union." I took the precaution of leaving several notes and affidavits indicating as firmly as I could that, any statement to the contrary "uttered" by me in the Soviet Union, I loved my country and wanted to return to it. While it was cold comfort, I had the feeling that any "forced confession" out of me would look a little silly and certainly dubious in the light of those carefully prepared "last thoughts on leaving."

CHAPTER 2

Journey into Moscow

ON OCTOBER 11 I left New York aboard a four-motored American-made plane flown by the Scandinavian Airlines. It was the usual de luxe ocean flight familiar to so many Westerners—a forty-passenger plane, two uniformed stewardesses, excellent food and drinks, comfortable reclining chairs and even some berths. It was to seem like Utopia as I later crawled about the Soviet Union in the battered little two-engine planes with their shabby and worn furnishings; their stiff chairs, lacking any straps; with no food aboard except on two occasions, and then only a miserable little box lunch; the dozen or so passengers; the luggage piled on the seats or sprawled in the aisles; the occasional stewardess in rough clothing, often wearing a shawl.

I stayed overnight in Stockholm and Helsinki. Anyone going to the Soviet Union ought to spend one night in each of these cities on the way in and again on leaving. These two countries, so close to the U. S. S. R., so small by comparison, seem by contrast to be as far away as Mars—and the contrast sharpens one's impressions of Russia.

Stockholm, which escaped the war, has some of the most striking and varied modern architecture in the world. Compared with that, Moscow is a city of worn, tired old buildings,

Journey into Moscow

decorated with eight new skyscrapers, all looking like the Woolworth Building, but not so well made. There is also another, quite different contrast. I walked about Stockholm in the evening after dinner, and there was almost nobody on the streets, no activity, no amusement. It was like one of those mystery movies in which all life in a city has been destroyed by a strange plague. This memory pointed up the first vivid night in Moscow, where the streets pulsed with animation and the stir of hundreds of people walking about till well past midnight. In Stockholm I was afraid I would meet a ghost. In Moscow that first night, it seemed a ring of people would have danced around any ghost so foolish as to be abroad.

In Finland the contrast was to be more vivid after I left the Soviet Union. This was a country which also had suffered from war, a very small nation without Russia's vast resources. But here, after a couple of months in the U. S. S. R., every well-dressed Finn—there appeared to be thousands of them—in his dark Homburg, carrying his brief case, seemed a cabinet minister, a man of extreme wealth, compared with what I had seen in the Soviet Union. The variety of autos, their many colors, the abundance of the shops, the smooth finish of the rooms and furnishings in the hotels—surely this must seem a land of milk and honey—and gasoline—to a visiting Russian. Coming into Helsinki from Moscow is like having a light shine on your face in the middle of the night. You can only blink in dazzlement at the apparent material wealth. Yet by our American standards, Helsinki is merely another Western city, distinguished by two or three buildings of interesting architectural design.

In Stockholm, as I was getting off the bus at the airport to continue on to Helsinki, I noticed several men standing at the entrance to the terminal. They were staring at the shoes of each of the passengers getting off the bus. One look at these men and I knew intuitively that they were Russians. The cut of their clothing, the little metal badges on some of their lapels, the bones of their faces, the shortness of their stature, the way they were huddled together—well, how does one recognize an accent? You know it without identifying each distinguishing feature. Certainly they were more poorly dressed than other travelers in Western Europe. And a glance at their shoes would tell you why they followed the footsteps of each bus passenger so wistfully.

One man had on a sports jersey under his suit, and I could see the middle two letters of what I guessed stood for U. S. S. R. (the Russian letters are C. C. C. P.). I walked over to him, put my fingers on the letters, and asked, "Russki?" He muttered assent and told me his group was a track team which had been competing in Scandinavia.

While I speak practically no Russian, and limping German and French, it is surprising to me how much one so limited can communicate with Russians. There are a number of words in Russian and English with common origins. This fact, plus a maximum of gestures and attempts at various words and tongues, somehow establishes a measure of understanding. Once on this trip I was with an English reporter in Moscow who knew quite a bit of Russian. Just as we were about to get into a taxi, a soldier came up to us. The Englishman said the soldier wanted to ride with us; but almost by pure guesswork I said, "No, he's trying to sell us a ride in his car." Sure enough, it was a Russian GI seeking to pick up some extra rubles by illegally peddling the use of his officer's car.

But another time I was not so smart. I saw a long line going into the building opposite the Kremlin, which was to be Moscow's newest and biggest department store. I thought I was getting a preview and so I joined the line, which was about four abreast. About five minutes later as I patiently progressed down the stairs in the middle of the line, I noticed some young girls laughing, apparently at me. I said in English, "What's the matter?"

They replied in Russian, "*Zhenskaya tualetnaya.*" Again I recognized the words; it was the line to the ladies' room. I felt a little better later when I saw other girls laughing at Russian men who were making the same mistake.

Journey into Moscow

The Russian track team rode with us to Helsinki.

On the plane the Russians acted like any American group of athletes, except that each had to be shown how to attach his seat buckles. Two started playing cards. A couple went off and sat by themselves in the back of the plane. One went to sleep. Another read a book. Two girls, a "sprinter" and a "shot-putter"—and they looked it—sat talking. One Russki was writing letters. The others picked up the magazines in the plane's rack. I watched them openly pick out and exchange *Time* magazine, some British illustrated weeklies, and several Scandinavian papers. Most of the Russians were sitting in the front of the plane, and I took a seat just behind them.

Shortly after the take-off, one turned to me and asked in English if I was an American. He pointed to a photo in *Time* of a young woman contestant for Mrs. America, a mother of nine children shown with her brood, and he asked me if this was true and if it "happened often in America." After giving him a Yes and a No in that precise order, I asked him a few questions about his team—it turned out he was the manager —and then I moved into the seat alongside of him and we conversed, mostly about his athletes, for the rest of the short flight. He apologized for his English, which he said was from books because he had had "not much practical." I was surprised at the way the team was openly reading foreign magazines and the way he had initiated the conversation with me, nor had he shied away when I joined him.

At the Helsinki airport Finnish officials made a phone call and confirmed my reservation for the next day on the Russian plane to Moscow via Leningrad. I was told just to get out to the airport a little before starting time. There was no bus and no Russian ticket office. I was not to see a Russian until I reached the plane.

The next day I boarded the plane with a Turkish diplomat, a woman secretary from the French embassy, an Italian, a Swede, four South Americans, and a couple of Russians. The announcement of the start was made first in Finnish and then in English by a woman; this was followed by a shorter Russian announcement spoken by a man. Promptly at four the pilot warmed up the engines of the little two-engine plane. Two passengers and a local girl friend stopped for a last picture; a Russian bystander in civilian clothes and leather puttees, wearing a peaked hat with a red star on it, stepped up to them and offered in English to take a picture which would include all three. Just as he clicked the camera the pilot zoomed the motors, and everybody bolted for the plane.

Inside were eighteen seats for passengers, all covered with a dull white cotton cloth; the chairs were of cracked leather; there was a threadbare striped carpet running down the aisle; overhead were tiny stringed racks for magazines; in the back was a toilet (in the past Russian transport planes often did not have one) and a little service cabinet used by the stewardess, a plain girl in a plain cotton dress; and perched on the rear two seats were my duffel bags.

Contrary to all I had heard elsewhere, the pilot took his time warming up the motors, and there was a no-smoking sign (this regulation was rigidly enforced on the many flights I took). But the take-off was hair-raising. No sooner did the plane start moving than the pilot lifted it off the ground and then flew a great length of the runway just a few feet above the surface, a procedure which always scared me lest he dip a wing. I am told it is standard practice where runways are bad, to prevent wrecking the undercarriage. Since most Soviet airfields are pretty primitive, the pilots seem to make this take-off a standard one even on good airstrips.

The trip was uneventful. We flew high above the clouds. We were given a box lunch consisting of one caviar sandwich, one bologna sandwich, some cookies and candies; and the stewardess prepared tea. The only function of the stewardess was to hand out the lunch and hot tea and then, at journey's end, to collect her silver holders for the tea glasses and stow them away properly. Nobody talked to anybody else. I glanced through some picture magazines and a copy of the Soviet satiri-

Journey into Moscow

when I started to leave the plane. This was not the West. This was Russia, and I felt disturbed and a little lost.

As we climbed down the ladder in the dark of night toward a group of waiting men, a little man, a Tatar, I later found out, stepped out of the crowd, ignored the two or three Westerners descending in front of me, and suddenly addressed me in English. "Are you Mr. MacDuffie?"

This strange land already gave me a peculiar feeling again. A little man starts it all off, plucking me out in the dark. But after the first shock I felt good, and relaxed. There was somebody to whom I could talk in my own language. I did not feel lost and helpless. I felt like myself.

I have made two journeys into the Soviet Union. Each time, unaccountably, I have become grim and tense and a little worried and uneasy as I approached my first Russians. Each time at first glance they seemed chill and forbidding. All of a sudden, after a moment of talk, of being recognized, possibly the first reply in English, and then one feels relaxed, at ease, at home there as anywhere. After that, as during the first trip, my struggle sometimes was to prod myself with a reminder of opportunities ahead, saying, "Hey, I'm in Russia."

CHAPTER 3

On the Intourist Chainbelt

THE GREAT Russian novelists have created the illusion of reincarnation. Their pictures of the steppes of Russia, the brooding skies, and snow-mantled Moscow are so sharp that a visitor who may have forgotten he has read their books almost instantly feels at home in Russia, among familiar sights and faces. Only now the streets of Moscow resound with the honk of auto horns and the pace of traffic as big black Government limousines, passenger busses, and great open trucks roar by. Beginning to loom over old Moscow is the sight of eight new "skyscrapers," sixteen to thirty-two stories high, all white and ceramic-shiny, each dominating a separate area of the city. Their peaked towers are supposed to be a modern derivation of the Kremlin turrets, their gleaming encrusted white façades an improvement over the flat dirty-gray imitation–Le Corbusier style of Russia's "modern" buildings of the thirties. The effect to me, however, was as though a giant had sown some Woolworth Building seeds, so that Moscow, with its lovely old, crumbling yellow buildings was starting to look like a dusty wedding cake with eight tasseled candles. But there still remain some of the finest and widest boulevards in the world, and that mysterious enchanting magnet which draws all Moscow visitors, which holds the attention of thoughts throughout the globe, the

On the Intourist Chainbelt 23

heart of Moscow—the Kremlin, Red Square, and Saint Basil's Cathedral. I wonder if anyone, when you mention Russia, does not have in mind among other images, a picture of the red Kremlin walls, possibly the tomb of Lenin (and now of Stalin, too), and those curious, ever-kaleidoscopic towers of Saint Basil's. And everywhere the crumbling, yellow old buildings, sleepy in the snow, like a dog by the fire, one eye open, his jaw on the floor.

There is one outstanding change: the imposing presence of Moscow State University named after Lomonosov, on Lenin Hills, which we could see as we approached the city. We drove from the airport for about twenty miles in a little Pobeda car, shaped like a 1950 Buick but of a smaller European size, along a four-lane highway almost bare of traffic. When cars approached, each would turn out its lights, and we would creep along nightmarishly. Outside other cities I was to have this same eerie experience, time and again narrowly missing black-coated peasants or a lumbering wagon heading in our direction when our chauffeur cautiously doused his lights. Until we reached the outskirts of the city, we saw only six cars and two trucks, and two of the vehicles had halted on the road for repairs, a sight never missing from any auto trip I took in the Soviet Union.

Another trip from the same airport on the same road in 1946 had given me a good illustration of Russian talent for improvisation. The gasoline feed-line of our engine became plugged up. In the United States we would have sought a garage and waited an hour while they took it out and cleaned it. There was no garage here. So the driver took a gasoline can, propped it under the hood, and let the gas run directly from the can into the engine—and we made the journey without mishap. Our driver had another good reason for improvising: the quality of the few service stations that did exist. Even seven years later a Soviet writer was still lamenting, "Many service stations work on one rule, give the least to the car and take the most from the owner."

This was a lonely road, with few buildings or signs of life. As we reached the outskirts of Moscow (an area which is largely a settlement of one-story wooden cabins, the window arches and doorways of which bear designs carved in an old Russian pattern), we glimpsed on the highest hills of the city the great thirty-two story Moscow University building newly completed, which houses some six thousand people. Its lights from a thousand rooms gleamed through a murky haze, with the center peaks and the two extended shoulders of the building bordered in red lights, ironically making a beautiful red but Christian-shaped cross towering on the heights above Moscow. Now this building and the Kremlin dominate the sights of the city, symbolic of the twin thrusts of Soviet Russia, the drive for universal education and the dictatorship of the Kremlin. Education rising to new Russian heights, and in the center of it all, the dark fortresslike dictatorship.

We drove to the National Hotel, facing on the square adjoining Red Square. Impressions rained upon me as from a machine gun. The uniformed policeman was at the doorway, no longer in worn-khaki with a frayed edge to his coat, as though he had cut its length with a penknife; now he had on a handsome rich blue uniform and coat, and a brand new blue peaked-cap with a red band. One thing was unchanged: They still stationed a policeman in front of the door of the hotel for foreigners, as much to keep away the Russian citizenry, I am told, as to protect the visitor. Swinging through the doors, I passed three visiting Chinese, and I do not recall seeing one in Moscow seven years before. As we ascended to my room, I observed a photo of Stalin adorning the first-floor lobby, one of Lenin at the second floor, and one of Lenin and Stalin together on the third floor. Soviet "art" had apparently not changed.

Last time I had had diplomatic standing, but I was berthed in the second-best hotel for visitors, the ancient, sagging Metropole, and I drew a room almost without heat, with worn red-plush furniture fit only for an ancient Victorian hostelry one-

On the Intourist Chainbelt 25

day removed from bankruptcy. This time I was given one of the most ornately decorated hotel rooms I have ever seen, and it had plenty of steam heat. Still grander was the view from my windows. I looked out across a vast empty square, where neither citizens nor cars could cross, directly upon the red walls and yellow buildings of the Kremlin. On a straight line from my room one's eye could travel farther beyond the Kremlin, up the street that led to Red Square, past the mausoleum of Lenin and Stalin, until the view ended with the colorful ancient Saint Basil's at the center of the horizon. The plush setup naturally raised my hopes as to what opportunities would be given me to see the country and its rulers.

Just after the war Moscow citizens were worn with exhaustion. There was a strained look about them, a weariness, an indifference. Moscow had seemed to me the dreariest city I had ever seen. So I came back to it with misgiving. I dreaded the inevitable gloominess of the atmosphere, which I am inclined now to blame on the oppressive brooding skies of Russia's winter.

But on my first evening, I was amazed. As soon as my bags were stowed, I rushed out of the hotel at about eleven at night and headed for the floodlighted Red Square and the Kremlin —behind the walls of which I could hear a pneumatic hammer chattering at that late hour—and after that up Gorki Street, the main thoroughfare, some 190 feet wide. What astonished me was the sense of life and vivacity, the numbers of people on the street, the bustle and gaiety, the improvement in quality of the clothes they were wearing (though they were still much shabbier than in the West), and the comparative multitude of goods in the shop windows. Conditions were still behind Western Europe generally, and many shortages were apparent, perhaps exemplified by the food stores which still grimly persisted in stocking their windows and counter displays with painted or wax cuts of meat, reminding one of Madame Tussaud's.

Of course I had seen Moscow at the bottom of its adversity, and this was all impressionistic. My conclusions may have been distorted by my previous grim experience; but certainly I sensed in the air a push and swing I had not felt before. My first quick estimate was that welfare and morale had greatly improved. At the end of 10,000 miles through European and Asiatic Russia that same first impression was confirmed; they were still poor, but much better off, and quite hopeful. That first night I walked about unmolested, and, I believe, unfollowed until almost two in the morning, and there were many people still wandering around at that hour. My spirits picked up, and I began for the first time to look forward to what might develop on this venture.

During my first days in Moscow I spent quite a bit of time with various people at the American Embassy, trying to avail myself of their knowledge and experience to guide my own sightseeing. Later I was to see a Russian review of a current play about the Revolution in which the writer referred in the present tense to the American Embassy as "that center of cunning and bloody intrigues."

Life in the embassy is pretty grim. Some of our finest citizens have served and now serve in Moscow, leading lonely, restricted lives which are often uncomfortable and unrewarding, and potentially dangerous. They work hard and with courage and persistence. On their painstaking efforts, the peace and safety of all of us may importantly depend. They are by any standards grossly underpaid. And they must dwell in a land where, by reason of an artificial exchange rate and huge material shortages, everything is fantastically extravagant. A lemon, when one is available, costs seventy-five cents. (The clowns at the circus underlined this shortage. One asked the other if he could spell *foodstore* with twenty lemons, and got the reply that it was more difficult to find one lemon in twenty foodstores.) An egg—one egg—ranged in cost while I was in Russia from twenty-five to forty-two cents. An American diplomat entertained a visiting Congressman one evening at dinner and the theater and it cost him $90. The wife of the

On the Intourist Chainbelt

ambassador and another lady took an extended weekend tour to Leningrad: cost, $600.

Our representatives live as in an armed camp or fortress. Outside the barricades are armed Russian police "guarding" them. Inside the walls are our own U.S. Marines, ever alert. A visiting American like myself, even one who has served in the Department of State, cannot walk from room to room without an escort. Once or twice I forgot myself and rushed from the room of one official to the room of some friend, only to have a deadly serious Marine pounce upon me and telephone both officials involved, in just rebuke. Nobody could step out of his room to the bathroom and leave me in his room alone. The necessity for such minute precautions inevitably creates a tense atmosphere.

On top of our own hampering security restrictions are the more frustrating Russian barriers. Around Moscow no ordinary citizen will have any but the most perfunctory dealings with an American official. Either close MVD surveillance or the history of what has happened to many Russians who associated with foreign officials in the past now makes most Russian citizens treat a visiting diplomat or correspondent like a leper in the Middle Ages.

Until recently diplomats were limited in travel to a few miles outside Moscow. Now they may go about the country (though many areas are still barred to all foreigners), but before each journey they must obtain special permission. More than that, the astronomical costs of travel hem in all but the most wealthy government-paid people.

When foreigners do travel, they have access for the most part only to public events. When I was there, the top American agricultural expert had not been able to visit one single Russian collective farm, though he could study the abundant published data and had a chance to observe the markets and the life of the city. After a year there he finally managed to see one farm. I have talked to wives of embassy officers long resident in Moscow who have never been able to go inside a school or clinic, a sight accorded the lowliest of tourists or businessmen. Of course none of them were ever invited to the home of an ordinary urban Russian, or, for that matter, of a top Russian. Occasionally one has visited a peasant's house. One Russian official who had recently been in America asked me to send him a good detective story and a current book on the American economy. When I said, "Why don't you ask the American Embassy?" he replied scornfully, "I wouldn't think of going near that place."

(This same Russian, named Bruslov, who had served in the Soviet Embassy in Washington—where he acquired a preference for Haig & Haig over vodka—thought that the worst thing in the U.S.A. was the press. He spoke glibly and critically of many of our columnists, disparaging in one breath the Alsops, Reston, Lippmann, Winchell, Sokolsky, and Pegler among others. When I suggested that it was a variable array to group together, he remarked, "What's the difference between a green and a yellow snake?"—indicative that Russian diplomats, when the chips are down, look upon all of us as infidels. I asked him what he did as second secretary in Washington. He laughed and replied, "The same thing your men do here; I read the papers all day long!"

Bruslov had an answer for everything. I complained that on my trips from hotel to embassy the Russian taxi meters ranged from four rubles [$1.00] to twelve rubles [$3.00] for the same trip. He responded with a story about a man arriving in New York City at the Pennsylvania Station who hired a cab to go to the Statler Hotel [just across the street]. According to Bruslov, when the driver charged the American six dollars, the passenger from out of town complained, "This is an outrage; last time the same trip cost me only four dollars!"

Since he seemed to attack everything American, I finally asked what he liked best about my country, if anything, and he promptly answered, "American practicality.")

But this restraint toward embassy personnel and toward official correspondents—they seem to consider Associated Press men as much government agents, as we, for instance, consider a Tass pressman in Washington to be in the pay of the Russian Government—does not seem to apply to businessmen and tourists who manage an entrance to the Soviet Union. It has been my experience on two extensive trips to that land that the average Russian has about as much curiosity as anyone I have ever met. Almost without exception, no ordinary Russian citizen has ever shown hostility towards me or been rude, despite the constant vicious official anti-American propaganda. Yet even this hostile line carefully draws a distinction between the American people and their alleged exploiters—"the politicians, the magnates, and the press." So if you are not a foreign-office representative, a military officer, or a correspondent, the Russian citizens apparently assume they will not be punished for talking to you. Then their natural friendliness swings into action. One expert on the Russians, speaking of this trait, acknowledged, "If the Soviet Government took all restraint off their people, our embassy would be knee-deep in Russians, and we would have to change ambassadors every six months from exhaustion."

It took me some time on this trip to meet ordinary Russians. First it was the English-speaking manager of the hotel, a dark, handsome lady, dignified and sensitive, sitting at her desk in her rich ancient shawl; the bustling, ever-cheerful maids, with their stocky bodies and broad, open Russian faces; the trim, pert waitresses in the international dining room, with brand-new uniforms and brand-new make-up (frequently including mascara), and now sporting fingernail polish; the tough old watchful madames on each floor of the hotel, looking for all the world like grasping French landladies; the puttering elevator operators in their shiny serge suits; the ancient waiters, whose baldness is accentuated by completely shaven heads, tottering about with a skill and dispatch they learned before Lenin was born; and then Rogoff, in charge of Intourist's office at the National Hotel. Almost all foreign visitors to the U.S.S.R.

are in the hands of the Government's Intourist Bureau for all arrangements as to hotels, tickets, travel, and appointments with Russians. Sometimes Voks, the Society for Cultural Relations, also takes a hand.

I liked Rogoff very much. His was the Russian face to end all Russian faces. Bald, broad, bland; patient, friendly, a little weary; a little unhappy, and persistently hopeful and quietly friendly. He told me one day he had been away to his grandmother's ninety-fifth birthday party, a gay affair. When I congratulated him on the best approach to a long life—long-lived forebears—he smiled with Russian resignation. "I will not live any length like that," he said wearily. "I had two severe wounds in the war; one bad one to my head . . . and sometimes . . . well, I do not think I will live so long. . . ." He smiled, and something about his eyes suggested to me what many Russians endured: all the normal struggle in that tough land, and on top of that, the harsh pressure and wounds and losses of war which swept drastically across so much of their land and people.

Rogoff led a harried life. All the visiting foreigners, and their number was increasing, were descending upon his hotel. I never entered his office with my own new requests that he was not sitting there patiently conversing about similar demands with a Chinese, or an East German or a Scandinavian, and once even with a slim French lass.

His idea of protocol was quite different from mine. One day I told him I thought I might not use some theater tickets he had procured because I had a tentative date to dine with the American ambassador. He told me firmly that it would be impolite not to use the tickets—and I meekly followed his hint: "When in Russia, do . . ."

If he had good news for me, he seemed happier than I ever could be. When he had no answer—as so often was the case—he did not appear sly or evasive, just unhappy and dismayed. It was no laughing matter for him when he reported for a time, almost daily, while my residence permit was running out, that "the Chief of Police is still ill . . . I do not know when we will hear . . ." And he would look at me with hurt eyes.

Now and then while we were waiting for a reply to some phone call or request, we would chat about affairs of the world. Rogoff had liked Mrs. Perle Mesta. "A very simple woman." He was surprised when I told him she rated the appellation "capitalist" if anybody did. One day he confided happily, "Yes, now every day more and more people come to us from many lands." Though it meant more harassment for him, he was pleased about it. Another time we discussed Senator McCarthy. Rogoff surprised me with his vocabulary (not until some American students told me they discovered he liked to pick up current American expressions did I realize where he learned this one). He said in English, "I think Senator McCarthy is a witch-hunter; everybody who is against him, he calls a Communist." Rogoff said this as though it was his own measured conclusion. Other Russians talked of that prickly subject somewhat differently. They always seemed to me to mention "Senatore Muh Kahteee" with a chuckling glee. From my experience, I would take an oath that the top officials loved him.

Rogoff, who was the son of a peasant, probably had the average Soviet citizen's ideas about the United States. He said that the Russians knew that the Americans had great productive skill, and they believed that the Americans didn't want war. The Russians knew more about war, since they had experienced more of it. "But the bosses in America, because there is no planning, no State planning—when there is overproduction in America, for example of automobiles, they need wars to take up their production." He blamed the U. S. newspapers, too, because they were "owned by big capital." All these things contributed to the present troubles, but the difficulties between our two countries, he remarked in a conciliatory tone, were also "because of misunderstandings."

Rogoff sent me on my first encouraging sally, accompanied by Zorya Novikova, one of the three main English-speaking interpreters in his employ. I swung through the neighboring shops with my flash bulbs and camera, permitted to take inside shots in the stores—a fact which astounded every American in Moscow and myself most of all. In each place Zorya would ask the manager for "an O.K." (English-speaking Russians love to use the word "O.K."), and on each occasion he or she always granted it. Nobody objected among those we photographed. On the streets a few people would glance askance at the big Rolleiflex hanging from my neck. In the shops, girls who had never seen a camera flash would scream in fright and then titter in embarrassment. Now and then a citizen would ask me questions about the camera and how it worked. One woman asked why I was taking pictures, and when told that I was an American tourist with permission, admonished me to "take very good pictures." Small boys inevitably hung at my heels (one day two of them followed me for four hours until I reached my hotel), and an elderly citizen went around collecting my used bulbs, explaining that they were for a friend of his interested in electrical matters. I strongly suspect that the "friend" was himself, who was going to show his neighbors an illustration for a new tale about "the American."

Next Rogoff teamed me with two visiting Britishers, an English canon and a charming, irrepressible businessman. With them I visited a school, a hospital, and a church. We also got the standard Intourist treatment, all of which I had experienced on my previous trip: the huge Lenin Library, the excellent museums, the main art gallery, the justly famous subway, the fantastically dazzling Bolshoi ballet, even a tour of the Kremlin, which I had seen twice before. Much of it makes up a splendid museum, full of czarist treasures going back to the fourteenth century. Since most travelers to the U.S.S.R. see only Moscow —chiefly the above items, all of which have been written about endlessly—I need only add my echoes to the tributes which have been lavished on them. My willingness to go to the Soviet Union this second time was in the hope of seeing something other than these familiar show places.

But my third trip to the Kremlin did have two small innovations for me. First, I saw a gang of workmen painting the

On the Intourist Chainbelt 33

belfry of one of its ancient churches. On the very top of the belfry, presiding over their activity, was a soldier with a rifle and bayonet. Secondly, I seized a rubbernecker's opportunity to speak from the rostrum in the great hall of the Supreme Soviet, where Stalin had so often addressed the Soviet Union's leading officials. I tested the acoustics with the first words of Lincoln's Gettysburg Address. On other occasions I spoke to real Russian audiences: to a couple of hundred English-speaking students at Kiev University in 1946, and in 1953 to almost 2,000 Russian Baptists, mostly women, when I preached a three-minute sermon on freedom of religion in America from the pulpit of Moscow's Baptist Church. This "freedom of speech for foreigners" is a new tourist treat, for a number of visitors have been led recently to that same pulpit.

The two Englishmen and I also went to see the Soviet's three-dimensional movies, which we agreed would never hurt Hollywood—just the viewer's eyes.

The canon's approach to all poor Russians who did not understand him was what I believe has been the standard British way since the Middle Ages. He would raise his voice and shout in loud, slow British tones—with never an attempt at the foreign language—the same unvarying words. If this did not work, he would raise his voice and try, syllable by syllable, again not varying a word nor trying any foreign substitutes. If even this did not work, he would show that he was offended.

Once I watched him bait the patient Rogoff. The minister insisted he was entitled to an interview with the Patriarch of All Russia. He pressed his point, always in English, and clipped English, to Rogoff, who understood a fair amount. The canon concluded: "The Archbishop of Canterbury personally desires that I see the patriarch. *If . . . I . . . do . . . not . . . see the patriarch . . . the . . . Archbishop . . . will consider it . . . a* SNUB!" Rogoff just blinked, saying nothing. I seriously doubt if he ever heard the word "snub" before; but he always tried to co-operate, and so eventually the good canon did see the good patriarch. And the rumor spread in Moscow that the patriarch had given the English canon an ancient gold-embossed Bible. At last I got a glimpse at it. It had been printed in Indianapolis, U.S.A.

One evening we watched some dancing in a Moscow hotel dining room. As at home, some citizens are very good dancers, but most are pretty poor. There it is an accepted custom for strangers to ask a woman to dance, and often women dance together. (The U.S.S.R. is reported to have lost in the war 25 per cent of its men in the group who are now between twenty-five and forty-five.) The general tempo of the dancing is what I call pump-handle jazz, but now and then I saw a touch of jitterbugging and an occasional rhumba. What surprised the Englishmen with me were the number of drunks, more, they asserted, than they had ever seen in any public place in England. There were a lot, but I believe I have seen just as many at American college fraternity dances. While I saw many drunks in Moscow, there seemed to be fewer elsewhere in the country. Friends told me about Moscow's sobering-up stations. If you fall on the sidewalk you are carted off for the night to receive a sort of compulsory Turkish bath treatment. Gossip has it that vodka tends to hit the knees first, and that the reason you always see one Russian drunk desperately holding another up is to save him from the sobering-up station.

After we had toured the town for some days, I asked the canon my usual questions, what did he dislike most about Russians and what did he like best. "The way they fob you off" was his first reply, and, "The excellent care they take of children" was the second. This exceptional care of children was praised to me by several women of the diplomatic colony, and I agreed strongly.

The British businessman was one of those chirrupy little fellows, bright as a whip, with a main eye on the pound to be made—"I'm here for filthy lucre"—but seriously concerned about world peace. "Trade makes friends. Trade makes friends," he would recite to himself at breakfast, to hearten himself for the day, and off he would bounce on his somewhat frustrating rounds. His problem was simple. He was ready to pay a good price for something, but it required inspection of the goods. First the Russians couldn't find the goods. Then they couldn't find the official he was dealing with. Then they thought they couldn't find the Britisher. Finally, when all that was lost was found, they said the material was at Leningrad's port and he could not go there. So it went. . . . He, however, was bubblingly irrepressible, and his observations often were illuminating. He said he had been in twenty-two capitals of the world and never had he seen so many men in military uniform. An accurate statement, I believe, from my experience.

He was generous about what he liked. He pointed across the beautiful square as we looked from the dining-room window. "In America a sight like that would be all fouled up with an electric advertisement for so-and-so's beer. On those buildings we would read about somebody's cigarette puffing longer. It's puritanical in aspect, but still it's better than the Babylon of Times Square." He added, "These Russians have another advantage. No vested interest can block the improvement of a view, the setting up of a boulevard, the beautifying of a square. If the Government wants it, that's all there is to it." This was probably one of the best things ever said about statism, but what he did not take into account was the thousand and one bureaucratic blocks that might also have been thrown into the slowly grinding decision to create a new square.

What didn't he like? Soviet women. "They're such a mess. They have no *élan*. A man likes to see a beautiful woman, elegantly dressed, at dinner." He went into the justified complaints of every foreigner who looks at Russian women—their frizzy unkempt hair; either their lack of make-up and powder or their having all the high polish and odor of a five-and-ten-cent store; their squat builds and solid legs; their earnest manner; the cheap, drab melange of clothes.

He didn't blame their poor clothing on their taste, but on their government. Said he, "I have an idea they'd swap a few statues of Uncle Joe for some silk panties next to their skin instead of the cotton stuff one sees in the stores." He, too, however, had to expand on the other clearly observable facts: essential aspects of figure which need no artificial dilation, and the general sweetness of almost any Russian woman. We agreed that the Soviet Union did not have the startling beauties of the world, but on the other hand, neither did it have so many ugly women as in America, England, and parts of Europe—especially Germany. Many Russian women are pretty, we agreed, and a great many are good-looking—so why should a man complain?

We also gave them good marks for never making up their faces in public. By contrast, Russian men are constantly combing their locks in public—in hotel lobbies, in theaters, even in restaurants.

As for the clothes of Russian women, they cannot easily be described by one mere male, though I did know enough about their quality to identify two groups of women sitting in the hotel dining room. One group was clearly Russian. As for the other group, I speculated to myself, "They're better clothed than the Russian women, but not up to Western Europe's standards." Afterwards I learned they were from East Germany.

The questions of the young girl in charge of Moscow's Fashion Show were also revealing. She told us she had seen some American fashion magazines and asked, "Are American women really that slim? . . . Don't you think too many pictures of bathing suits exist? . . . Don't you think American dresses are either too tight or too voluminous with all those petticoats?"

I owe the British businessman a debt for my favorite pictures from the trip. We visited a Muscovite grammar school together. In two classrooms for eight- and nine-year-old girls—where competitiveness, especially for marks, was highly stressed—he went to the blackboard and drew in Disney fashion swift, amusing cartoons of himself and his two boys, all chased by a buxom wife with a rolling pin; and, while the little pretty Russian girls shrieked with laughter, I shot a dozen photos of

On the Intourist Chainbelt 37

them. The girls seemed so pretty and neatly dressed that one or two of my friends who have seen the pictures claimed that this was a select school planted upon me. I think this can be disproved by a double argument: other pictures of the drabness of much of the school with its ordinary beat-up look (about on a par with some old New York City public schools) and a strong argument that all little girls of that age look exceptionally lovely in any country. Now the Russians are requiring Moscow school children to wear uniforms. While we might argue that this is government regimentation, they look upon such a move as "democratic"—for children of varying wealth are dressed "equally."

Even this friendly Englishman, however, fell afoul of a Russian. We were inspecting the Lenin Library together. One of the top librarians gave us a long and boring lecture, causing me to remember Walton Hamilton's line: "There is nothing like the passion of a functionary for his function." He showed us a list of last year's foreign acquisitions, mostly, of course, scientific works, though two others caught my eye: one by my old teacher Theodore Sizer entitled *The Works of John Trumbull, Painter of the Revolution,* and *The Verbal Syntax of John Dryden's Prose,* an obviously subversive document. It was rather paradoxical to learn that among the most treasured items in the "godless Soviet's" chief library are its oldest manuscript in Russian, the Archangel Bible, from 1092, and their oldest printed book, *The Epistles of the Apostles,* printed in 1564.

Finally the librarian mentioned that he had some books by Sir Walter Scott, whereupon the little Britisher intervened helpfully and said, "I find him a good sleeping pill—read him anytime I can't sleep—doze off in two minutes." The Russki librarian looked aggrieved. Last year he had made a great coup. He had purchased one hundred first editions of Scott from some Leningrad citizen, who apparently relinquished this family heirloom under present-day stress.

CHAPTER 4

Russian Justice

In any large city it is not easy for a stranger to get close to the real life of the citizens. In any foreign city it is much harder, especially in Moscow. But there is one place where people of all lands publicly recount certain intimate details of their lives —in the courtroom. My first escape from plain Moscow tourism came when I managed to spend a couple of days in the district courts. Later I was in a similar courtroom in Baku, a thousand miles to the south, and I also interviewed the chief judge of the Alma-Ata Regional Court, out in Kazakstan on the edge of Sinkiang.

In the normal Russian district court each case is tried before three people who have equal power. One is the judge, the permanent member of the court, who is elected every two years by the people of the district. The other two are "jurymen" (people's assessors) also elected by the district. Seventy-five jurymen are elected to serve ten days each year for two years. While doing jury duty, they are paid their normal wages. (A judge told me that in the Soviet Union they "encouraged people to control the State, and that is why persons are elected to serve as jurors.") In special types of cases a public procurator also participates, questioning witnesses on both sides and making a final recommendation to the court. A clerk of the court

Russian Justice

is always present also, but seems to note down bits of evidence only when occasionally ordered to do so (I heard of one case where the appeals court refused to rule—the only "record" was the name of the case on a blank piece of paper). Plaintiffs and defendants and procurator all may appeal cases to the next court. Court costs do not seem too high; in some cases none are assessed. The procedure in all cases is very informal, with little of the careful distinctions as to admissibility of evidence which prevail in our courts.

Though it is a rough justice, I must admit that in all the cases I observed, I was in general agreement with the verdict. It is also fairly swift justice. In two cases I noted dates: Events occurring in September and October were before the courts for litigation in mid-November.

Here are some of the cases I witnessed in the Soviet Union:

THE CASE OF THE DRUNKEN DRIVER

Ivan Grechnikoff, "a chauffeur for an enterprise" who was born in Smolensk in 1924, was in trouble. He was charged with driving without a license and, while "in the middle stage of drunkenness," steering across the street diagonally and running into a building, injuring the auto belonging to his "enterprise" to the tune of 965 rubles. He was summoned to appear before the district court presided over by a rather severe-looking woman judge of about his own age. In this case Ivan's fate was entirely in the hands of women. The two jurors drawn for his trial were also women, as was the only other official he faced, the clerk of the court. In the courtroom sat still another woman official, Mrs. Maculova, the State Inspector of Courts. The judge wore a suit of blue serge, a little on the masculine side. One lady juror, her hair parted in the middle, sat there in a traditional woolen shawl. The other juror wore one of the best tweed suits I was to see on anybody in the Soviet Union. The little secretary was using an old-fashioned nib pen.

The courtroom was small, dully painted, and dully lighted.

The lower half of its walls were painted yellow, the upper part a dull gray-white. Two chandeliers with five bulbs each hung from the ceiling unlit. Four male spectators idled about the back of the room.

First the defendant was requested to give his name and address. Then the judge instructed him as to the law and told him that he must sign a paper that he would tell the truth, that if he lied he would be sentenced to two years in jail. She apprised him of his rights: that he could summon witnesses in his behalf, that he had the right to request the withdrawal of a member of the court. Thereupon she gave him her name, the names of the jurors and of the clerk of the court, and again told him he could have anyone of them withdrawn. Then she asked him four questions: "Do you trust this court? Are you a member of the Communist Party? What is your military record? Have you ever been before the court before?"

The defendant, having accepted the jurisdiction of the court, stated that he was not a member of the Party, that he had never been "before the court," and that in the war he had been awarded "two orders and two medals." He testified as follows: "As to the charge against me, I do not quite agree. I am a driver of the first class—I've been a driver for six years. I never had any charges against me in all that time before this accident. Before the accident I had been all night at a wedding party. After the party I was driving out into the country when a policeman stopped me for just a little mistake. Because of the smell of vodka he took my license and papers away from me. But I was not drunk, I know. I was just sleepy because I had been up all night."

Ivan continued: "Then in the afternoon I met my friend Danilkin—who is here to be my witness—and we had a few more drinks. After that, while driving home, I fell asleep. I had not had any sleep the previous night because of the wedding—and then I ran into the building . . ." Grechnikoff, throughout, was most earnest. The court received all his answers deadpan. Nobody smiled once.

The defendant concluded: "I was not drunk, definitely; I was mostly tired."

The judge opened up: "Do you agree you were drunk according to paragraph such-and-such of the charge?"

A. "I don't know of any such paragraph."

Q. "How do you explain the smell of vodka?"

A. "I had had nothing to eat, that's why I smelled so strongly of vodka. I might have been just a little drunk."

Q. "If you weren't drunk, then you wouldn't have had the accident?"

A. "I had a sleepless night."

Jurywoman: "Do you agree that 965 rubles ($241.25) was the amount of the injury?"

A. "Yes, I agreed to that, and I paid for it." He handed up a document which was swiftly perused, first by the judge and then by both jurywomen.

Jurywoman: "Were you drunk after you met your friend or after the wedding? Why were you so easily ready to drink while you were driving?"

A. "I was angry with the policeman. I took the second drinks with my friend because I was angry with the policeman who took away my documents."

Second Jurywoman: "How did the first policeman learn you were drunk? Were you driving badly?"

The witness, bumbling as ever: "There was a special place in the country where policemen were inspecting after a picnic to control what drivers were drunk." (Some picnic!)

Second Jurywoman: "Why didn't you go to the garage? Why didn't you get something to eat?"

Defendant, lamely: "I was mad at the policeman."

Then Danilkin, the defendant's witness, took the stand—that is, he stood up before the court. He was about thirty also, a tall slender man with dark curly hair.

The judge asked the witness to give his name and address and state what he knew about the case.

Danilkin began: "I met Grechnikoff the afternoon of the accident, and he suggested to me that we go to a pub (so translated to me) and have a few drinks. I remember entering the pub, and then I don't remember anything more. But I do recall getting into the car—and then I fell asleep."

Q. "Who drove?"

A. "The defendant."

Judge: "But he was asleep."

Witness: "I don't know . . . during the accident and for a long time after that I couldn't realize what had happened . . . for a long time."

Judge: "What do you think about asking a driver to drink with you, and do you know what results happen?"

Witness: "Yes, I know about the injury to the car."

Judge: "How long were you having a few drinks together?"

A. "Four hours."

At this point the judge turned to Ivan, the defendant, and asked him if he had any questions of his witness. Ivan for once was swift and clear. "No questions whatsoever," came the ready response.

Judge: "Do you have any additional statement to make?"

Defendant: "I was not drunk; I was just sleepy. . . ." Here he began to repeat all that he had said before, but the judge cut him off impatiently.

The judge read aloud a written statement from the factory for which Grechnikoff drove. This said that Grechnikoff had "always represented the factory well," that the factory "never had any complaints against him nor were there ever any charges of bad driving."

The judge requested the defendant to make a final plea. He arose and addressed the court: "First, I hope this is my first and I hope my last default. I hope you will make it easy because I am young. I hope this is my last mistake."

Thereupon the judge and jurors filed out to debate his fate. The pretty court inspector, who had once been a judge, leaned over to me and said that in her opinion it was a mistake of the first policeman ever to let Grechnikoff go on. If he was drunk,

Russian Justice

the policeman should have held him. If that had happened, there would have been no accident. She smiled tolerantly and said, "I think they will be easy on him. He is so young." I asked her what record they had of the arrest, and she told me that the cop had sent in the arresting papers, that Russian courts did not require the arresting policeman to appear.

Finally the court reappeared after about a half hour. All spectators and participants stood when judge and jury entered and while the judge, standing, read the verdict. The decision was lengthy, for the judge recited all the charges and summarized the evidence at length (this document apparently was the chief evidence in any appeal), and then the court found Ivan guilty and sentenced him to one year in jail. We all quivered a bit, but the judge continued that the sentence was suspended, conditional on two years of good behavior by the defendant. This was interpreted to me to mean that if he had a comparable traffic accident, the original penalty would go into effect plus any additional punishment.

THE CASE OF THE ERRANT COLONEL

The only divorce case I saw was one brought by an Army colonel in the Sverdlov District Court, seventh section, before Judge Micronov and jurors Chernova (a cashier) and Switzer (a metallurgical engineer). A divorce suit is now a special action. The person seeking a divorce has to advertise his intentions, then go through a lower court, where an effort at reconciliation is made, and then on to a higher court before a decree is granted. This was the lower court of the two-court process. The colonel was rather tall for a Russian, just beginning to go gray and bald, about forty years of age, wearing what appeared to be a brand-new uniform. His wife, about the same age, was rather well dressed. She was on the plump and short side, like so many Russian women, and very ruddy. To me they looked like a couple of stubborn characters; I had the feeling I would not want to be on the opposite side in a domestic argument with either one of them.

The colonel was connected with the Military Engineering Academy in Moscow. The wife was "an engineer" at the Moscow Economic Institute.

The colonel rose to testify first. He said, "We were married in 1939, but we grew apart during the war and because of my work, which takes me away a great deal. I admit that I have many faults, and therefore my wife has stopped trusting me. But my wife has a bad temper and she has been very hard on my daughter by my first marriage. Her mother is dead." He finished, "We have not lived together for two years."

Q. "When did you part?"
A. "September, 1951. Now we live in different cities."
Q. "Have you any children?"
A. "Yes, a son twelve."
Q. "Where is the child?"
A. "With my wife. My wife has no claim for any payment. She has made no claim for any payment."
Q. "What is the reason you have decided to divorce her?"
A. "Because there was an absence of trust—and I fell in love with another woman."
Q. "Is this the first time you have separated?"
A. "No, this is the second time."

The judge then asked the jurors if they had any questions, but none were forthcoming.

The judge addressed the wife, who remained seated. "Do you have any questions?"

A. "No."

The husband sat down and the wife stood up to testify, beginning by stating her name, address, and occupation. Her face flushed, and she spoke in a tremulous voice, now deliberately, now in a gush of words, intermittently dabbing her eyes with a handkerchief.

"Before and during our marriage my husband was very fond of women. He had many women in his life, and in 1943 we parted. In a year he came back." She began to weep. "He said, 'Now I return to you.' And I agreed only because of our son.

Russian Justice 45

It was my duty to educate my son, and because I realized the years of war may have caused my husband's faults, and because he broke with that woman, we became man and wife again until 1950, and we lived well together. My son was my main aim in life.

"Then he left suddenly." And she wiped the tears away with the back of her hand in a broad gesture. " 'How can you leave?' I said. 'You have a son.' I tried to keep my family together, but I failed. In a month he left. One morning he refused breakfast, and he left that same morning. . . . In ten days he came back, and he asked my pardon, and again we lived some time together. Then this woman where he works began to make all possible trouble for me. Three times in 1951 he left."

She raised her hand again to brush away the tears, and I noticed that her nails were painted a deep dark red.

"We spent the summer in the south, and we were all very happy. All was good. And I believed that he loved me again. When we returned to Moscow, however, I learned that that woman had followed him to the south, and had been there, too. The year 1951 was horrible for me. Several times he left, and several times he returned. He is a good man, fond of his son. As a Soviet citizen, as a member of the Communist Party, he must first of all be a good father, and I am quite sure he will in time realize his faults. I am sure it is too early to break."

As she concluded she turned away from the court, directing her words passionately, urgently, to her husband, who sat impassively.

Again the colonel rose to testify: "All she said is quite true. But she doesn't take into consideration other details. Since August, 1951, I left my family forever. First, she is right that it is my fault."

Judge: "Do you insist on breaking your ties?"
A. "Yes."
Judge: "Why?"
A. "From our experience. It is necessary."
Judge: "What about the son?"

A. "I want to educate him. I live in Moscow. But my wife won't let me see him."

Juryman: "In 1943 you had some reason for returning. Maybe you will return again."

Judge: "So you say you have separated for two years because there is no trust?"

Wife: "I don't understand what he means by 'no trust.' If it's trust of me, I was faithful to him always. If it's trust of him, I trust him in everything. Before me he had other wives, and with each he did not live for more than five years. He lived longer with me than any other wife." She turned in her pleading to the judge, to each of the jurors, to her husband, and raised her voice as though to plead with the onlookers, to enlist their support as well.

She continued, "He had two former wives with children. He's not such a young man now. It's time he understood he is a father. He has a son twelve. A son of that age needs a good father. It is necessary to have a father."

On these words she sat down alongside her husband, and the court adjourned. The wife, talking low, continued to plead with her husband, who, as throughout the case, stared rigidly in front of him. He did not pull away, but just sat there, unyielding.

The court was out only a short time, and the decision was brief. "The court considers the case finished here. The colonel may now address the City Court of Moscow." I expected the wife to become hysterical, judging from her earlier actions, but now she too was impassive, and she and the colonel walked out silently, side by side.

MRS. SMIRNOVA GETS HER JOB BACK

The third case I watched was in a very small, dark courtroom, with two little windows in the rear and one small three-bulb chandelier in the center of the room. To add to the gloom, the walls were painted a dark green. The inevitable picture of Stalin hung over the judge's head. There were seats for only twenty spectators, which was more than enough, for there were only five or six observers at most.

Almost every foreigner who has written of a trip to Moscow has described the heavy-set peasant-type women, often of middle age, who do all sorts of very arduous manual labor—lifting cobblestones, sweeping the snow on the coldest nights, chipping away at ice on the pavements, their gloveless hands raw from the cold. There is always speculation as to how they live, where they come from. Mrs. Smirnova, the plaintiff, was one of these women, and she was suing the Road Supervision Section of the Moscow Soviet to get her original job back. In her case the judge was on vacation, and she appeared before three lay jurors: a man of about forty-five who was an architect; a girl of thirty who was a store clerk; and a woman of forty who was an engineer. The only member of the Communist Party was the young clerk; apparently this is why she was acting as the judge instead of her older associates. Also present in this case was a pompous official, called the procurator, all dressed up in a shiny brown uniform with brass buttons and green piping on his sleeves. The Moscow Soviet was represented by a young executive, a man in his thirties.

The plaintiff, Mrs. Smirnova, probably had on her best clothes for the occasion. She had on a pretty good black cloth coat with embroidered decorations and a small caracul collar, and she wore a white shawl of fine wool. She wore black horn-rimmed spectacles, a rarity in Moscow according to the satirical magazines, which were riding the Health Ministry because of the shortage. Mrs. Smirnova testified that she was a street painter who had the job of painting white broken lines across the streets of Moscow, that she had been earning about 650 rubles ($162.50) a month (I estimated the average wage rate for the entire country to be about 750), that she had been fired by the Road Supervision Section, and the local Dispute Committee of her enterprise had refused to restore her. (Such a Dispute Committee, they told me, is composed half of trade-union members and half of employers' representatives.) She said that she then took her case to the Regional Trade Union Committee and that the Trade Union had overruled the Dispute Committee and empowered her to present her case in court.

Judge: "What are you seeking?"

A. "I have two years to go on this job and I will be entitled to a pension. I am fifty-three now. I want the same job I had before until I earn my pension."

Mrs. Smirnova went on: "I was quite suddenly removed from street painting on the pretense that I spoiled part of the work. I was so disturbed and upset by this that I became ill and I went to a clinic, and while I was absent, I was fired. I had been removed only from that particular work; but then later I was fired. I was fired when I was absent. I have been in the same job since 1934. All I ask is that I be restored to my original job and that I receive my pay for time lost. I want payment for the time since I was expelled. I do not want to have to go and live with my daughter. My daughter has her own family. My husband was killed in the war. All I want now is my own job. I do not want to live with my daughter. I want my own job for two years so that I will earn my pension and can live on that."

Judge: "Do your glasses prevent you from painting the street crossings?"

A. "No."

Judge: "What about the job as a night guard near the store? You were offered that job."

A. "I'm afraid to be a night watchman. I prefer to work with the group that I have been working with in the past and paint streets."

Judge: "How old are you?"

A. "Fifty-three."

Judge: "When did your husband die?"

A. "He was killed at the front." (Anybody I ever heard mention the war always referred to it as "at the front.")

Judge: "Do you live in the building of your enterprise?"

A. "No, I live in a room which belongs to the Moscow City Soviet, but it is not connected with my job."

Judge: "Have you any reprimands or punishments for your work on your record?"
A. "No."
Here the procurator intervened. "You were offered another job before you were fired?"
A. "Yes. Washing the floor of the office. I refused it."
Procurator: "Maybe you are too old for this work that you have been doing?"
A. "No, I have friends doing this work who are older."
Procurator: "But this work is hard to do, and you feel badly when you are working?"
A. "No."
Procurator: "When you were expelled, did you have a discussion with the Administration or trade union?"
A. "No."
Juryman: "What was the reason you were fired?"
A. "I am not so quick as some of the young people."
Procurator: "Have you received your labor book and your expulsion money?"
A. "No."

The defendant's man then rose and spoke. He was wearing a brown overcoat and the only white silk scarf I had ever seen in Moscow. Everybody dresses up when they appear in court, as in other lands. He said, "She has high blood pressure. She could fall on the street and endanger traffic. It is the conclusion of the clinic that it is impossible to use this woman on the streets. She cannot work there. She can only work on . . ."

He was apparently reading excerpts from the clinic's report, but the judge interrupted him and asked to see the entire document. The judge read aloud, "Mrs. Smirnova cannot work on roads according to the state of her health. She can be used only as a worker, not on her feet and not at night."

The Street Section representative took up his rebuttal: "I offered her a job to clean the room and to wash the floors or to be a guard near the storeroom. For a month we paid her without her doing any work, but then, according to an order from the chief, we offered her the same jobs again, and again she refused them. I therefore ordered her fired, with two weeks' notice. This is why we don't agree with her. According to our rules for the protection of labor, we cannot restore her to the same type of work."

At this point the architect-juryman bore down hard on the Government representative. "Why did your office ask the clinic to say she had high blood pressure? She made no claim of having high blood pressure. You decided she was ill, and only then did you add the conclusion of the clinic. She didn't claim she was ill."

The defendant retorted: "You have the medical conclusion. You have it. It doesn't matter who requested it." He was standing there calmly, his arms folded, rather sure of himself.

The architect went back to the attack. "So you think she worked for twenty years and became ill, so now 'good-by'?"

A. "You don't know the technique of our work." The defendant then told how lines were painted, by machine on the broadest streets in the center of the city, but by hand on narrower streets. He concluded, "Do you understand?"

The architect charged back: "I am not satisfied with your explanation. Have you any information that she felt badly during working hours?"

A. "Yes, I had signals from her associates."

Procurator: "Your order says she was expelled because of her bad health. Did you get permission from the Trade Union Committee to expel her?"

Defendant: "The chairman of the Trade Union Committee said that as we had the sanction of the medical commission, we did not need the permission from the trade union to fire her."

Procurator: "If she changed jobs, she got 360 rubles ($90) a month and not 650 ($162.50), correct?"

A. "Yes."

Judge to Mrs. Smirnova: "Do you have any questions to ask the representatives of the office?"

A. "No."

Judge: "Do you have any additional statement to make?"

A. "My comrades who work with me say they need a woman to sweep ahead of the person with the paint, and this is easier work and the same pay. I would like to get that job. I have always fulfilled my quota, and they say I did not do my work. The younger workers make trouble on the job and they spoiled some of the markings. I didn't want to say anything about it; I didn't want to harm them. Ask my comrades. They will tell you that I do my work adequately and well enough." She concluded, "I have only a little pension, from my husband's death, just 49 rubles ($12.25) a month."

The procurator, who was very conscious of the visitors in the courtroom, now rose for his summation; he took off his glasses and held them in his hand, gesturing with them like lawyers the world over: "Article Two of the Code of Civil Procedures states that the procurator has the right to interrupt at any time. Under another special paragraph the procurator must make conclusions on cases involving labor, injuries on jobs, and in the taking away of living space and the expulsion of people from work. She is fifty-three. She has worked without a break in this office since 1934. She even got some presents from the management for good work. She needs two more years' work to earn her pension." He held up a paper which he read from: "She was expelled in September, 1953. According to her, she had no notice of the expulsion. She considered herself healthy enough for this work. The administrative order expelled her because of bad health. After the Dispute Committee approved the discharge, she addressed the Regional Trade Union Committee, which overruled the Dispute Committee's decision and permitted her to address this court."

Said he: "It is my conclusion that she was not expelled from her job in the correct way." He held up a law book. "According to our laws, a man can be expelled from his job for some reasons, including bad health. But before suspension for bad health, the administration must ask for the agreement of the worker. Only with the official agreement of the Trade Union Committee and of the office in question, and only with the agreement of the worker can this be done. They have no agreement from the Trade Union Committee of her office and none from her. They should have given her a test time, say two weeks' controlled time, to see if she could fulfill her job. So, according to our laws, without permission of the committee, it is impossible to expel a worker. She can go to court and be restored with pay for time lost, but not more than twenty days." He put on his spectacles and buttoned the brass buttons on his coat.

The court adjourned. In about a half hour it returned, read a long summary of the case, duplicating the procurator's remarks, and, following his suggestions, awarded her the job and twenty days' back pay, with the defendant taxed 15 rubles' ($3.75) cost.

CHAPTER 5

A Case of Socialized Medicine

About a month later I visited a court in Baku in the Republic of Azerbaijan and walked into a courtroom whose furnishings were identical with those I had seen in Moscow, only the room was larger and more pleasant. Here the judge, Iskanderov, was a young man of twenty-six who had originally worked in a chemical factory and had, as I recall, studied law at night. The two jurors were women. One was a distinguished Armenian lady, an opera singer named Dorfman. The other, Abdulaeva, was an engineer, and she looked very Persian. In another age one could imagine each of them as harem beauties, definitely Oriental in style. Here they were, stern distributors of justice, and rather acute, too. This court had one additional innovation. All statements were translated through an interpreter into Azerbaijani, the language of the republic, though in one case all parties involved, including those on the bench, understood Russian.

Here a young doctor of about twenty-three years of age was complaining against the Baku Civil Aviation Department, which was represented in court by an official not much older than the plaintiff. The doctor was suing to be re-transferred to his original job, and he had brought along a lawyer to speak for him. This was the only case in which I was to see an attorney appear.

When the doctor arose to testify, he was asked to sign a statement that he trusted his own lawyer! This was one of the few items I ever saw directed to be put into whatever record there was. Then the doctor was notified of his right to challenge the court and jurors. The doctor said that he was employed in internal medicine by the Civil Aviation Department, where he had been for almost three years. He said, "I am a specialist in internal medicine, but recently I was transferred to the laboratory without my agreement. This changed my profession. I wrote to the Chief of Medical Service of Civil Aviation that I didn't agree. In the laboratory they need a doctor of hygiene. This is not my specialty. I graduated in internal medicine. I ask to be left on my job. If there is no possibility of getting my job back, I ask the court to cancel my labor contract with full expulsion money. (Russians told me that if you quit on your own, you get no termination pay; otherwise it amounts to two to four weeks' pay.) In my previous job, I had been working in the field in which I had studied. I am a therapy doctor and I aid people. I am accustomed to helping sick people in their homes. I refuse to work in the laboratory at all."

Judge: "What does each job pay?"

A. "Eight hundred rubles ($200) a month."

Question: "If the salary is the same, why didn't you go to the lab?"

A. "This is not my specialty. To work in the lab, a man should be educated in the hygiene or sanitary department of a college. I graduated in internal medicine and I want to stay in internal medicine. The management persists in transferring me to the lab."

Then the procurator rose and took him through the same ground: "Why did you refuse to transfer to the lab? It was a new lab and needed workers."

A. (Same as before.)

Procurator: "Who replaced you?"

A Case of Socialized Medicine

A. "A woman doctor was transferred from another department, and now we are both working in internal medicine."

Q. "Do you have your job still, and how do you get paid?"

A. "I get paid on the lab pay roll. But I am still working in internal medicine because I won't go to the lab. Now there are two of us there."

Q. "If your office cannot restore you to your job, do you agree to leave?"

A. "Yes."

Q. "In your three years, has there been any complaint filed against you by the administration?"

A. "No."

Q. "Does the person who replaced you have training in internal medicine?"

A. "I don't know. I think so. She was an eye doctor."

At this point the actress-jurist cut in and brought the cat out of the bag. Q. "Why were you transferred to the lab?"

A. "This woman is the wife of the chief of the airport, and they wanted to find a place for her."

Jurywoman: "Is she a recent graduate or an old doctor?"

A. "She's an old doctor."

Q. "How do you know she is the wife of the chief of the airport?"

A. "Everybody knows it."

Then the defendant asked a couple of questions of the doctor, apparently to imply he owed them some special loyalty. Q. "Didn't we give you a special trip to Moscow to improve your specialty during the war?"

A. "Yes."

Q. "And how long did you work in the famous Semashko Clinic?"

A. "I worked there evenings. I don't know how many hours."

The doctor's lawyer now barged in. "Is this lab attached to your clinic?"

A. "No, it's thirty kilometers away. My clinic is in the center of the city."

Lawyer: "What are the lab duties?"

A. "They are sanitary. They are concerned with food, with living conditions, with the examinations of pilots before flight. But there is no treatment of sick people. There are no sick people. I have never had anything in common with healthy people. I want to treat sick people. I am a doctor."

Now the defendant rose and said that the doctor had described the lab work incorrectly. He started to read the official job description, that doctors were "to study and analyze the diseases of the pilots, to control the health of the pilots during and before flight."

The judge cut in: "Why did you replace him?"

A. "He specialized in electrocardiography in the clinic and then he studied internal medicine for five years in Moscow. The staff of the lab requires an excellent specialist in internal medicine. That's why he was sent there, in the interests of the airport. He gets the same salary. He has only changed departments from the clinic to the lab, but the work is the same. We refuse to release him because he has not worked the full three years. He was in Moscow for five months of study. He violated the civil aviation instructions when he rejected the order of the chief. We sent him to Moscow to improve him. We had big expectations. We want to use him for this work. We consider the jobs to be the same, and we need a specialist in the lab."

Judge: "Who replaced him?"

A. "We did not bring anybody from outside to assist him. We put somebody in his place from our own system."

Judge: "So you put in someone from your own system. Why don't you put the woman doctor in the lab? She has a twenty-year record. The lab needs an expert."

A. "Internal medicine is important, and he specialized in it. She hasn't got such specialization in internal medicine."

Judge: "Why did you send him to Moscow?"

A. "The chief of the medical services recommended him for this study."

A Case of Socialized Medicine

Q. "Why wasn't she sent to Moscow to improve her specialty?"

A. "I don't know why he was sent and not her. He's a young specialist—he didn't refuse the request." (The judge spoke emphatically, gesturing with a pencil, pointing it at the defendant like a gun.)

Q. "If you represent your organization, you must know why he was sent."

A. "He was sent as a young specialist. He was given the rank of Captain in Civil Aviation. Such people can be released only by an order of the Chief of Civil Aviation. We cannot release him."

Judge: "If only Moscow can release him, how were you able to move him from the clinic to the lab?"

A. "The Chief of the Baku airport can transfer him, but does not have the power to release him."

Here the actress cut in with a question which was a major point in the decision. "Did you get his agreement?"

A. "No, it was the same work."

Judge: "Any claims against him since 1950?"

A. "No, except this case."

Q. "Couldn't the woman doctor work in the lab?"

A. "No, she doesn't have enough specialization. She cannot work there."

Judge: "He came to you from college?"

A. "Yes, from Moscow. This was his first job. His first job was in internal medicine, to aid people in their homes."

The procurator now intervened: "Are there any complaints against him by patients?"

A. "No."

Q. "Will there be a change in his work?"

A. "No. He has the same patients. It's only a change of office."

Q. "The woman is an eye doctor. In your opinion, can she work in internal medicine?"

A. "Yes, because she once practiced that at another airport. But she hasn't specialized, and we need a specialist in the lab."

Procurator: "It was a mistake to replace a therapist with an eye doctor, and a sanitary doctor with a therapy doctor."

Defendant: "She worked in internal medicine also, at the Schroth airport."

The doctor cut in. (Anybody seemed to speak at any time.) "All I know is she is an eye specialist. But I don't know where she worked."

Procurator: "Is it correct that he was replaced without his agreement and that she is the wife of the chief of the airport?"

A. "I don't know who she is. I don't know about her. We have thousands of people. I don't know whose wife she is."

Judge: "If you represent your office, you must know whose wife she is."

A. "I don't know."

Then the doctor's attorney started to earn his fee. "Can the defendant show instructions that the lab doctor must treat (and he emphasized these words)—*treat sick people?*" The defendant started to talk about the analysis of diseases. "But," said the attorney, "what about *treatment?* You're talking all about analysis, not treatment."

The defendant started to read some more excerpts from the job description, and the attorney turned to the court and said, "I demand that the defendant not read parts of the job description, but all of it, including the hygienic aspects." The judge himself then read the full job description aloud, and the attorney immediately chimed in: "All this applies to the lab, but not to my client, who was sent to Moscow to study internal medicine." (Throughout the lawyer was sitting while the witnesses stood.)

Doctor's attorney: "You said the jobs are the same. I will now compare . . ." For the first time in any court, I saw a judge enforce some rules of evidence. Perhaps because this was the first time an attorney was there.

Said the judge: "Don't speak to him. You can ask questions."

The lawyer, like lawyers of other lands, slipped in something

A Case of Socialized Medicine

anyway. Said he: "In his job, the doctor treated sick people. In his new job, would he treat sick people or healthy people?" The judge cut this question off. (Later in chambers he told me he did so because this had already been brought out in the evidence. He added that the judge had power to cut off any question he chose.)

Then the doctor's lawyer made his summary, emphasizing that the job instructions did not call for a doctor who treated sick people, that this was therefore a change of specialization, and that by law such a change without consent of the doctor was unlawful. He asked that the doctor either be released or given his job back with compensation. He also got in some praise of his client, asserting that he had been sent to Moscow to study because he was so good.

Cheramov, the procurator, followed with his summary that their law courts could correct mistakes made by managers of enterprises. "According to all of our laws, it is necessary for a person to give his consent if his type of work is changed or if we transfer him from his place of work. It is quite impossible to do this without his consent. The main task of our country is to encourage young specialists. The airport sent him to do what he doesn't like and which cannot help him develop as a good doctor. The procurator is against his release, which was his second request. He was sent here by the Government and he was given a good job. The office should give him back the same job." (My interpreters informed me that student specialists during the three years' paid compulsory service after graduation could not have job or salary or type of work or place of work changed without their consent.)

The court's decision was that the doctor should be restored to his job. Afterwards I was introduced in chambers to the judge and jurors. I said, "I would guess the wife of the chief of the airport was the key to this case," and they all laughed, but said nothing.

TEACHER LICKS THE BUREAUCRACY

In another case in Baku a woman zoology teacher named Kambarian sued the Lenin Teacher's College for 1,060 rubles ($265), which she claimed were owing to her for extra hours of teaching. The government institution was represented by the assistant director of the college. In the testimony it was admitted that she had taught the extra hours. The college lamely contended that she did not have the appropriate signed authorization from the director of the college, and insisted therefore that her own "chair" should pay her. I think the college representative meant that the funds should come out of her dean's budget instead of the college budget. It was obviously a technicality, and judge, jurors, and procurator beat him heavily about the ears. The teacher had filled out hourly slips which were each certified by her dean. She, too, apparently worked "by plan," and when the court asked her if she "fulfilled her basic hours," she replied, "The basic is eight hundred and forty hours—I did about eight hundred and sixty."

At one point, when the assistant director started to criticize her teaching ability, the judge quickly cut him off: "That's not pertinent. What we're after is why did you not pay her for the hours worked?"

The problem of the college also was revealed when the defendant testified, "The Ministry of Culture of the Soviet Union allows not more than five hundred additional hours to the college per year." Finally the court awarded her the full amount, 1,060 rubles for 106 hours, and assessed the cost to the college at 21 rubles ($5.25) or 2 per cent.

CASE OF A SLIP ON THE STAIRS

I glimpsed part of one other case in Moscow where a woman doctor, newly working for a factory, had rushed to the home of a patient suffering from a heart attack. When she started home, she tripped through a hole in the stairs, fell, and broke her leg. She was suing everybody in sight: her employer, the factory;

A Case of Socialized Medicine

the City Department of Space Control; and the manager of the building. She sought salary lost while ill, and cost of a month in a sanitarium plus the cost of transport to and from the sanitarium. But she did not seek the additional heavy damages for permanent injury and mental suffering often sought in our courts. The doctor testified that she had no social insurance because she had just transferred to a new job, revealing that all Government protection is not perfect in the Soviet Union.

The factory's representative made an ingeniously naïve argument and gave some illuminating information on what happens in Soviet courts. Said he, "I know in the majority of cases the decisions are in favor of the injured man, but in this case it was the doctor's fault. She went up the stairs and saw the plank and forgot about it on the way down. It was not the fault of the factory. It was not good, I admit, but she didn't notice it and therefore it is her fault. It's like a case of walking on even space where somebody falls and breaks her leg—it's her own fault."

CHAPTER 6

It Pays to Advertise

I DO NOT recall seeing much advertising in 1946. All over the country the chief decorations had been political slogans in white letters on red banners and portraits and photos of its political leaders which were seen everywhere, on buildings, in theater lobbies, at railroad stations, in hospitals and classrooms, wherever you turned, and always, of course, at parades. Lenin and Stalin, particularly Stalin, predominated, but there were many, too, of the dozen or so members of the Politburo, later called Presidium. Just after the war, pictures of a number of marshals of the Army could be seen on occasion, but these were much less numerous and much less conspicuous. The bearded portraits of Marx and Engels were seen rarely, and then usually along with Lenin and Stalin. About the only public display of pictures of individuals was of honored theatrical "artists," shown in the theater arcades, of crack workers (Stakhanovites) displayed on "honor-roll" boards in factories and farm clubs, and art-gallery portraits of painters, ballerinas, and conductors. (One Leningrad conductor seemed Stokowski's twin.)

On my return to the U.S.S.R. I was again to see similar innumerable slogans and portraits of its political leaders, without increased emphasis on current-day rulers, except that now and then Malenkov's portrait would appear a little more often than his fellows'. And there was one newcomer—Mao Tse-tung. The public display of military leaders had practically disappeared. I saw only a little bust of Marshal Budyenny at a tank-town airport in the East and wall portraits of several marshals of the Red Army in a Palace of Culture and Rest of a southern city. (Russians love the words "palace" and "culture." What we would call a Y.M.C.A. becomes a "Young Pioneers' Palace," and a plain park is a "Park of Culture and Rest." One "Palace of Culture" I visited included billiard tables and a gymnasium. Apparently anything which is nonpolitical and noncommercial is "cultural." And the word "noncultural" is a real insult. A Westerner directed this adjective at the manager of my hotel; hours later when she saw me to complain about the remark, she burst into tears.)

On this trip to Russia, however, among the first things that caught my eye upon my return to Moscow were the colored neon signs and advertisements on many buildings once one left the center squares of the city, where there were no signs at all. Now there are a good many such signs in the rest of the city, but the number is still less than a twentieth of New York's or London's. One night in Moscow I went around copying down some of these ads. On the front of the Moscow newspaper *Izvestia's* main building is an electric sign with moving words like the news sign on the Times Building in New York. The text was quite different. It ran: "Mineral Water—Moscow Mineral Water is hygienic. It is used also for sick stomachs and liver ills—drink Moscow Mineral Water. . . . Repair your watches in the shops labeled True Time, quality guaranteed. (Later I read a Trade Ministry booklet which said: "Wind your watch in the morning, not in the evening, because then its springs are better able to survive the jolts of the day.") . . . Wine produced from grapes and berries. Buy fruit-berry wine. . . . Drink champagne, produced sweet, half sweet, half dry, and dry. Drink the best grape wines. Drink Soviet Champagne. . . . Prepare cold dishes from gelatin produced by the Moscow

Gelatin Plant. Gelatin is on sale in all food stores. . . . Natural tea has very good aroma and good taste. Buy natural tea in the farm shops and food stores. . . . Beer is a good and healthful drink. Beer helps to raise the appetite. Drink beer of the Moscow Glovino Plants. . . . Buy always fresh products in the special fish stores. . . . Buy fruit jelly from our Moscow Jelly Plant on sale in all food stores. . . ."

The main neon signs to catch one's eye, a few blocks from the Kremlin on one of Moscow's great squares, is a sign about fifty feet by twelve feet, which has neon autos, seemingly moving, as they flash on and off alternately in green, the word "taxi," in red, "most convenient traffic," and in blue, "call for taxi by telephone, numbers (listing five of them)."

Another large sign with a red border and blue script says, "Smoke," and then in red letters: "Astra, Pamir, Ducat, Prima." It's as though the mayor of New York City put up on Fifth Avenue: "Smoke Chesterfield, Lucky Strike, Old Gold, Phillip Morris, Camel."

Others announced: "Don't forget to insure your home and furniture in the State — . . . Wines and liquors of Georgia. . . . Drink natural coffee. . . . Drink tomato juice. . . . You can win 100,000 rubles in a 3 per cent loan. . . . Buy ice cream. . . . Buy Moscow sausages. . . . Keep your money in — . . . State insurance of furniture and of life. . . ."

Those were on the sides of buildings, on roof tops, and in similar places. In addition, many stores had signs announcing their products in one neon color. They read simply: "Meat. . . . Radio and Music. . . . Mosclothes. . . . Books. . . . Cakes and Breads. . . . Consumption Goods. . . . Restaurant. . . . Foodstuffs. . . . Cans. . . . Barbershop. . . . Café—Ice Cream. . . . Theater Tickets. . . . Milk. . . . Fruits. . . . Wines. . . . Shoes. . . . Women's Shoes. . . . Industrial Goods." About the only variations were in the colors of the borders and of the words, the use of script and print, and the shape.

Soviet newspaper advertising, which has greatly increased

It Pays to Advertise

lately, is hardly any more inspired, though it does give some insight into the Russian way of life. One paper in Moscow, *Evening Moscow*, carries the bulk of the city's ads, which occupy almost all seven columns of its fourth and last page. Here are sample contents:

About half the first column listed what was going on at twenty-seven different theaters—operas, operettas, serious plays, and a musical satire. Among the foreign authors' works were Dickens' *Dombey and Son* and a play by Lessing. Another theater was giving Chekhov's *Uncle Vanya,* and the Gorki Theater announced *Anna Karenina* for one day and immediately following that an opus bearing the title, *The Guardian Angel from Nebraska*. Among the theaters listed were: Musical Theater of Stanislavsky, Theater of the Lenin Young Communists, Central Theater of the Soviet Army, Central Theater of the Railroad Workers, Theater of Satire, and the Moscow Gypsy Theater. A concert hall announced a musical program including Tchaikovsky and Rachmaninov, and the circus had a small ad. Each of these was only a line or two.

Next to them was a section TODAY IN THE MOVING-PICTURE THEATERS, two columns wide, four inches deep. This listed two films, *No Peace under the Olives* (an Italian film) and *Servant of Two Masters,* each playing at twenty-one houses. About twenty-three other films were listed, most of them showing at one house. The names of the theaters did not seem inspired—Sunbeam, Aurora, Peace, Change of Guards, Hermitage, Salut, Dynamo, Storm, and Barricade. A few were functional: Theater of Young Onlookers, Science and Knowledge, News of the Day, and Chronicle.

Scattered about the page were fourteen divorce ads. (I have seen thirty-six in one day.) The person bringing the action (half were brought by women) states his name and address and the name and address of the defendant and where and when the court action will take place.

In the upper right columns were twenty-four little ads announcing graduate students' "Defense of Dissertations." One read: "Philosophical Faculty of the Moscow Order of Lenin Governmental University named after M. V. Lomonosov, Moscovaya No. 11, house No. 5 on December 26, 1953 at 3 P.M. in auditorium No. 55, seeking the scientific degree of Candidate of the Pedagogical Sciences, Karpova, S. N., on the theme, 'The Development of the Consciousness of Words in the Preschool-age Child.' "

Some of the theses resemble Ph. D. theses the world over: "Ground Taxation Policy of English Colonizers in Bengal in the Middle and Second Part of the Eighteenth Century"; "The Grasping Policy of the American Imperialists in Turkey during and after the First World War, 1914–1920"; "Dysentery in Groups of Very Small Children"; "Genetical Differences in the Tissues of Potatoes"; "The Adverb in Contemporary Uzbek Language"; "Verbal Forms in Moscow Business Letters of the Fifteenth Century"; "The Rise of the Workers' Movement in England from 1911 on"; "The Development of Czech Musical Classics"; "Scandinavian Adaptation of Words from the English Language"; "Functions of Predicate Constructions in Old Russian Literary Languages"; "Influence of Egg-white Nourishment on the Secretions of the Stomach."

These ads indicate the normal way to obtain a doctorate. Here, too, all is not perfect in the U.S.S.R. I saw a drawing entitled "After the Formal Dinner." Two older men are going out the door. Seated at a table covered with the remnants of an elaborate meal, including several empty wine bottles, are two younger men. Says one, "Well, comrade, you can say that I defended my thesis."

The other replies, "But how is that? You haven't even finished work on it."

And the first answers, "But I worked on the examiners!"

Help-wanted ads appear occasionally, such as: "Editorial office requests a Chief of a Planning Section; call number . . ." "Moscow Film Studio requires electricians, chemical laborers, plasterers, stonemasons, coal shovelers, call —." "Moscow Experimental Factory of Musical Instruments seeks engineers-

It Pays to Advertise

constructors, wood experts, and a radio technician." "The Moscow Shipbuilding and Technical Organization wants a teacher in mathematics." "Wanted by an organization:—chauffeurs for light cars and typists, call —." "Moscow *Izvestia* seeks a Manager for the Planning Section."

Among the people sought in various ads during one week in December were: chief mechanics; electrical *monteurs* (for temporary and evening work); laboratory experts on ventilation; technician-calculators for experimental mechanical shop; construction superintendents (a place to live offered for them); wall painters; builders of stoves and heaters; chemical laboratory workers with knowledge of colors; secretary-typists; bricklayers; forestry specialists; and chief accountants. And one foodstuff trade office wanted a slew of workers—"seeks people for permanent work, workers for handling, loading and unloading, service workers, cleaners in shops, drivers, sellers of meat, grocery, and vegetable goods. Payment according to piece rate."

In the few papers translated to me, I did not find any ads by persons seeking positions. Occasionally competitions for skilled jobs and opportunities for advanced study would be announced. "The Lenin Military Academy of Tanks and Mechanical Arms of the Soviet Union announces a competition for positions as teachers of geometry, graphics, details of mechanics, and mechanical technology of metals and machines. Docents and candidates of technical sciences can take part. Last day of competition, December 24."

"The Institute of Internal and Foreign Trade announces opening of eight-month courses for chief bookkeeper. Eight persons will be admitted to these courses who have had higher education or who have finished middle school and have had at least five years' bookkeeping experience in a production organization. Students are assured of a scholarship in the amount of the remuneration which they had on their previous work."

They even carry out this approach with respect to what we might call athletic coaches. "The Stalin Institute of Physical

Culture announces a competition for the position of Director of the Chair of Swimming. Put on the application the following documents in two copies: autobiography, copy of certificate of higher education, copy of diploma of higher education, copy of diploma and attestation of defense of scientific degree as doctor—must be certified—references from last place of work, list of scientific works and inventions."

In these ads I did notice that living space often would be offered and that they had "dormitory space available for bachelors." The space problem was apparent in many ads. Firms sought office space frequently and always said they were willing to remodel and make major redecorations at their cost. One company asked garage space for an auto. The puppet theater sought storage space for theatrical supplies, and a theater group wanted rooms for its "artists."

A number of concerns advertised their products or the service jobs they could perform, and some were looking for materials (I remember in Stalingrad on the Volga an ad which read: "Co-operative steel docker takes all kinds of loading and unloading work from the population."): "Consumption cooperative will buy iron, steel, and nonferrous metals, bones, rags, old paper. Gather and sell to village consumption co-operatives and district offices, metal scrap and utility refuse. There are millions of tons of iron and steel for the production of tractors, cars, agricultural machines and consumption goods." A fur plant offered to tailor and restore furs for coats and collars, etc., "material to be supplied by the orderer." An institute announced it would do blueprinting. An artificial-leg plant proclaimed it took orders for complicated and simple special shoes, and sold women's medical bandages.

The manufacturing division of the Central Art Store was all ready to make statues, fountains, garden jars, and memorial plaques and said it had some of the best masters of art for this work. Bookbinders had masters who would bind anything, by contract or single job. Bookstores announced some new books hot from the printer. A knitting factory advertised that it

It Pays to Advertise

accepted cotton and woolen goods for dyeing, and in the same ad said it needed a chief mechanic. Another factory offered to repair felt boots and assured the reader it had very good material and thread. Moscow Plant for Iron and Concrete Goods No. 5 said it sold concrete twenty-four hours a day. The Co-operative for Invalids of the Great Patriotic War declared it made appointments for the repair of typewriting and calculating machines and sought contracts or individual jobs. Somebody unidentified except for a telephone number wanted grand pianos and upright pianos, and a co-operative wanted some ribbed pipes. Almost all of these ads were about one to three inches high.

There were also a variety of feature ads as large as six or eight inches in height and two to four columns wide, occasionally illustrated. These were chiefly announcements by department stores or chain stores selling consumer goods, or institutional ads urging consumption of certain food and drink. A couple of these larger notices advertised the feature film of the city, one listing the names of the producer, four authors, the photographer, the composer, two sound operators, and the five lead players. (While I was there, the film featured this way was from Lux Film of Rome.) A big ad for men's and women's shoes listed forty-two stores and thirteen market stalls where a "very large choice" was available. Another ad listed a number of universal (department) stores, and said, "You must economize on time. Use the stores in your district." A five-inch by two-column ad inserted by the Ministry of Trade, showed a cartoon of a girl happily pouring a glass of beer, and announced: "Beer. Beer has a very pleasant taste and increases the appetite. Fresh beer is available in all beer halls, pavilions, and restaurants."

Another day a three-column by six-inch ad proclaimed Soviet Champagne. "Soviet Champagne is an excellent wine, the pride of the Soviet wines,—Soviet Champagne, the best decoration of the table." Under these words was a drawing of a bottle in an ice bucket, some cut glasses and fruit on a table, and a group of seemingly convivial people around the bubbly stuff. Beneath the drawing was some bureaucratic advice: "It is best to serve the Champagne cool."

One ad urged readers to drink "Natural Tea." Another showed Father Frost, the Russian Santa Claus, with a horn of plenty, out of which poured New Year's tree (Christmas tree) decorations and toys, and this ad said that a large illuminated tree was at the central store. The department stores listed, without illustrations, quite a variety: all kinds of clothing, wall clocks, ice skates, radio parts, musical instruments, gramophones, china, electric refrigerators, electric vacuum cleaners, electric calculating machines (though I never saw anything but abacuses in use), electric irons, lamps, crystal goods, and wall paper.

One even offered vacation facilities. "The All Union Resort Office of the Ministry of Health is selling resort tickets in the House of Rest 'Sunflower' situated in a very picturesque environment not far from Seneshsky Lake. Direct auto-bus connections from the White Russian Station. Railway connections from the Leningrad Station." The ad also instructed readers, as did many others, how to reach the advertiser's office by subway.

A few revealed customs or innovations different from our life. One announced the drawing of lottery tickets of the governmental "3 per cent loan." (The individual really gets no interest by right, but 3 per cent of all the "loans" is given away in huge lottery prizes to some lucky "lenders." Eventually lender-citizens may get their principal back. State-encouraged gambling.) A railroad advertised it would deliver railroad tickets to homes within the city limits if orders by postcard or telephone were made ten days in advance. A trolley-car company (in Stalingrad) advertised unlimited season tickets at 72 rubles ($18) a month for the general taxpayer and 18 rubles ($4.50) for students at regular schools and at factory schools. And the Dynamo Central Stadium said it would pay for unused tickets for certain games up to a specified date.

There was also a column announcing the nightly television

It Pays to Advertise

show, usually one event, sometimes two. For successive evenings it scheduled: "A performance from the Moscow Theater of Drama. . . . Concert of composer Dunaevsky from the Hall of Columns. . . . Transmission from the Tchaikovsky Concert Hall—an evening with the composer V. P. Sedoi. . . . New film *Marriage with Dowry* and concert by the Russian Folk Chorus. . . . Drama from Central Theater of Transport Workers entitled Armored Train No. 1469. . . . Transmission of Bulgarian ballet from the Musical Theater of Stanislavsky. . . . Opera *Boris Godunov* by Moussorgsky from Bolshoi Theater."

One day, right under the happy TV announcements for the day, was the only death notice I saw, a one-column statement about two inches deep with a black border around it, reading: "The Collective of the Workers of the Apparatus of the Presidium of the Supreme Soviet of the Russian Federated Republic of the U.S.S.R. sadly announces the death of its member since 1947, Alexei Myemilinov, which took place on December 14, and expresses its sympathy to the family of the deceased." Apparently less prominent citizens die without benefit of proclamation.

In other large cities newspaper advertising was similar, though in other ads there was some local chauvinism. Minsk plugged its own factories in several large signs. For instance, one on the top of its newest apartment house urged: "Buy candies and sweets of the Minsk factories."

Kiev had a few new ones: "Buy Fish Food in State Stores of the Ministry of Fish. . . . Buy Perfumes in the Perfume Shops —Scents of all kinds. (In a Soviet magazine I saw a drawing of a woman testing out perfumes. "I don't like this fragrance," said she. "Don't worry," replied the salesman, "it won't last long.") . . . Buy Kiev Glass." This sign was pretty fancy. The word "buy" was in dark red, the other words in blue, and then there was a picture in blue and red of twelve cut glasses and a thermos bottle. One other sign read "In case of fire, ring zero-one." A billboard with a picture of an auto which alternately flashed on and off warned: "People should take care while crossing the streets." Another sign, all in red, was: "Buy all kinds of margarine. It is very good for health and nutritious, made by Kiev Butter Plant. It is made of the best kinds of milk." And one uttered this stirring exhortation: "Buy cigarettes in our shops."

The city of Kharkov had another new one: "Health—Eat Vitamins Because They Are Useful."

A rash of advertisements had also sprung up in the countryside. On an automobile drive to Poltava in the Ukraine I saw a number of colored billboards, about six feet by six feet square, stationed on either side of the road at irregular intervals. These were not parallel like most of our billboards, but faced the driver like our traffic-warning signs. On each side of a billboard was a picture with a slogan. I jotted down as many of the slogans as I could. The first one said, "Keep signs along the road in good order," and the next one, "The task which was set to us by our native land will be fulfilled thoroughly." After that stern beginning, they became more diverting. A picture of a truck and child and the warning: "Take care of little children." One of boy and girl with the slogan: "To the new and big successes of our young people." And another: "Glory to those who won the great October Revolution." A factory worker proclaimed, "Let's salute glorious toil." Some soldiers and sailors announced, "We grew up under Stalin."

A picture of a truck on a highway warned: "If you don't change your lights at night, there may be a catastrophe." A young man carrying a banner declared: "Our way is the way forward to communism." A little farther on was the advice, "If you stop, drive your car to the side of the road," and almost parallel with the sign was a truck in trouble, standing smack in the middle of the highway. Then a sign: "50 kilometers to the next gasoline station." A peasant, "Let us increase the crop." A man with a banner with one word on it, "Peace." Stalin towering over a great dam affirmed, "We are reaching communism by the Lenin-Stalin Plan." Another read: "This road was built by the Road and Railway Department of the Ukrainian Republic." (A self-laudatory plug which kept cropping up every few miles. What I wondered was, Who else there could they imagine might have built it?) I was to see some more peace exhortations: a girl holding a paper in her hands saying, "We demand peace," a red banner with the inscription, "For Peace," and still another declaration, "If the people take the cause of peace in their hands, peace will be preserved and upheld."

Other themes were: "Glory to the Soviet mother. . . . Collective farmers, it depends on you to make our crop rich and our country wealthy. . . . For the wealth of the people. . . . To the brave, heroic sons of our land."

A number of the billboards were repeated quite frequently. On this trip I saw no signs promoting the sale of any products, but I have seen a few such ads on roads in other parts of the country, including one in Azerbaijan promoting "corn flakes." On one finely made road running up a mountain overlooking Tiflis, I came across three huge billboards advertising beer, defacing a lovely mountain view as much as any billboards of the capitalist world.

CHAPTER 7

The Road to Minsk

A LENGTHY journey on a Russian train is more like a picnic than any other traveling I know. Usually there is no diner, so you must prepare your food and bring it along, or forage for it as you go. Being pampered by Intourist, I would start out with a whole cold chicken, some caviar, a loaf of bread, a bottle of vodka, some hard-boiled eggs, pickles, and assorted cakes. The trains generally amble along at less than thirty miles an hour, so that you have time to look at the scenery. There are frequent stops at stations and in-between. And the stops are long. At almost every station half the passengers descend for a little stroll, especially in mild weather when it is sunny. It is not exceptional to see a man climb out of his berth and wander around the station platform in his pajamas, shopping for a bit to eat. At each station there is the same line of peasants hawking their surplus goods—a few eggs, some milk, a glass of sauerkraut, now and then some meat cakes or other delicacies, and occasionally a chicken or a duck. I have a photograph of a conductor purchasing a string of fish. People aren't in a hurry because they can't be. You just relax and enjoy it.

The trains are built on the European style, with each car having a series of compartments in a row. "Soft" cars are a little like our Pullman cars. "Hard" cars are harder—you sit and

The Road to Minsk

sleep on wood. On most soft cars each room has two upper and two lower berths. It is not unusual to have men and women who are strangers share the same compartment. In the daytime a soft compartment may hold six people, but four is customary. Restless passengers stand in the corridors hours on end. It all leads to conversation with strangers, and can be very enjoyable.

The cars are equipped with radio loudspeakers, and the newer trains have a radio receiver in each compartment. The trains always conspire to start the journey from Moscow to the tune of a snappy, cheerful march. This adds to the holiday spirit. Most men, as in my compartment the night I started out alone from Moscow to Minsk, take off their shoes and coats, but sleep in their clothes, and again, it is like camping out. On this ride my compartment began to seem more like Grand Central Station than a Russian train. An old man and I slept fitfully in the lower berths, but the uppers were really "hot beds." The two first occupants slept an hour or two, then departed. Two soldiers next climbed in for a couple of hours, and out they staggered into utter darkness. Two other people were there in the morning. After breakfast they left us.

But the old man and I did not stay alone long. The radio was blaring away very loudly, and neither one of us could find the gadget to turn it off. A helpful citizen rushed in, reached under the table, and silenced the noise. Then Mr. Helpful sat down and started to talk to the old man. The newcomer never left our compartment, though he had no ticket for it, until he left the train late in the afternoon. After the first short conversation, Mr. Helpful sat the rest of the trip in stony silence.

I have prided myself on an ability to get any Russian to talk to me, but not this one. I tried various languages, offered him vodka and food, brought out some gadgets from home and tried to lure his attention. About the only remark I got out of him was when I showed him my Swiss scout knife which he said was "for children." Compared to Mr. Helpful, Gromyko would have been the life of the party. Yet at every stop my friend would come to life. He never failed to alight when I did, and so far as I could observe, he seldom took his eyes off me while we were at a station. When I asked if I could take his picture in the compartment, he declined, a rarity in my experience. Finally I asked him point-blank if he was in the MVD. His face was grim, as he abruptly said, "*Nyet*," and his eyes shifted away quickly.

Although anybody might have acted the same way, somehow I felt he was a policeman, and I am not one normally to imagine I am being followed. In fact, I say that during my UNRRA travels, I was almost never followed by the police.

He stayed with me. Eventually, at a station where we stopped late in the afternoon, a younger and shorter man wearing an identical dark blue coat and blue cap, both of fine material, met him. By chance I witnessed their meeting; they walked away from our car side by side and started to talk. At one moment both turned their heads to look back toward me, and at exactly that instant I snapped their picture, whereupon both abruptly turned away again. When the train started, Mr. Helpful was on the platform; Mr. Little Helpful was standing in the corridor of my car. Twice after that when I went to the diner, the only train on which I was to see a diner, I found Mr. Little Helpful standing outside my compartment, and each time he came into the diner and sat at the next table, back to back with my chair. That's all I know about those two.

Later when I had dinner in Kiev with some Ukrainian cabinet members whom I had known before, I twitted them about their secret police and said I could tell these two a mile away by their good "official" clothing. To which one Ukrainian vice president smilingly replied, "Do you think we should not clothe our police well?"

There was another fellow on the train who was either a general nuisance or a lower-order policeman. This one, who was tieless, and who had long blond hair cut in German fashion, said he was a "chauffeur for an enterprise." In the diner I was invited to sit with a colonel, two majors, and the wife of one of the majors. We had struck up a conversation in German and in English, speaking across the aisle, whereupon they invited me to join them, and they insisted on treating me to a bottle of beer. In our talk I showed them a little note in Russian which explained a bit how I happened to be there. After one major left, this "chauffeur" slid into the empty seat and almost immediately interrogated me in good German about the note I had been showing the officers. A few minutes later, at the next stop, I went out of the car to get some pictures. When I returned, all the people who had been sitting with me had left the table, though they had not yet finished.

Afterwards, at another stop, just as I was about to photograph some peasants with their wares, this fellow shooed them off, and dashed off to another car before I could ask him what he was up to.

I went back into the diner. He came in and sat opposite me and again began to question me. I got up and left.

A little later I came back to the diner. The original group of officers with whom I had been eating were there again, but though all had been cheerful and pleasant before, they did not speak to me, and acted as though they had never met me. I sat down alone. Two young lieutenants seated themselves opposite me. Again both spoke some German. They were young, gay, and most courteous. One had a couple of extra drinks; as he drank, he became more proper, more punctilious in his manners. The colonel at the next table finally called over to him and told him to shut up. The lieutenant made a brushing-aside gesture and snapped back at the colonel, who flushed but did nothing, and the lieutenant remarked to me, "It's a democratic army; besides, he's not my colonel."

At length the soldiers left, and two more people sat down opposite me. About this time the little "cop" came along, sat down right behind me, half turned in his chair, and began to talk to us. I was fed up. I took him by the shirt and said, "You've been following me, and I'm sick of it. Now get out of here."

He said, "I'm not following you."

So I laid my passport on the table and said, "If you're not in the MVD, then show me your papers. Show them to me." He made some stumbling protests and fished out a picture of his wife, pretending to misunderstand me. I finally said, "Show me your papers or get away from me. I don't want to talk to you." He got up and left.

Aside from the skirmishes with these "civilians," what impressed me on this trip was the number of soldiers I encountered everywhere. I did not bother generally to distinguish between soldiers and officers, though in all my count of the military in restaurants, hotels, and theaters, as well as on trains, the large majority were officers. The train's little diner was near my car, and I would slip into it frequently. In the evening I counted 7 soldiers and 6 civilians at the tables. At eight the next morning, 11 soldiers were sitting there and only one civilian. About an hour later when I went to get breakfast, there were 22 military men and 4 civilians. At noon there were 24 in uniform and 3 civilians, and this time I noted that all but 2 of the military were officers. When the train stopped at Smolensk, I counted on the platform 70 soldiers and 3 "Wacs," and among the civilians, 36 men, 17 women, and 3 children. Later, in midafternoon, when I entered the diner once more, there were 7 soldiers, 4 Russian civilians, and 8 Chinese. It was at Smolensk that a soldier, standing below the platform, started talking to me in halting English as I was taking a picture; pretty soon there was a ring around him of 7 soldiers and another ring of 10 soldiers and officers around me up on the platform, all listening to this GI and me shout back and forth, with many of them volunteering questions for him to translate to me. All were curious and friendly in manner. I remember that they asked me why the United States was in Korea, and that when I told them we had shot down some MiGs, the soldiers denied there were any MiGs there. Also at this station I watched two well-dressed women carrying suitcases cross to the opposite platform. Without a moment's glance of hesitation, they just stooped and walked underneath our train.

After all the men in military uniform that the Englishman

The Road to Minsk

and I had noticed in Moscow, the sight of the great numbers of them on the train and on the railroad platforms began to fill me with somber speculations, to see this vast country which we fear so heavily militarized. What were they preparing for?

I had made this very same journey seven years before. At that time a Russian colonel-general from the Far East had joined us in our compartment, bringing with him some pepper-vodka and bread "baked by his wife." I remember his glancing through the pages of a copy of *Life* magazine. He objected to one ad showing four or five neckties. Why show four or five, was his argument, when a man only needs to buy one? Another ad really shocked him. It was one by a Canadian paper company showing woodsmen standing on floating logs in their bare feet. The general thought this barefoot business was too primitive. He couldn't believe that the United States didn't have some more modern method. When I said, "Well, anyway, it's Canadian," he replied, "Then you shouldn't print it in an American magazine!"

I seem to have an affinity for off-beat Russian generals. One sat next to me once on a plane from Kaliningrad to Berlin. He spoke good English, but with quite a stutter. American abbreviations and slang were his "h-h-hobby." He knew what "snafu" meant all right, but "what was this 'ss—oo—pp'?"

These fellows, like most Russian generals, were short and stocky. But General Grechko, who recently became the Soviet commander in Germany, is at least six feet two and quite slender. When we first met him in Kiev, he was wearing a full-dress uniform, his golden jacket covered with all his many medals. My secretary exclaimed, "What a beautiful hunk of man—and all wrapped up!"

This time I had only my grim MVD man for company. But the countryside was more cheerful. In 1946 it was pitiful. I had inspected the ruins of cities in Germany, Poland, and Czechoslovakia, and, except for Warsaw, this area was the worst of all. The brunt of battle and destruction had fallen on Byelorussia, which was never too rich a land anyway. Almost no stone building had been left standing, and there were no railroad stations left. People were living in caves and rubble shacks, and the roofs of trains and their outer steps were crowded with wretched Russians, unable to pay a fare. At every stop there were beggars, and everywhere the pinched faces of ragged, filthy, possibly homeless children, always holding out their hands for something to eat.

Now there was none of that. I did not see a beggar at any stop, nor were there any free-loaders clinging to the train. Every city had its new railroad station. Throughout the countryside you could see from the windows of the train good solid homes, and many more being constructed. In tiny villages I saw brand-new caterpillar tractors time and again. Here and there I would see those new blue or red Soviet busses, all Greyhound-shiny, just like in Moscow, and at each station substantially fed peasants were hawking their surplus, this time selling with a smile, where before you sensed a sale was one of desperation. It is still not a rich land—drab and sparse and looking something like poorer parts of rural America in the first years of this century—but it is a thriving land by comparison with the aftermath of the war. There are still many shortages. I saw, for example, on an abandoned siding, a string of German *Schlafwagens*, now fully outfitted as homes, complete with smokestacks, curtains, and telephone lines. I had seen few bicycles or dogs in the big city. Now there were many peasants wheeling along the roads, and here a collie, there, what seemed an Airedale, and there, what seemed, and was, only a mongrel. It was all summed up for me when a valiant trolley car kept up with us for several miles. Poor little beaten-up Byelorussia was determined to match the not-so-advanced rest of the Soviet Union.

Some of Russia's headaches also became clearly visible. Everywhere a sea of mud which makes much of the country impassable so much of the time. The pressure for manpower, exemplified by the sight of seven women working with pickaxes on the railroad under the supervision of one man. (On another journey I saw a gang of soldiers doing similar railroad-

The Road to Minsk

repair work, and when I asked why soldiers were doing that kind of work, a Russian snapped, "What would you prefer that they do?") The freight cars of maddeningly variable sizes—15, 18, 20, 30, 40, 50, 57, and 60 tons—all in the same train. One can only imagine the problems of ordering and scheduling, the waste of hauling capacity, resulting from that little imbalance.

When my train pulled into Minsk that evening, there were three men on the platform awaiting me: a young interpreter, the chief of the local Intourist organization, and the head of the local cultural-relations organization. They drove me to my hotel, asked me what I wanted to see the next day, arranged for my meal to be served in the double suite which had been given to me, and then departed. Each time these officials came to my hotel room, their chauffeur would tag along and freely join in the conversation.

The suite they had given me was certainly large enough, for there were two double bedrooms and two living rooms, plus a bathroom—in which there was no hot water or soap or toilet paper. The chief ornaments of the suite were four rubber plants, one of them over six feet high, an orange lampshade, and a huge painting of Stalin and Molotov. As you drive through the streets of the cities of the Soviet Union, you will see through window after window the inevitable potted rubber tree, and in the center of the rooms a red or orange lampshade suspended from the ceiling, normally the only light in the room.

The painting could only be called spectacular by one who has seen many real-life photos of Stalin and Molotov. They were depicted traipsing through the spring fields together. Uncle Joe wears a plain gray uniform without medals, and on his left arm he carries a tiny girl in a red shirt. Next to him gambols his Foreign Minister in a white open shirt and white pants. He is smiling angelically and, instead of the customary brief case, he also is carrying a little girl who has her arms around his neck in adoration. In front of them scamper a little girl with a butterfly net and a small boy in swimming trunks. The most idyllic scene since *Pippa Passes*.

For pedestrian contrast, a spittoon sat in the corner. No Russian hotel room seems up-to-date without one, but I have never noticed a Russian chewing tobacco, and certainly not gum. (In 1946 some of the UNRRA food packages purchased from the U. S. Army contained sticks of gum. A little Ukrainian boy told me it was "charming chewing rubber—all my friends love it.")

The key to the door was one of the standard heavy old-fashioned type. Six keys and one hairpin would open all the rooms in Russia.

I sallied out to explore the city. Minsk when last I had seen it was like a house wasted by a devastating fire, just after the smoke has died down from the ruins. Now even by night I could see I was in the midst of a gleaming new city, accentuated by brilliant lofty street lamps which burned all night long.

I worked my way back to the railroad station. There the entire waiting room was jammed with soldiers; not only were all seats taken, but there was scarcely room to move through the crowds of them standing shoulder to shoulder. Across the street were two brand-new skyscrapers, and on one a colored neon sign advertised a new restaurant. As I entered it, seven officers swept out the door. When I advanced to the check room, eight more officers were grouped about the harried attendant. The restaurant had two floors. On the ground floor were about twenty tables, all occupied, and not a civilian in the room. Upstairs were a similar number of tables and in the whole room, again crowded, were only six civilians. I walked out into the night and home to bed, shaken and troubled. I began to feel that far more than half of the men in the Soviet Union were in arms. The smell of war was in the air.

With the sunshine in the morning these dark forebodings evaporated. I would never again in thousands of miles see so many soldiers or anything remotely resembling such concentration, though I was to see in many towns a good number of officers. Khrushchev himself explained to me that Moscow was a center of transportation and that there was a main training

The Road to Minsk

base near Minsk, but it was some time before the impact of those early impressions wore off. If I had flown out of the Soviet Union then, I would have sworn that the entire Soviet Union was a teeming armed camp. While this may not be so, those first vivid jolts will never let me forget that, at the least, the Soviet Union is extensively militarized, far more so, I would guess, than the United States.

With the morning came a happy vision of prodigious peaceful construction. The first view in my life of a Russian city had been from an airplane over Minsk during the first winter after the war. At that time Minsk was just a burnt black stub of hollow buildings in a white wilderness. They looked like empty craters on the moon, with no life visible. Now I walked down some of the most spacious avenues in the world in the midst of a brand-new shining city of 400,000 souls, as though some genie had touched a magic wand and a city of palaces had appeared. The contrast was the most stupefying experience I have ever had.

The most dramatic fact of Soviet life today, in Minsk and elsewhere, is the tremendous amount of construction that is going on. Wherever I went, I saw row upon row of offices and apartment buildings being erected, and in a single street in one city I saw eleven giant cranes at work on a group of workers' flats.

When I had last seen Minsk, more than 75 per cent of it had been destroyed by the Germans. Today, one of the happiest persons in all the Soviet Union must be the chief architect of Minsk, a man named Matzkevich. For five hours he escorted me about the newly restored city. His job is to rebuild and extend an entire city. He has plenty of money and manpower, and his plans have been approved. So far he is doing a magnificent job. The new Minsk has miles and miles of new apartment houses, department stores, schools, and office buildings, all radiating off spacious tree-lined boulevards, some of which are 210 feet wide. There are squares galore to provide light and air, and an eighty-five–acre Park of Culture and Rest.

The same kind of reconstruction is going on elsewhere in the U.S.S.R. The chief architect of Kiev, for instance, charged with rebuilding 42 per cent of a city of 900,000, told me, "It's a pity the day is so short and life so brief."

There's one great problem though: Soviet workmanship on buildings is very bad. I noticed recent constructions with the paint chipping, doors sagging, and bricks out of line. Throughout the country the newest buildings often look at least twenty years old. The Russians are aware of this shortcoming. A cartoon in *Crocodile* depicted a decrepit apartment house with tenants practically falling through the gaping walls. A man is asking the janitor, "Hasn't this building ever been repaired in all these years?" and the janitor replies, "Why of course not. It's a brand-new building."

Later I visited Moscow's Museum of Construction to find out how the nation-wide building program is being carried out so fast. I was told that much building is now done on a prefabricated basis—that whole stairways and sides of buildings are built as units and transported to the site on special trucks, permitting a single crew to work on fifteen buildings at once, piecing together the prefabricated sections as they arrive. The Russians claim they can erect a 4-story 48-apartment building in 29 days. One result, of course, is that monotonous uniformity all over the Soviet Union, with the same windows, the same set patterns of rooms, the same exteriors.

CHAPTER 8

Factory-Farming

AFTER THE heavy-duty tour of the city, we swung out into the country to visit a collective farm. Soviet agriculture was in a bad way. Government officials had just admitted that there were actually fewer cattle in the country than there were before the Revolution in 1917. Between 1940 and 1952, while industrial output was rising 230 per cent, farm production was up only 10 per cent. A number of specialists believe that the major flaw in the Soviet economy is its serious failure to solve its agricultural problems, resulting in widespread poverty, high food prices, a continuing shortage of meats and dairy products, and prevailing imbalance of diet—though there appeared to be no starvation.

The Soviet farmers were being subjected to an incessant shrill nagging in the public prints, aimed at increasing production. I remember a *Pravda* article in October lecturing readers sternly on the subject of fodder, and a Stalingrad newspaper railing interminably against "the shallow, impractical running of agriculture," the "weakness of some party organizations," and "serious failure in fulfilling plans of farm workers." Out in Uzbekistan I saw a statement which solemnly declared: "The fight for cotton is the fight for peace."

The attack went far beyond just the poor farmers. Said Moscow *Pravda*, "Take for example the Kuibyshev Publishing House. In 1952 and 1953 it did not publish a single book on potatoes and vegetables!"

Also, chairmen of collective farms were being shifted around, machine-tractor stations were being reorganized, and thousands of additional technical experts were being sent into the field.

Apparently the tractor stations needed a shaking up. I saw a cartoon in a Russian magazine depicting a soldier walking through the snow, pausing to ask two children, "How do I get to the machine-tractor station?" and they replied, pointing to the snow-covered, rusting machines lying about, "Just follow the trail of those abandoned machines and you'll get there all right."

This is typical of the present needling. I saw another showing wistful humanized little potatoes, peeping out of a snow-bound hut labeled "Storage of Vegetables," addressing a man peering at them, "But Comrade Chairman, we are supposed to be fried, not frozen!"

The formation after the Revolution of the great collective farms, supposedly on a gigantic mechanized factorylike basis, has magnified the fundamental conflict between the peasant and the Government. On each farm the peasant must in effect punch a time clock, serving so many hours a day on duties for the collective farm. For this he is paid in "labor days," a unit of value for each kind of work, computed by the farm each year on the basis of the over-all profits for the year. Payment for a labor day is in rubles and in quantities of different farm products. In addition, most peasants have their own small individual plots, on about an acre or an acre and a half, which they now may use about as they please. On this land they raise potatoes chiefly, but also cabbages, carrots, beets, onions, and now and then some fruit. Most own pigs and chickens and possibly half the peasant families have a cow. The State takes heavy compulsory deliveries of products from the big collective farms, and the machine-tractor stations exact additional amounts from the collective farms in payment for the use of tractors and

Factory-Farming

combines. This setup has a tendency to make the peasant slow down on the enforced shift and speed up on his own time, where he can use the results directly for his family or peddle any surplus on the free markets. Through the years the Soviet Government has struggled with the farmers, trying to get a maximum output, trying to run them like factory workers, alternately squeezing and wheedling the individual peasant.

As part of the intense program to boost output, individual peasants were permitted by the new regime to own more livestock, taxes were eased on the individual farmers, and payments by the State to the collective farms for the required delivery of the bulk of their farm products were increased. In the case of meats and potatoes, the collective farms were receiving under the new arrangements amounts equal to about 10 per cent of the Government's retail price to the consumer, whereas previously the collective farms got about 1 per cent of the retail price. (In America farmers were receiving about 35 per cent of the retail price for the same products. Thus one can see that the Soviet Government's spread between cost of payment to the farms for their compulsory deliveries and price to consumer is enormous. This and the existence of a turnover tax on transactions make it unnecessary to have a high direct income tax—which runs from 2 to 13 per cent—for the Government has already exacted its very high share from both farm and consumer.)

Some idea of the size of their farms may be had from these statistics: in a country of over 200,000,000 people, about 100,000,000 are classified as agricultural. Their activity is conducted on 94,000 collective farms and about 12,000 State farms. The United States, which has a little less than 80 per cent of Russia's population, has 5,232,000 individual farms and a farm population of about 25,000,000.

Until recently the State Department had two farm experts in Russia, studying this great agricultural land. By comparison, the state of Iowa alone has 150 voluntary crop reporters; at the same rate this would require 21,000 crop reporters in the

Soviet Union. Yet under a bureaucratic economy drive requiring transfers according to seniority, known as "riffing"—reduction in force—our embassy, while I was there, was compelled to cut its agricultural staff in the Soviet Union in half. This left the United States with one specialist for the entire U.S.S.R.

I managed to visit about a dozen collective farms scattered throughout the country. Their vast acreage, however, made it impossible for me to do little more than ask pertinent questions of its executives, wander about some of their barns (those I saw were in excellent shape), observe briefly a few of their other activities, and occasionally talk to a few peasants. To grasp the underlying facts about such farms, one should live there for days. Until some qualified visitor approaches the farms in that way, I do not believe we can get a complete estimate of what is the true trend of life on them. I could only hit the high spots.

At the Minsk collective farm (formerly called "Soviet Specialists" and now named after Gostello, a war hero), we met the chairman and one Valkovich, the deputy chairman, both, it was revealed, members of the Communist Party. Like so many executives I was to meet, they unraveled yards of statistics, all without notes. The farm had 4,450 acres on which 400 people worked, half of whom were men. The farm owned 1 auto and 6 trucks, and it had 327 cows, 127 calves, 20 bulls, 212 horses, 765 pigs, and 1,800 fowl ("all the birds," said my interpreter). They raised rye, wheat, potatoes, cabbages, tomatoes, a few other vegetables, and apples. Then they proceeded to tell me the output of each product per hectare (2.2 acres) and the amount of land devoted to each product. The omission to consult any record made me think there was quite a bit of loose generalization. (Throughout my entire trip all executives always reeled off all their statistical answers without consulting a note. Therefore I developed a special fondness for the director of the Kiev Resthouse, a native of Omsk, Siberia, who carefully checked his books before each reply.) They went on to recite that the cows averaged 3,550 liters (3,751 quarts) of milk per year, and 4.2 per cent of butterfat when standing and 3.8 when

Factory-Farming

in the fields. I learned that they gave the cows vitamin D and the pigs fish oil, but that no antibiotics were used as yet.

I asked them how their average peasant made out. Against an estimated average wage, rural and urban, for the country of 750 rubles ($187.50) per month, on this farm, they said, one person in each family earned in the past year: 3,500 rubles in cash, 1½ tons of wheat (worth 4,000 rubles), 4 tons of potatoes (2,000 rubles), and ½ ton of vegetables (1,000 rubles) making a total value of about 10,500 rubles per year or almost 900 rubles ($225) per month, not counting amounts earned on the farmers' private plots. Furthermore, individual farmers got a share of the rye and wheat and pigs when the output of these items "overfulfilled the plan." Against all this, the peasant paid 350 rubles ($87.50) tax annually. This put these peasants, I judged, well above most.

In the Soviet Union, on farm and factory, wherever output can be measured, they seek to pay on a piece-rate basis. From the above figures, so variable, depending upon the weather and the output and nature of a particular farm, it is extremely difficult to estimate what the average peasant earns. Once I asked some highly placed Russians in what category the average farmer could be placed. They denied first that there were any categories in the Soviet Union; then they admitted that a farmer on a good farm would be in the top rank of Soviet life, and a farmer on a poor one in the bottom rank. From all the poor peasants I saw at free markets, which I inspected in every city, there must be still a lot of very poor farms.

Two other items of information about the Minsk farm were revealing: Communists and race horses. They had almost the same number. Out of four hundred workers, thirteen were Communists, and five of these served on the nine-man bureau which was the executive committee for the farm and which chose the deputy chairman. They said the chairman was "elected" by the members of the farm. All the newspapers were then carrying talks by Government leaders and editorials that better "chairmen" must be put in office, and I got the clear impression that any election was a formality, more a ratification by the peasants—who had no other choice—than a spontaneous election.

Of the two hundred and twelve horses on the farm, twelve were race horses. When I asked whether they bet on horses in that locality, the chairman smugly retorted, "We have no such habits." Well, that could be. This is a northern and western part of Russia, the soil in places is as rugged as Vermont's, and there may be similarly a touch of Puritanism. I do know that Moscow had an intricate betting system whereby bet payments were calculated in split seconds on old-fashioned abacuses, and thousands of miles away in Kazakstan, one of the leading citizens told me that often men "suffered very heavy losses" from betting on horses, and at times a man "would spend his entire wealth" just to own a race horse. He said it was in their blood.

After the lecture on the output of the farm, we made a brief tour of the main buildings. It was getting late in the afternoon, and sharp fall winds were blowing. Hardly a person could be seen as far as one looked in any direction. Near the pigsty we came across a group of seven women just finishing the day's stint. I asked them about their education and earnings. Each had had the minimum of seven years' education, and they claimed that their earnings averaged 800–900 rubles ($200–225) monthly (which substantiated what the chairman had told me; frequently the first workers I ran into in a factory or farm would be earning less than the director's estimate to me).

One of the women remarked, "We have seven years' education now and soon ten will be required," which was true according to all statements I heard.

And another added in sturdy peasant fashion, "It is necessary to have an education so that nobody takes advantage of you."

Then came the first questions I received in the U.S.S.R. this time from a peasant. She was a girl of about twenty, standing in the cold fall twilight of a farm near Minsk. "Is it proper to ask a question? Do you have racial discrimination in America?" I had made a long journey to face up to that question from a poor Russian peasant. They asked me about education in America, whether it was free, and how much was compulsory, and then how much did workers on farms make in America. These questions were to foreshadow many that I was to hear throughout the Soviet Union. The first one from the girl exemplified the politeness of those to whom I talked; the second from her illustrated how the Soviet Government spreads the news effectively of our defects; the third revealed the universal interest, almost an obsession, of the Russians in education and its opportunities; and the last, about the economic status of people like themselves in America, was a question to be given to me by Russians in all walks of life, revealing a very human preoccupation with their own station in life and what their chances would be elsewhere. The latter question also possibly indicated a discontent with their lot or a disbelief in what they were told, for they in effect sought to get the story, while they had the opportunity, from a flesh-and-blood American. This was emphasized, I thought, by the question I often heard: "What is your *personal opinion?*"

After this we talked to the woman in charge of the pigs, who told us she made 4,000 rubles ($1,000) in the first half of the year and that her husband, who was in charge of some horses, had earned about the same amount, again substantiating the chairman's figures. Her family owned one cow and four pigs, and they had a small apple orchard.

This picture of Soviet agriculture was little different at the other end of the country. Three thousand miles from Minsk I later visited a collective farm called Rays of the East Collective Farm near Alma-Ata in Kazakstan, run by a giant Ukrainian. This farm seemed to include an entire suburb of the city. It was the largest I was to encounter, with some 10,000 people on the farm, which owned 25,000 acres of land and which was yearly assigned 150,000 acres of grazing land by the State. On this farm were 30,000 sheep, 1,200 cattle, 1,300 horses, 450 pigs, 4,500 fowl, and even 135 camels.

The farm raised prodigious quantities of apples, grapes, vegetables, potatoes, wheat, and fodder. It had 52 accountants and its own branch of the State bank. Its 1952 income, according to the director, was equivalent to $1,820,750. It maintained fifteen stores throughout the city where it sold its produce.

The statistics were dizzying. If the farm sold through cooperatives, it paid a tax of 5 per cent. If it sold on the free markets, it paid taxes between 10 and 13 per cent, depending on the particular crop. The farm paid these taxes in money, but also was required to deliver large amounts of its crops to the State. In addition, it paid machine-tractor stations for the use of tractors and combines. When using combines to gather wheat, it paid 9 per cent of the crop. When using machinery to prepare the land for planting wheat, it paid on an agreed schedule, 10 to 80 kilograms of wheat for every acre, according to the crop. Peasants were paid according to a complicated "labor day," giving them so many rubles plus a share in half of any overfulfillment of plan for any crop or animal production upon which their brigade had worked. The chairman's payment was a Wall Street operation. He got credit for a basic number of "labor days" according to a State schedule, depending on the size of the farm. He also got additional pay for number of years on the farm; 5 per cent for 3 years; 10 per cent for 5 years; 15 per cent for 10 years; and 25 per cent for 20 years. On top of this, he got additional percentages for number of years he had been chairman, as distinguished from just working in other positions on the farm. Then for each 1 per cent that the farm overfulfilled its total plan, he got 10 per cent of his base pay. Furthermore, on each particular crop or animal product which was overfulfilled, he got an additional percentage. For instance, on a certain grass crop he received 5 per cent of the total value realized over the plan.

When these figures were recounted to me, I said, "That makes you a kulak or a capitalist."

He laughed and replied, "Yes, of course." He continued seriously, "All is based on the same principle. If you work

Factory-Farming

better, you get paid better." I heard such remarks all over the country. Many Westerners do not realize that the famous Karl Marx dogma, "From each according to his abilities, to each according to his needs," never has been adopted in the Soviet Union; that's the communism at which, theoretically, they claim they may someday arrive.

Some of the chairman's figures revealed one of the basic injustices of the Soviet social-security system, which some foreigners think protects everybody equally. In reality, only urban workers are protected by the State. Farmers have to depend upon the conditions on their particular farm and partly, I suspect, on the local whims and politics of those who control the farm. Here the elderly and invalids got their help from the Collective Farm Mutual Aid Fund, which was run by an elected board of five men. The chairman said that last year the farm had sent 12 farmers to a sanitarium, 35 children to a sanitarium, and 60 children to a Young Pioneer's summer camp. Out of a farm population of 10,000, this seemed small indeed. One of the strangest figures that came out of this was the salary of the local Communist Party secretary. He got 800 ($200) rubles a month for that job and only 330 ($82.50) as chairman of the Mutual Aid Bank. But his wife, who was a veterinarian, earned 1,800 ($450). The farm chairman himself was making close to 5,000 rubles ($1,250) monthly.

All these farm calculations seemed a little like the *Crocodile* cartoon of one farmer at the door of the collective-farm office saying to another, "Let's report that we have fulfilled half of the plan by 100 per cent."

CHAPTER 9

The Play's Not the Thing

FROM THE farm we crept through the evening darkness, dousing our lights for every oncoming vehicle, back to Minsk to attend a "concert" at the local opera house, a very handsome structure. Soviet opera houses and theaters are among the most magnificent buildings in the country. Each is built like a palace of the czarist days, with great classic columns, luxurious red, gold, and white *décor* (the historic treasures in the Kremlin reveal that these were also the favorite colors of the czars), and handsome creamy-white ceilings from which hang ornate chandeliers. Fortunes obviously are spent on the theatrical productions.

On my earlier trip I had gone as often as possible to the opera and ballet. There is little that I can add to the fame of Russian music and the Bolshoi Ballet other than to put in my uncritical view that the virtuoso ability of the dancers is superlative, the precision of some of their dance troupes a match for the famed Rockettes, the lavishness of the State-financed productions overwhelming. At the Bolshoi Theater in Moscow I saw moving scenery at least five times the width of the stage pass in front of and behind the principals to give the effect of movement by a boat on a mountain lake.

This time I concentrated upon local productions and upon

The Play's Not the Thing

the plot of the satires and plays I saw. Listening through interpreters, I did not feel competent to judge the acting. It seemed adequate and not hammy.

The "concert" in Minsk was a modest show, a sort of vaudeville performance, consisting of a few musical numbers and a series of short dances, often duets, notably a violent and thrilling sword dance to Khachaturian's famous music. The audience gave the most applause to this and to what purported to be a Spanish dance. I have also seen alleged Spanish dancing in Moscow, and the dancing made clear once and for all that there is not a drop of Spanish blood in the Slavic temperament. The Russians have magnificent dancers, but they lack the fire and snap of the Spaniards, and the imitation can be about as ludicrous as a Boston church choir trying to sing Memphis blues. But Spaniards trying a classical Russian ballet might be still worse.

In the lobby of the theater was an exhibition of paintings by Minsk's best artists. Out of forty-eight shown, fifteen had individuals as the subject, three were still lifes, and seven were nature paintings. The rest were what I call "modern Russian heroic"—what they term "Soviet realism"—somebody operating a combine on a farm, young pioneers at a meeting, decoration of workers for overproduction, people preparing for an anniversary parade—all about current activities in pursuit of progress, in that same uniform "happy-life" style. There was nothing remotely resembling the modern schools of the West.

The Minsk concert was full of mechanical stage effects which Russians delight in and contrive so well. This one had a witch disappearing into the floor with a cloud of steam rising above her; a woman came eerily out of a grave and began to dance; there was a scene of a boat moving on a lake (as I had seen more elaborately in Moscow); and the inevitable flames broke out. A circus is not a circus anywhere without a clown, and I believe that a show is not a show in Russia without a fire. In one very serious play I witnessed in Tashkent, the plot did not call for any fiery eruptions, but stage directions took care of that.

A man entered, complained of the cold, opened a wall stove to warm his hands, and flames a foot long flickered forth!

In Kiev, the next city I visited, I went to another local concert which was more like a review. Two very talented Ukrainians, a lanky skinny man and a little short clown with one of the most lugubrious faces I have ever seen, guided the performance. They did everything: announced the acts, danced, sang, cracked jokes, and pulled some sleight-of-hand. In-between their stunts we cast our eyes upon three of the heftiest female artists in the world, a singer, a xylophonist, and a pianist. There were also a couple of folk dances—as at every Russian variety show—and, similarly, a couple of short ballet numbers.

The two clowns pulled a trick that still baffles me: one lit a match to his cigarette, and the other's cigarette lit up and he began puffing on it. In another skit they squatted on one leg, with the other crossed as though on an imaginary bench, and when the audience applauded, one cracked, "It's an easier stunt than getting China a seat in the United Nations."

Their satiric jibes provided the most fun. They announced a series of dances: a Ukrainian folk dance, a Byelorussian folk dance, a sword dance, then something from Greater Russia, followed by two dances "of the future." In each case they went through the identical steps. After all the seemingly identical folk dances I had witnessed on two trips, I was ready to get up and cheer.

Next, one told the other "a story" about two young children who gave their seats on a trolley car to an old couple. "Is this a true story?" said one.

"No," answered the other. "I told you it was a story."

Other satires were aimed at bureaucrats. One depicted two men in conference all day who never did get to their work. Another was about executives who spent the first part of the month in relaxed talk about their families and their sports, then went crazy toward the end of the month trying to meet their schedule, and ended up by falsifying their figures as the only remedy. Lastly, they performed something which seemed

The Play's Not the Thing

straight out of Menotti's, *The Consul:* a man sought to get a permit from two Government departments, and each one kept him bouncing back to the other, the first saying he must have an O.K. from the second, the latter insisting that to get the O.K. he must first have a written paper from department number one. It seemed to me from the relaxed laughs of the audience that these were evidently ordinary events in that land.

In Zaporozhe we went to see a play called *Port Arthur,* in four acts and nine scenes, adapted from the best-selling novel of the same name by Stepanov. Waiting for the show to start, we chatted briefly with the director of the theater, who told me that greenhorn actors got 800–900 rubles ($200–225) a month, but that stars received as high as 5,000 ($1,250). He himself "got enough—1,000 ($250)."

The play was a real Pearl-White *Perils-of-Pauline* melodrama, with fireworks in every act. I didn't need any translation, the action was so clear. There are a couple of czarist scenes full of old world costumes and *décor*, and an elaborate ball, interrupted by the booming of cannons. One other scene shows the interior of a Chinese night club where a can-can is danced, realistic only as to stockings and a red wig for one dancer, but with the mildest of knee flexing. This is interrupted by an attempted assassination.

The remaining scenes are not so peaceful, as they all portray battle action, mostly on the Russian side, but including some brutality by a toothy Deadeye Dick Japanese commander at his GHQ. The play is full of sound and fury. Flares burst overhead; guns pop off; whistles blow; soldiers come in always on the dead run; a nurse is carried in on a stretcher and decorated on the battlefield; another nurse is shot in front of us and rolls down an embankment almost into the orchestra pit; men kiss each other dramatically and charge off over the hill; wounded heroes toss aside their bandages, gulp a vodka, and charge back; a nurse slaps a coward, but it's no slap, it's a roundhouse swing with all her buxom weight behind it. Finally the curtain comes down in a Fourth-of-July series of explosions, while the reformed heavy-drinking hero towers mid-stage, brandishing his sword for a suicidal charge. Oh yes, they had a seductive woman spy in it, too. She wore long-sleeved black gloves and was slim and dark. (FBI please note.) Incidentally, Russian drama critics are not satisfied with their portrayal of spies. Said *Pravda* of one Russian actress portraying Sylvia, an American woman agent (at the time of the Revolution): "The agent was in fact more resourceful and more enterprising and clever. Why indeed belittle the strength of the enemy—this weakens the conflict and weakens the tension."

On my later trip to Central Asia I concentrated on seeing the Eastern dancers (who were charming) and listening to Eastern music (which was generally delightful), but I went too far when I spent a painful evening listening to *Carmen* in the Kazak language. The Kazaks must have had a similar opinion of this *Carmen*, for there were about 40 people in the cast, 30 in the orchestra, and less than 200 in the audience out of a city of a half million.

In Tashkent I saw one of the most popular shows in the country, currently being enacted in all the major cities. *Not to Mention Any Names* played to a packed house of about 1,000 at the Tashkent Gorki Drama Theater.

The plot is one of those typically moralistic Soviet businesses, depicting the decline of a Ukrainian cabinet minister because he indulges the whims of his spoiled wife and daughter who live only for luxury and pleasure. Along with his downfall, it displays the concurrent successes of a few hard-working Soviet-type men and women.

The language, the by-play, and some of the scenes and incidents cast some revealing lights on Soviet life.

The play opens at the country home of the minister near Kiev. The mother, the daughter, and the daughter's girl friend all wear clothing such as I have seen only in Russian fashion shows. The daughter, for example, is dressed in a red and white jersey and gray slacks, and she wears long ivory earrings. There is an upright piano on which they play jazz and some

The Play's Not the Thing

"Spanish songs." One says she has managed to get a blouse from Paris, and her friend says, "I have a beauty of a record from Canada." Apparently they wallow in luxury, for the servant sets the table with "five champagne bottles."

In the first act the daughter spurns her country fiancé who wants her to go off to little Poltava, where he is trying to improve the tomato strain. She says, "How can I live in a city without the opera and the circus?"

In their parting quarrel he bitterly charges, "Your mother checked on the flat I have and on my salary and the fact that I have no Pobeda automobile." (These remarks seemed to confirm my impressions as to three of the chief concerns of the citizens—money, living space, and the to-be-attained car.)

The old peasant father comes for a visit, bringing with him the gorgeous country cousin, a flower of simplicity. Grandpa is all earthy peasant. When they tell him about his brat of a grandson, who runs around climbing trees and shouting, "Tarzan cannot fall" (the Soviet papers have been complaining about the Tarzan craze, all a result of three Weismuller movies taken by the Russians as booty from Berlin)—the lad has been called a *wunderkind* by his teacher—the old man modestly remarks, "Sometimes it happens, even in our family."

When the tired cabinet minister comes home and complains that the trade union objected to his efforts to fire his secretary and that his fellow cabinet members have quarreled with him about it (inner secrets of Soviet Government revealed), the old man suggests that maybe the trade union is right, and cracks, "I thought ministers never quarrel," which gives the audience a big laugh.

The official has a rough time in the bosom of his family. His daughter wangles a secretarial job from him for her girl friend, who, as a trained doctor, was about to be sent to the country. This causes Pop to remark, "For each sick person in Kiev, we have three doctors."

Then the wife, appearing in a velvet dress, complains that other officials seem to have more money, and when an editor telephones, she is sirupy on the phone and then nags her husband for not publishing popular articles instead of wasting his time on Government reports. In the argument she gets a round of applause when she declares, "You may be boss in your ministry, but at home I am the boss."

The daughter's new fiancé, an architect, arrives with the news that he is to build a big new city far from Kiev, and the daughter faints as the first act ends. All the cast takes bows at the end of each act.

The second act has scenes depicting the erection of a power station by the architect and showing the cabinet minister's family on vacation near by. Old grandpa now works as a bricklayer and complains he has too many chiefs and not enough bricks, and they give him three different quotas a day. A foreman gets into a terrific row with his all-girl crew. They want to put wallpaper of different colors in different rooms, and he laments that their fussing is ruining his production percentages. What amazed me was that a State inspector, who later goes to jail for embezzlement, is represented as extremely effeminate. The high point of the act occurs when the spoiled grandson throws a piece of bread away. The old grandfather's voice booms out, and a hush fell over the audience. "Don't ever throw bread away—" says the old man in a voice of doom, and then very solemnly and slowly, "This is labor of the people."

In the third act the family learns in the newspaper of a decree by the cabinet firing the minister for surrounding himself with relatives and for "committing bureaucratism," whatever that may be. One pun gets a laugh. The wife remarks, "But soon our guests will arrive, and we shall sit at the table." The husband, repeating the phrase (which in Russian is a colloquialism for sitting in jail), says, "Yes, soon we shall sit."

Act IV shows a marriage-registry office where the daughter now works as a clerk. The young architect comes in and marries the pretty cousin. The bumpkin ex-fiancé arrives with some new big tomatoes, which the hungry daughter eagerly grabs. And we learn finally what becomes of ex-cabinet ministers in the

The Play's Not the Thing

Soviet Union. In this play, the cabinet minister is now manager of a brick factory in the little town of Poltava.

Last item: In Russia the part of adolescent boys is enacted by women.

For comparison with this current popular hit, I went to an Uzbek folk drama called *Golden Lake,* which had been enacted off and on since 1939 in glorification of the Soviet life. I could smell it was a turkey when I saw an audience of 65 to listen to a cast of 30 and an orchestra of 20. This seemed to be a double illustration—the persistence of the bureaucrats in putting it on; the resistance of the proletariat in avoiding it.

The plot, which runs from spring to fall, deals with the attempt of a collective farm to get a good cotton crop. A couple of ne'er-do-wells prefer to roister and drink, and desert the farm. The sweetheart of one of the bums carries on as a brigade leader. Eventually she wins the deserters back, and they atone for their sins by extra work, which brings a record crop. The play has a few of the customary peasant dances plus scenes of happy workers and scenes of earnest workers chiding the negligent. Production figures and banners and slogans are as dull as in real Soviet life. Even the inevitable bookkeeper is there to check their crop collections.

The play concludes with the presentation of an award to the hero—a copy of one of Stalin's works—and they all sing a song entitled "Long Live the Results of Peaceful Work," which ends as they turn to a statue of Stalin highly spotlighted under a banner proclaiming, "Long live the great Stalin, who is the champion for peace." The curtain falls with the last line of the song—"that great man who showed us the way to happiness."

In the intermission we had a short chat with the theater manager. He told me that this Tashkent theater had about 200 actors, a chorus of 30, a ballet of 72, and some 35 soloists in addition to some 30 musicians. The top salary was 3,000 rubles ($750) monthly, the conductor got 2,500 ($625) and the average was about 1,000 ($250). Actors were required to perform ten times a month and got additional pay for extra performances. The manager established salary standards, and if the theater overfulfilled its plan, all got a bonus. The plan, by some hocus-pocus, called for a box-office "take" of some 5,040 rubles ($1,260) a night, though now and then they took in as much as 20,000 ($5,000). He apologized for the current production, saying it had been originally produced in 1939, but he said they had a new play for which there had been 15,000 applications for tickets. The audience, I noted, treated the play as we treat a Victorian melodrama, and seemed chiefly to sympathize, a bit raucously, with the sluggards, especially when they went off and got drunk. Nobody seemed embarrassed to sympathize audibly with the slackers. It illustrated to me that a lot of Soviet propaganda must bore the citizens to tears.

In Stalingrad I saw another of the Soviet's latest "morality plays" entitled *It's for You to Decide*. The theme is contemplated adultery. A big Soviet boss wants to abandon his family and take a pretty widow off to the north, where he must build a big new city. After four acts of moody Russian pondering, they abandon the plan for elopement, and the hero sighs manfully, "It is difficult to be a Communist from all sides." Then he turns around, full of sudden spiritual zeal, and persuades the widow to follow along anyhow so that she may teach school purely in the new great life to be built in the north. This play I learned was being shown at that time in Moscow at the Theater for Children.

In Baku, the Soviet's largest city after Moscow and Leningrad, I turned to the ballet, for a very good reason. I had been personally invited by Lena Vekilova, a prima ballerina whom I met one evening along with a tenor, a music critic, two composers, and a playwright. (During this brief meeting I apologized for the informal, worn tweed suit I was wearing, saying, "I call this my collective farm suit," to which the playwright tartly responded, "Our collective farmers have better suits than that!") Vekilova had graduated from the famous Bolshoi Ballet School in Moscow where, she told me, they practiced dancing three hours daily; half the time on basic lessons and half on

The Play's Not the Thing

specialty dancing or "supporting lessons." There they also studied French, for most of the ballet terminology is in French, and in addition they studied the history of music, the art of acting, the history of the dance, and the history of the theater. She asked me whether we had ballets in New York, and ballet theaters and ballet schools, and whether we produced Russian ballets; and then she remarked as I was leaving, "You have seen me to talk to, and now I invite you to see me dance. I shall dance in a ballet called *The Seven Beauties*."

Like any fatuous male I was pleased and promptly went to the next performance, being given an aisle seat in row one.

In the best Russian ballets, the scenery, the staging, the elaborate costuming are so rich and romantic that it all seems like the most elaborate fairyland one could imagine. It is truly an *Arabian Nights* atmosphere, and often the plots seem to come from similar tales, as did this one, which dealt with shahs, viziers, ancient battles, and romantic paintings of women who came to life and danced in diaphanous robes. As in most Russian ballets, it was contrived to have a scene where beauties of many lands dance, giving composer and choreographer a chance to throw in some variety from many lands. Here the beauties in a magic carpet came to life (new device) and gave in succession dances labeled Indian, Byzantine, Eastern (Dance of the Houri), Slavonic, Spanish, and Chinese, in that order.

While my ballerina friend was whirling in high style, I smugly admired my role as her guest in the front row, only to see her stub a toe and collapse ignominiously on the stage, skirts flying, pink-pantied rump inelegantly exposed. Except for this disillusioning blow to romance, I must say that she was very good.

I did not realize how good she was till we were back in Moscow, when one day my interpreter remarked, "Do you know who I liked best on our trip?" I wondered what Asiatic official he meant, only to hear him say, "The ballerina from Baku." I asked him whether he had told his wife and he answered, "A little bit, but not my private thoughts."

In Tiflis we tried another type of ballet with somewhat disastrous results. The theater had a typical Soviet name: Tiflis Order of Lenin Palashvili Theater of Opera and Ballet. The ballet was entitled *For Peace* and dealt with the sudden attack by the Germans, the operations of the Russian guerrillas, and the capture and torture of some of them by the Germans, including the blinding of the hero. Just as all are to be exterminated, Russian tanks arrive, and Russian doctors restore the hero's sight.

It was a "benefit" evening for Georgia's Master of the Ballet, one Chabuckiani, one of the great dancers of the Soviet Union, who was the star dancer as well as author and choreographer; and the house was sold out to its sponsors, the local co-ed medical college. The opera house was constructed as so many new Russian theaters are, with a tiny balcony, but with an orchestra which gradually slants up a hill, so that you enter on about the second or third floor level and descend to your seats (which have a slight forward tilt, literally keeping one on edge). Before the show the enthusiasm of the audience was electric. It was certainly the most excited audience I ever saw in Russia. The hero, no longer a young man, did some virtuoso leaps, even for the Soviet ballet, during the three hours of the show.

When it was over, about eleven-thirty at night, a presentation ceremony took place. The whole cast lined up on the stage with the hero dead center. A wreath about the size of the one we put on the winning horse at the Kentucky Derby was hung on his neck, and for one hour and a half speeches and poems were read in Russian and Georgian, first by a leading citizen and then by six boys and girls of the medical college. All this time the whole cast stood under the spotlights and the great dancer wore his wreath like a noose. (Once Ambassador Bohlen, after I complained to him about the length of a show in Moscow, remarked jokingly, "Everything in Russia should be cut in half," and I certainly felt so that night.) They called old Chabuckiani "god of the jumps" and a "fighter for peace," and one little girl even cited *The New York Times* in his praise as saying some twenty

The Play's Not the Thing

years ago when he went to America that "his dancing created a revolution." My favorite was a lovely Georgian lass who delivered a lengthy and impassioned poem and then wound up with an "old Russian proverb: Let all your sins be transferred to me." We slept soundly that night.

This ballet had one innovation for me—the first sexy stuff on their stage that I had seen—supposedly a night-club dance in a decadent German café. The girls wore only bras and short pants, one long black-sleeved glove on their right arms, and black stockings. They also carried fans and wriggled "wickedly." It was about the way I would imagine a convent lass might dance after having secretly read a lurid description of a burlesque show. Interesting in an off-balance way. As for nudity, it just doesn't exist, except for girl acrobats in the circus, who appear in shorts and bras. Even in Moscow's most famous art gallery I saw only two paintings of nudes. One was placed so high on the wall it was hard to see. The other, called "Sword Dancer," featured a female figure about ten inches high. It was at eye level, all right, but it was roped off—the only painting with a rope around it—and three Russian GI's were eyeing it steadily.

In Moscow I found the most enjoyment watching Rykin, their famous satirist, who looks like a younger edition of Eddie Cantor, even to the pop eyes.

Rykin put on practically a one-man performance in a series of skits. The show began with a man coming out of the audience and quarreling with the actors. He said he was a critic, but he didn't need to see the show since he had already written his review. This was ironically prophetic. When the Russian ballet later went to Paris, its performance was canceled at the last moment because of the French crisis in Indo-China; but a sympathetic French paper had already gone to press describing the stirring performance and the ovation the ballet received.

One scene, called "Steps to Power," showed a bureaucrat rising and becoming more and more haughty, till he comes a cropper. One aspect of his rise was his conversation about his autos, beginning with the tiniest Soviet car, ascending to the best Soviet car, a seven-passenger 42,000-ruble ($10,500) auto, and winding up at the pinnacle of his power with a Chevrolet!

Two skits were rougher on the Soviet way of life than I expected to see. In one Rykin plays a lifeguard at the beach. A bystander rushes up to him and informs him that a woman is drowning. The lifeguard ponders while the drowning woman yells, "Help!"

The bystander asks, "Why don't you throw her a life preserver?"

"I can't," says the lifeguard. "I don't have any authority."

By this time a crowd has gathered, and several people urge, "Go on, throw it anyway."

"I can't," insists the lifeguard. "It's government property, and I'm held responsible for it."

"Then why don't you dive in and save her yourself?" demands one of the crowd.

"Impossible," replies Rykin. "I'm only a lifeguard by verbal authority. I haven't received my written authorization yet."

In the second one Rykin, as chief executive of a clothing factory, stands behind his desk in a presentation ceremony in honor of a Stakhanovite prize worker. Rykin gives the worker a package as a reward. When the worker opens it, he throws it in the executive's face, saying, "Why, this is a swindle. This is the suit I worked on."

Rykin blinks at him and says, "What do you mean? We are all satisfied with our product. I am proud to wear the products of our plant." At this point he steps out from behind the desk, and the lower half of one pant leg is missing.

The current theater also plays a major part in Soviet radio and television programs. In addition to numerous news broadcasts and a great deal of music—classical music and folk songs, including quite a bit from foreign lands, but not any jazz or works of modern Western composers—the radio has for years broadcast the latest shows and operas directly from the main theaters. Soviet TV, available when I was there only in Mos-

The Play's Not the Thing

cow, Leningrad, and Kiev, devoted itself primarily to their best theatrical and cinema productions. The programs ran for a few hours each evening and on Sunday afternoons, showing primarily, direct from the stage of the chief theaters, the leading plays, ballets, and operas, often during their opening week. There were some sports programs, some feature events like a Red Square parade, but no regular news telecasts, no special features written just for TV, and, of course, no commercials.

There were reported to be between 150,000 and 300,000 TV sets in the country, and these were expensive, running close to 2,400 rubles ($600) for sets which had much smaller screens than in the West. Technicians say their images are clearer than in America, since they have 625 lines to the picture, to our 525. Listeners have many of the same problems as do Americans: sets are costly, repairs are frequent and expensive, and neighbors complain about the noise. Broadcasters have fewer problems. The director of the Kiev station told me he had no idea how many people listened; his only concern was to put on the programs and transmit them so many kilometers. He added for my benefit, "We do our very best, while we understand that in America television is widely used to upset people, such as by the use of comics and murder mysteries and so on." But he has his problems too. I read a complaint in the Kiev papers that citizens were receiving strange images and weird noises on their sets, all because the station and its electrical matters were under a Ministry of Construction, and the managers and broadcasters were under the Ministry of Culture, with bureaucratic failure of co-operation between them.

Children had the hardest luck with Russian TV. Programs were put on for them mostly on Sundays, and instead of blood and thunder and romance, they were shown programs about how-to-make and how-to-do some practical things. One evening while I was watching, at the start of the program, a woman appeared on the screen and sternly warned that the film to follow was "not suitable for children."

CHAPTER 10

Minsk Automobile Plant

SUNDAY morning I drove to the Minsk Automobile Plant which, surprisingly, was in operation that day. For the most part factories shut down on Sundays, while stores remain open so that workers can do their weekly shopping, it being their only day off under the Soviet forty-eight-hour, six-day working week prevailing in just about every walk of life. (Soviet propagandists tell their people the United States is on a forty-hour week because there isn't enough work to go around.) This factory, I was told, manufactured 5-ton, 7-ton, and 25-ton trucks, with an output in 1952 of "about 15,000 trucks," size otherwise unidentified. This was as close to a factory output figure as I was ever to get. Having been disillusioned or baffled about such figures on my previous trip, this time I concentrated on salaries, prices, and cost of living, with a little more success.

The entrance to the plant provided a typical contrast in that land. The buildings were surrounded, as are many factories, by a very thick brick wall about ten feet high with little towers about fourteen feet high, spaced every sixty feet around the factory. But the gate itself was a thin, rickety wooden barrier, tended by a little old woman. When we arrived, a line of a dozen six-wheeled trucks, each carrying a giant tree, were waiting to enter the dusty-looking plant. The buildings, which were of

Minsk Automobile Plant

brick, looked chipped and dirty, and I guessed the plant was about twenty years old, only to learn it had been erected after the war in 1947. We walked down a long and very dark corridor where there was no heat, up a flight of stone steps, through an anteroom occupied by two secretaries surrounded by about six telephones, an abacus, and one typewriter, and into the director's office.

This room was much like all the offices of chief executives that I was to see throughout the land. Even Khrushchev's was on the same pattern. On the left was a long table covered with green cloth. Around it were about forty straight-backed chairs. At the end of the room was the large dark desk of the boss, and behind him on the wall were two paintings, one of Lenin and one of Stalin. On his desk were three telephones, a marble desk set with two inkwells, some nib pens, and a jar full of knife-sharpened pencils. To his left was a complete telephone switchboard. In the corners were two emblems, a figure of a basketball player—a prize won by a factory team—and a metal bull—the emblem of the plant which they stamped on their trucks. The wastebasket was a simple wicker one. The walls were half paneled, and the upper halves and the ceiling had painted decorations.

The graphic non-Soviet symbol of a bull for the plant's output was unique in my experience. The flock of telephones on the desks of the secretaries and on the chief's desk was typical of all offices, even in the Moscow Communist Party Headquarters. I never saw the multiple-switch telephone system which so many of our executives use, nor did I ever notice a buzzer to summon a secretary. I never heard a communication between the two offices except in a play. There, the secretary just bellowed to the boss through the half-open door. Since everything else in the play was realistic, even to the clouded windows badly smeared with putty, I assumed this was standard procedure.

In this office we met Meyboroda, the director, Zafronov, the deputy director, and Ilchenko, the chief engineer. First they gave me the history of the plant and told me some figures about its operations, revealing that it covered 420 acres and employed between 10,000 and 15,000 people, 30 per cent of whom were women. The plant at that time was operating on one shift. I learned that workers, as in all other plants I was to visit, were paid on a piece-rate basis wherever one could possibly be computed. They got two to four weeks' vacation, depending on the arduousness of the work done. This extra vacation goes to workers who do the heaviest physical labor or work in unpleasant or dangerous physical surroundings. Persons in the higher-paid brackets also always got four weeks' vacation. The director told me that the average wage for their unskilled labor was about 650 rubles ($162.50) a month, and the top three men in the plant to whom I was talking received 4,000 rubles ($1,000), 3,000 ($750), and 3,000 per month respectively.

(As I said, the average wage in that country is about 750 rubles [$187.50] per month. A ruble is worth twenty-five cents. It is difficult to compare Soviet wages, prices, and standard of living with our own. First, the exchange rate for the ruble has been artificially established by the U.S.S.R. Then, the Soviet worker must put in a forty-eight-hour week; he is pressured to contribute one month's salary to "state loans," which are repayable years later; and he lives in an economy where consumer goods are both very scarce and very expensive by Western standards. But he has no medical expenses; his rent for the poor housing he has is exceptionally low—often as low as nine or ten dollars a month, at the current exchange rate—and he pays very low income taxes—2 per cent on incomes above 260 rubles a month up to a maximum of 13 per cent on incomes above 1,000 rubles per month. For older people, pensions are often an important item. Eligible pensioners, who may continue to work, draw from 50 to 80 per cent of their last base pay. In some fields pensions start at age fifty for women, fifty-five for men.)

I managed to get Meyboroda to tell me about his career, just how he rose to become director of a big factory. After graduating from a technical school in Kremenchug in the

Minsk Automobile Plant

Ukraine, he first worked as a locomotive driver. Next he studied at the Kharkov Institute and at a tractor institute in Moscow. On finishing his studies, he went to an automobile plant in Gorki, where he served successively as an engineer, section head, chief inspector, deputy chief engineer, and chief engineer. Following this, he was transferred by the Ministry of Auto Industry to his present job. In the course of our conversation he showed quite a bit of knowledge about operations of Studebaker and Mack-truck factories in America, and, while discussing his record, he remarked, "Sorenson (for years a key Ford executive) had a simple biography. To be a director a man must not only be educated, but must also be a good organizer and show the qualities of a leader. Advanced people everywhere have a natural respect for workers. The director of a plant in the Soviet Union is not free from criticism; his job is to serve the people and every worker has the right to criticize him at plant meetings."

He did not mention the Government, but two months later I read in a leading Moscow paper, *Trud*, for December 13: "Matters are still worse at the Minsk Automobile Plant. Expensive equipment is being used wretchedly here. In the first and second ten-day periods, the people work leisurely in the shops, but in the third ten-day period, rush and overwork is the order of the day. During twenty-five days in November the plan was only fulfilled by 40 per cent. In these conditions, can it be a question of the correct usage of equipment, of high volume of output from each square meter of each production site; executives of the enterprise are supporting only in words advanced experience, the initiative of participants in competition, *et cetera*." At least nobody can claim I was taken to a "show place."

After they told me about their plant, I induced them to ask me a few things. The questions came in this order: "What do you think the political and economic situation will be after the Korean War? . . . What will the United States do with respect to automobile production? . . . Do you think there will be any overproduction and unemployment? . . . What do you think the chances are for trade between the United States and the Soviet Union? . . . What is the current agricultural situation in the United States? . . . How are you dealing with the current unemployment? . . . What increase in population have you had in recent years? . . . How many people live in your larger cities?"

One asked me, "Which do Americans think is better, state industry or private industry?" When I said that many Americans thought the ills of bureaucracy made state-owned industry inefficient, he replied, "As to bureaucrats, we remove them as quickly as any private institution!" ("And no doubt put them farther away," thought I.)

Then we wandered in a rather aimless fashion through various buildings of the plant. It was spread out over a vast acreage, and since I am not technically trained, I was interested mostly in a general impression and in speaking to the workers. As in almost all Russian factories, I saw a number of machines which were American or English or German, and occasionally one from Budapest or Austria, but most of the stuff was Russian. There was no spit-and-polish finish to anything, but the lighting was fair, there was plenty of space, and none of the workers were hanging onto a lathe in exhaustion. I thought the yards had an unusual amount of debris, though all factory yards get that disheveled abandoned look. This, however, was a little extra. A Russian satirical drawing put its finger on this aspect. It showed a factory yard in which there were two jumbled piles, one of cabbages and one of miscellaneous pieces of wood lying in a mixed-up heap. The boss said something had to be done. Next the pictures showed the "accomplishment." In the piles were sticks with signs: "Storage of Vegetables" and "Storage of Lumber."

Going through the plant, I noticed a couple of slogans in the shops. Sometimes I think Rotary International ought to sue the Russkis for plagiarism. Plastered all over the country are slogans and quotations and exhortations. In the pressing section I saw one which read, "Peace will be preserved and consolidated if the peoples of the world will take the course of preserving peace into their own hands and will defend it to the end.—J. Stalin." Another said, "Long live the Soviet Trade Unions." But some were more domestic. Over one spot a banner in the inevitable white letters on a red background proclaimed, "This is the place of the brigade of excellent quality. The head of the brigade is Comrade Nettkov." In a way this is no different from some of the ideas of our industrial psychologists who display the name of the operator of an elevator, or who announce achievements of star workers in the industrial "house organs," except that on banners it seemed possibly cornier.

As we walked through the shops, I would collar workers who seemed the least busy, since I did not want to be the ultimate cause of the failure of the next five-year plan. First I spoke to two plump young girls who were waiting for a truck into which they were going to load spare parts. They said they averaged between 600 and 800 rubles a month and that they paid 19 rubles a month rent for single rooms, a little less than a day's wages. They asked me whether women worked in American automobile plants and how much they made, and, after that, how much education they had. At that moment their truck arrived and off they rushed.

A little while later I stopped to talk to two men who did not seem very busy. Within about a minute workers were gathering from all over the shop, and soon there was a tightly packed ring about me of over twenty men. Throughout the questioning by the men, the deputy director and chief engineer stood beside me smiling, unhurried and unperturbed. The questions came thick and fast from the knotted group: "How many hours a week do men work in American factories? . . . How much money do they make? . . . How do they live? . . . How many rooms do they have? . . . What sort of education do they get? . . . How many are unemployed? . . . What vacation do they get? . . . Can workers get an opportunity for education? . . . How many years education do they have in

America? . . . How much education have you? . . . Who paid for your education? . . . What do you do now? . . . How much do you make? . . . How many rooms do you have? . . ." And one volunteered, "I go to school at night—I was a simple worker and now I'm going to get a degree as an engineer. Can a worker do that in America?"

The questions came so fast I had little time to ask any of my own. This was one of the most eager, persistent groups I ran into. I did ask a number of them how much education they had. All had at least seven years and a couple had a few years more. Three of them told me that their rent was thirty rubles per month. I foolishly asked whether they expected more consumer goods under the new plan and got the inevitable Soviet response, "Naturally."

All the time we talked, the word was spreading, and more and more people were stopping work and flocking round me. Finally I said, "I'm keeping you from your work. I don't want you to lose valuable production and money from your income." To this one of the fellows in the front row within a couple of feet of the top executives in the plant replied in a bellow, making a sweeping gesture with his hand, "*Nichevo* (It's all right). It doesn't matter. We'll fulfill our plan. Don't worry about that." They all laughed and went on pressing more questions on me from all sides, but I had to move on reluctantly, for I had a plane to catch. In that group there was certainly only curiosity and a general friendliness. In all honesty, there was nothing beaten about these men. They were healthy, full of bounce, eager, friendly, wide-eyed with interest as they stood there in their grimy clothes, and there was no fear in their faces when the "*nichevo*" rolled forth at us.

I have no admiration for the Soviet philosophy of government, and I know the Soviet standard of living is far below ours, but we still must get rid of the misconception that every worker there is a pitiful case, starved for food, dying of exhaustion, with the spirit of a whipped dog. We deceive ourselves. Despite their obvious poverty, these people are strong and vigorous and

Minsk Automobile Plant

many seem happy. Some knowledgeable persons argue that the Russian people may be "our secret allies." As a people they do not seem to have that militaristic power lust which crops out so cruelly in too many Germans. I have traveled most of the world for years and I have been in every state and major city of my own country, and I would say that the average Russian is closer in character and personality to an American than any foreigner I have ever met. He has a vigor and confidence, a curiosity and general friendliness which I like to think typifies an American. The Russian rulers make a careful distinction between the American people and those allegedly "controlling" them, and similarly we must make a great distinction between the ruling Communists and the Russian people.

If the Russian workers deserve more credit than we give them, Soviet factory management deserves less than the Communists claim for it. Industry in the Utopia of the planned society suffers from unsavory ills often attributed to the evils of capitalism. In most factories the Soviet incentive system provides that the management may double their salaries monthly if the plant exceeds the plan. Russian papers are full of charges of exaggeration and falsification of figures. One can only imagine the incentive for juggling figures that must arise as a plant nears 99 per cent for the month, when the executives stand to double their money for just the tiniest more production on the books. And this is not the only evil of Communist industry. While I was there, I saw a picture in a national magazine of a factory executive debating with himself: "They say that in my organization there are too many unnecessary employees. If I discharge the relatives of my wife, she will have no mercy on me. If I discharge the relatives of those who are above me, they will discharge me."

After leaving the factory, we made a quick run through some of the State stores. The main general food store had only canned goods and two chickens and a few pieces of sausage for sale. A special vegetable store had a small amount of fresh carrots and some potatoes. In a meat store there were a few meager pieces of beef of low grade and no lamb, pork, veal, or chicken. In the free markets, where the collective farms and individual peasants were marketing their surplus, prices were very much higher, but they were selling large quantities of beef, a lot of potatoes, and the only fruit—apples—in the city.

At one of the stores I saw two women come to blows. Many doors to small shops are French doors, and for some perverse reason, usually only one is open, making half a doorway's entrance space by our standards. Two very short and very buxom Russian women got stuck trying to go through such a door simultaneously but in opposite directions. They wound up slugging each other with roundhouse blows. One other time in the U.S.S.R. I saw women punching each other, in a struggle to board a bus which was bulging like a New York City subway car. To their credit, I have never seen any hair-pulling. Nor have I ever seen Russian men fighting each other, though one night I saw a sturdy peasant girl in a real fist fight with a soldier, and another time I saw a drunken Russian stand off two cops. It was late at night on a main street in Kiev. Two policemen started to lead a big drunk off the main drag and down a side street. He became belligerent and refused to go with them. They remonstrated with him, then took him by the arm and started to pull him along. He gave one a push in the chest, sending the policeman spinning about six feet off the curb and into the gutter, though the cop did not fall. The drunk lurched off and the officers remained staring at him in shaken bewilderment.

After our shopping tour of Minsk, two Soviet officials escorted me to the airport. Since I had had no lunch and we had a little time, we went into the restaurant, where they asked me what I wanted. I ordered a "rumpsteak" and a bottle of beer. Then they ordered cookies and cherry pop for themselves. I ate in embarrassment, not knowing whether they were eating at home at a different hour, or were too poor to eat more and too proud to let me treat them. Maybe I just was oversensitive, but it was one meal that satisfied my hunger but provided no enjoyment.

CHAPTER 11

Kiev Seven Years Later

THE TWO hour trip from Minsk to Kiev was on a plane just like the one I took from Helsinki to Moscow. The cost of the flight was 200 rubles ($50). A corresponding trip from New York to Washington costs about $16.50. There were only two other passengers, and the three of us sat in the front seats, a woman on my left, and across the aisle, a man who turned out to be an engineer from Kiev. The rest of the seats were covered with baggage. The man spoke some German, and the woman spoke some English. We passed the two hours in a struggle to understand each other. The woman was on her way from Leningrad, where she taught shipbuilding mechanics, to Odessa, where she was going to finish a book with a professor with whom she had been collaborating by mail. I learned that she was a qualified architect and engineer. She was unmarried, about forty years of age, and rather attractive. She said that she earned 1,000 rubles a month and paid 150 rubles' rent for a three-room apartment which she shared with her father and mother and two nieces. (This was one of the highest rentals I was to hear of.) We compared prices in our countries, and in our limited pidgin-Russian-English she told me the cost of all she wore, and I reciprocated. What I call foreign-exchange intimacy. Her rather masculine blue serge suit cost 300 rubles, a very good silk blouse, 200 rubles, a little black necktie, 10, kapron stockings (like nylon), 30 rubles, black low-heeled shoes, 200 rubles, a small imitation-leather bag, 100 rubles, and a rather poor quality fountain pen, 10 rubles. One gold bicuspid, she said, cost her 10 rubles. (Many Russians use stainless steel teeth, and quite frequently I have seen men with a full upper mouth of steel.) I would guess the same materials of similar quality would be priced in America: suit, $25; shirt, $12; tie, $1; shoes, $15; stockings, $1; fountain pen, $1; and bag, $5—but the tooth might have been much more expensive in New York. In other words, her "outfit," except for the tooth, cost her about $212, at present exchange rates, whereas in America she might have purchased the same for $60. But her rent was about $12.50 per room in Russia's second biggest city, and it was a high rent for that country, probably comparing to New York rentals of $55 per room.

When I said their prices were high, the engineer fished out a pretty good lipstick for one ruble, or a U.S. quarter. He was quite proud of it, and he was bringing it as a present for his wife. He revealed that he earned 1,500 rubles a month and that he and his wife and two children had a two-room flat plus kitchen and bath for which they paid 80 rubles rent.

They assured me that there was plenty of food and they claimed that there was plenty of fruit and vegetables. I could agree only that there seemed to be enough food.

The woman asked me if the daughter of a peasant like herself could become an architect in America, how much such an education cost and how long it took, and then suddenly she asked me—no doubt as a necessary part of any education—how much aspirin and multiple vitamins cost in the U.S. In the Soviet Union 200 aspirin cost 8 rubles, while 200 vitamins cost 3 rubles. They also asked me how much I made and how many rooms I had, and, on hearing my answers, told me that I was very fortunate, as they might have said to thousands of Americans.

It was not surprising to find a woman working as an architect in the Soviet Union. Women do participate in a great many aspects of Soviet life. From the time I came into the country until I left, I saw women in the following activities: plane announcers, air stewardesses, doctors, customs inspectors, hotel managers, maids, tourist guides and interpreters, mechanics, street cleaners, clerks, waitresses, chauffeurs, taxi drivers, traffic policewomen, salesgirls, museum directors and guides, fashion-house directors, models, theater announcers, acrobats, watchwomen, hospital directors, nurses, college deans, professors, ditch diggers, train conductors, bank cashiers, schoolteachers, school superintendents, judges, jurywomen, court inspectors, architects, chairwomen of trade unions, airport managers, basketball referees (for a men's game), musicians, orchestra conductors, construction workers, railway repairwomen, crane operators, bus drivers, horse trainers, dog trainers, lawyers, dentists, writers, sailors, soldiers, radio broadcasters, TV announcers, dieticians, choreographers, gas-station operators, and slaughterhouse workers. I even saw a woman acting as "bottom strong man" in an acrobatic act, with men as the other performers.

Yet on my entire trip I met only one woman executive in a farm or factory—a leading engineer in the Baku Meat Combine. The other top-ranking women I met were: the director of a railroad-workers' hospital in Kiev, the dean of a faculty in Tashkent, a surgeon in Moscow, the prima ballerina in Baku, and the superintendent of a grammar school in Moscow. The Soviet Union makes a big fuss about the equality of women in all walks of life. But there were no women on the tomb of Lenin and Stalin the day of the annual anniversary; there were no women in the chief governing body, the Presidium; and at the Bolshoi Theater celebration of the Thirty-sixth Anniversary of the Revolution, only five women appeared among the forty-seven high officials present on the platform.

(It was probably a coincidence, but after I published similar observations in *Collier's,* Russian broadcasts in English stressed how many women served in the Supreme Soviet and in local

Soviets; a woman was promoted to be a deputy minister; and at a big celebration the following May, an unidentified woman appeared on the reviewing stand alongside Khrushchev and Malenkov.)

At the Kiev airport I was met by Victor Ionkin, a pleasant young man of twenty-eight who spoke fairly good English. He was to accompany me as interpreter on the rest of my trip through the Ukraine. The airport was greatly improved, with brand-new terminal facilities, and on a siding I noticed a four-engine transport plane, the only one I was to see in the Soviet Union.

Seven years ago I lived for some months in Kiev, where I had a two-room suite in the Intourist hotel on Lenin Street. One room was my bedroom; the other we used as a clubhouse for the mission. At that time there was only one small toilet for all the hotel guests on our floor, and baths were a sort of Saturday night ritual—requests had to be made days before, and the whole ceremony became a major event. My rooms had been sparsely furnished. Now some Russian with a touch of sentiment or propaganda had arranged for me to occupy the same rooms. They had been done over elaborately. A private bathroom had been installed and there was hot water at all hours. In the past we had shaved in cold water regularly except when we could find the floor maid to heat a little water in her kettle. The walls were newly decorated; the furnishings and paintings were brand new; only the old beds and their board-like unresilience remained as a reminder of the past. The blankets on the beds were made up in a familiar style, untucked, so that you can roll yourself up in them. Churchill in his memoirs tells an imaginative story about Molotov's sleeping that way so that he could easily leap forth from his bed, pistol in hand, to protect himself. The trouble with the story is that Sir Winston just hasn't slept in enough uncomfortable Russki beds. So far as I could see, all the help—the manager, the doormen, the maids—was new. But some things had not changed: there was the same little rickety elevator; the courtyard of the hotel re-

Kiev Seven Years Later

mained a dreary, dirty mess; and again, the liveliest spot in the hotel was the little restaurant on the ground floor with its still-woebegone band.

After we reached the hotel, one of the first things we did was head for the dining room. The linen, the furniture, the uniforms of the maids were the same as in the plush Moscow restaurants. Even the numerical proportion of customers was similar: 13 men in civilian clothes, 5 officers, 2 soldiers, 6 women, 1 child. The menu in four languages, Russian, English, French, and German, was quite elaborate and very similar to Moscow's Intourist restaurant. (Many visitors see just these two cities and just these two dining rooms, thereby getting a distorted impression that there is abundant food of great variety.)

I chose caviar with tomatoes and onions, accompanied, of course, by vodka. This was followed by Ukrainian borsch—all beets, carrots, potatoes, and lots of grease—and then the famous chicken-cutlets-à-la-Kiev, which I still think the best dish in the country. I had first tasted it in a Russian restaurant in Chicago years ago. On my previous trip this dish had been unavailable in Kiev; now I was to see it on almost every menu. My interpreter told me he had lived in Kiev for years, but first learned how to make these cutlets when he read, in English, a book written by a British ambassador's wife. Not being a cook, all I can say is that butter is melted in the center of a ball of white meat only, which is breaded, and that when you cut into this "bird," you have to be careful that the melted butter doesn't squirt all over you. Along with the cutlets came peas and carrots and the inevitable "French fried" potatoes.

After dinner I went to see the Kiev cathedral, which I had last visited at an Easter service (the Russian people wore willows on Palm Sunday as a substitute for palms) when the crush of people had worried several of us, as a number of persons fainted from the pressure. The Russian Orthodox churches are distinguished by a multiplicity of paintings and decorations and altars throughout the church. At whatever hour I entered one of them, a service was in progress, full of chanting, and with a great swinging of incense. There is a pomp and color and display worthy of the crowning of some medieval ruler. I visited about a dozen Orthodox churches in the Soviet Union, and the scenes in Kiev were typical.

My memories are necessarily impressionistic, and possibly prejudiced. The notes of any traveler must bear some personal bias, which others are free to criticize. I did not like the faces or manner of most of the priests I observed in the Soviet Union. They were usually pompous, sleek, and patronizing. I sensed something oily and cynical. Few of them were humbly pedestrian, and certainly none were martyrs or rebels. These, it seemed to me, were hucksters of religion, shill-men, dazzling the faithful poor and ignorant with their gaudy assurance. I have seen in many countries men whom I believed to be devout, humble followers of God. Most of the churchmen I saw here seemed of another kind. They were right out of an 1844 Russian painting by Savitsky called "Meeting the Icon in the Village," showing a cynical and wealthy old churchman too lazy to get out of his carriage to receive the tribute of the believing peasants. It is a fact that the head of every church of every faith in the Soviet Union signed a statement accusing the United States of using germ warfare. When I told one American specialist on Russia that many Soviet churchmen had informed me there was complete separation of church and state, he replied, "Yeah, like a razor's edge."

My attitude is possibly colored by a fantastic meeting I had seven years earlier with one of the leaders of the church, an archbishop, in Lvov. He resided in what seemed to me to be an old castle overlooking that lovely old-world city which had once been Polish. When we supped at his table, we were given the richest food and the finest wines we tasted in a land which was then on the edge of starvation. The vulgarity was underlined when the top priest's chief aide made aggressive and unmistakable, though ludicrous, homosexual advances to an embarrassed member of our mission. Throughout the meeting the high priest was "steered" by the local secretary of the Com-

Kiev Seven Years Later

munist Party. My American interpreters informed me later that time and again they caught the "Communist liaison officer to the church" prompting the ancient, almost senile, and somewhat drunken dignitary on how he should conduct himself toward us. But the priest had the last word; he whispered to my interpreter, "You think he runs me, but I will tell you a secret: his wife comes to my confession!"

To me the whole business seemed straight out of Chaucer; the medieval setting, the castle of the church, the towering view over the ancient city, the pomp and splendor of the clergy, the rich exotic fare in a land of hunger, the battle of intrigue between the powerful churchman trading on the honest beliefs of his constituents and the local barons, now not fat runty knights on horseback, but local secretaries of Communist organizations with similar powers: they ruled the land and held the serfs on it enfeoffed. Later this dignitary of the church was assassinated, allegedly by fanatics of a dissenting sect.

I wandered about the great Kiev cathedral for an hour and a half as the service progressed, and I counted and recounted the persons present. The number in the cathedral ranged between 350 and 500, for people were coming and going constantly, and the average was clearly between 8 and 9 women to each man. Almost all the women and men were old, and practically everyone was poor—by Soviet standards. (The price of women's hats in shops around the country ranged from 40 to 112 rubles, and only a handful of women present ever wore such hats; the rest were always in humble peasant shawls.) I counted 4 babies, 3 of them with what appeared to be grandmothers. About 5 children were under 5 years of age, 1 boy and 6 girls were between 5 and 15, about a dozen people were between 15 and 35, and a handful were between 35 and 50. The great majority were certainly over 50 and many of them, I would guess, over 60.

There seems to be freedom of religion, all right—but there's also evidence of an unrelenting opposition to it that apparently is very effective. There are fifty-five churches in Moscow for a population of five to seven million (there hasn't been a precise head count since 1939). New York City (population 8,000,000) has more than 2,600 places of worship.

One Sunday in Moscow I witnessed a mass christening of nineteen babies, who howled in international style. Only godparents could represent the family. Nineteen godmothers did their duty, but only five godfathers had been found willing to appear at the public ceremony.

I have never seen a soldier in uniform in a church, though I have seen a few men in the uniform of the railroad workers and of the post office, and once I saw a treasury man. In this cathedral I saw one woman who was very richly dressed by Soviet standards, and wearing a red hat. She was about thirty years of age, and she had two fat little children with her. She was an exception, one which I was to see in almost every church, but always singly and glaringly apart from the rest. I even saw one priest hover about one such woman, as though she might be a V.I.P., ushering her and her children into a special alcove before a special altar in that land of the common man.

As we stepped out of the Kiev cathedral, there were four women beggars standing at the door; one carried a baby, swathed in very good clothing.

One last item: some lay sisters circled through the audience seeking contributions. Victor, who clearly does not believe in "the God," chipped in his two bits anyhow.

In the evening I turned down *Prince Igor,* which I had seen so often before, and went instead to the new moving-picture theater, erected since the war. It was built on a lavish Cecil B. De Mille scale, with two main moving-picture theaters, an auxiliary theater for waiting guests, a children's theater, an art gallery, a restaurant, a soda-pop stand and a number of other lounges where production charts, five-year-plan statistics, and similar Government propaganda devices were on display. It is a Soviet custom to entertain waiting guests in movie houses, and here I watched 150 people seated in the auxiliary theater, having their impatience soothed by a forty-piece orchestra, which included eight women. In another theater in the Soviet East,

Kiev Seven Years Later

I entered just in time to catch the concluding words of an anti-God lecturer, "Nothing is permanent, all is change"—a moment before the doors to the movie opened and his audience rushed off for a change.

In nearly every Soviet building—museums, banks, offices, theaters—you are required to check your coat and packages, however brief your visit. (I even saw an old man employed to check coats at a snack bar which had only four tables.) For some eccentric reason this was not so in the movie houses, which were always overheated. There the audiences sat impassively, huddled in their heavy coats throughout a show. In some of the outlying cinemas, the men sit with their hats on until the show starts.

Soviet order of promotion puzzles me. The manager of the movie theater rose to that position from a job as head of Kiev's tourist bureau, which he got because he knew Chinese. He told me his theater showed many foreign films, English, French, even Chinese, and especially those "from all the democracies—Poland, Bulgaria, and Rumania." The last American film he recalled was allegedly named, *The Black Legion*, all about the Ku Klux Klan.

That night I watched two films, a Russian one in color about an admiral who fought beside Nelson, and an Austrian one called *My Little Friend*, a comedy about a lost and mischievous little boy. The Russian piece was what I would call "heavy drama." It was full of heroic scenes and sharp contrasts, with quick reversions from *Birth-of-the-Nation* battle scenes, to interior close-ups of Dostoevsky-like Russians grimacing in thought and grief. I remember some excellent outdoor color shots and some badly lit interiors in which make-up on actors was too plainly visible. I would have called it ponderous grade B stuff.

The Austrian film had the contrast of vivacity and prankish humor, and I thought the audience responded more favorably. I was chiefly interested in seeing what glimpses of another life were afforded to the Russians. In this picture, certainly everyone was better clothed than in the U.S.S.R., and some pictures of the interiors of stores showed an abundance not seen in Russia. But there were almost no full views of the life of the Austrian city, no general street scenes, just individual shots. There were, however, a couple of pictures of the inside of a country home, far richer than anything I ever saw in the Soviet Union. Even this one film must have revealed to Russian citizens that life outside their country was materially better than their own. I was surprised that the film was shown. Another time I saw a film from East Germany about a night-club singer. Whenever she appeared in slinky dresses, there would be a ripple of gasps and a rustle of excited comment in the audience, chiefly from the women.

After the movies I took a walk alone through the streets of Kiev, one Ukrainian city I know pretty well. At the theater I had seen, for the first time on this trip, a picture of Malenkov in a place of honor: on one wall were portraits of Stalin and Lenin; opposite them was one of Malenkov. Then I stepped down the street to the neighboring art store. In 1946 in its two windows were plaster busts of Stalin and of Khrushchev, then the top man in the Ukraine. This time there were two bronze busts—of two deceased leaders, Stalin and Lenin. The change from plaster to bronze symbolized the change I was witnessing everywhere in quality of materials and in standard of living.

Most surprising of all was the Kreshchatik, Kiev's famous broad main street which the Germans had almost totally destroyed. Now it was completely rebuilt with some skyscrapers fourteen stories high, prodigious in size alongside most of Kiev's low buildings. Once again it has become one of the finest streets in the U.S.S.R. Late at night, as in Moscow, there was a liveliness in the air; many people were walking happily along its streets, and again I remarked that the women of Kiev were prettier than those in Moscow. On our last trip I had christened the Ukrainians as "the Texans of Russia," and nothing has changed my mind about that.

One disappointment marred my first day in Kiev. In Moscow

Kiev Seven Years Later

I had made reiterated explicit requests that I meet certain persons in Kiev whom I had known before, notably Khomyak, the former head of the Ukrainian Government's UNRRA bureau, for I thought he could guide me to familiar scenes and faces. The Muscovites assured me that this would be arranged. When I arrived in Kiev, nobody had heard of such a request, but, as always, they told me they would try to find the gentleman in question. This is par for a Russian or Soviet course. Time and again they will assure you of something or promise a date or a trip, only to have all promises melt in thin air.

Sometimes I wonder if this derives from Oriental influence in their lives, for I have had many similar experiences in the Middle East and Far East. "Abdul, are you sure this suit can be pressed today, a holiday?"

"Yes sir, yes sir, yes sir."

Later: "Abdul, where is my suit?"

"Sorry, sir, today is a holiday, no shops open."

But then the Russkis can surprise you, too, by a belated full delivery of the goods, as they did subsequently in Kiev.

The next morning I visited the chief architect of Kiev. Here I learned that Vlasov, the former chief architect, whom I had met in 1946, was now chief architect of Moscow. This Kievan architect, whose name I neglected to note, no doubt out of irritation, was possibly the most assured man I met on my trip—and one of the highest paid, at 8,750 rubles a month. He and Khrushchev were the only two men whom I noticed wearing jeweled cuff links.

He told me that Kiev, which is the oldest city in Russia and which has been invaded many times, had been reduced during the war from a population of nearly a million to 300,000, and that now it was back to normal, with the 42 per cent of its living space which had been destroyed fully restored. He spoke of the five-year plan for essential living space and of an over-all twenty-five–year plan to beautify the city, with an emphasis on its "green carpet" of many hills. Now buildings were no longer built shoulder to shoulder in a straight line on a street, but were spaced so as to provide more light, air, and color. In the past the highest buildings had been only five stories; now some went up fourteen stories, and there were plans for an eighteen-story hotel; he added that this was not much compared with New York, but in Kiev they sought "an even and better skyline." He was also very proud of some streets which had been widened from 90 feet to 225 feet.

Planning for such a city is entirely governmental. The Construction Institute first devises the plans, and after approval by the chief architect and his staff, they are submitted to the Council of Ministers. When I remarked on the crumbling buildings I had seen elsewhere and the sharp Russian jokes about their construction industry, he retorted, "In Kiev we have ceramics which will be everlasting." It has always seemed to me that Soviet citizens, when you criticize them, invariably have some pie in the sky which is just about to be brought to earth.

In the afternoon I went to a number of shops I had been in before and priced a variety of items. The prices set forth are based on the official exchange rate of four rubles to the dollar. In a dairy shop butter sold for $3 a pound; eight different kinds of cheese were available at $2.50 to $4.00 a pound; and milk ranged from 50 cents to $3.00 a quart, depending on the grade. In a department store I noted down everything I could find with a price tag on it (most items would be rated as cheap to lower-middle grade by our standards): woolen blankets, $20 to $30, and a few for $40; cheap razors, $2.50 to $5; bath towels, $4; various silk materials, $21 to $24 a square yard; some good blue serge, $94 to $110 a square yard; men's suits, $325; women's rayon dresses, $13 to $15; a small lined-pad, 35 cents; fountain pens, $4 to $7; ordinary lead pencils, 40 cents to $1.70 apiece; penholders, 80 cents; rulers, $1; automatic stamps for dates of the month, $4; men's shoes, $59 to $89 a pair; women's shoes, from $59 to $115; men's rubbers, $5; babies' boots, $5; electric coffeepot, $20; aluminum teapot, $13; two ordinary desk lamps, $44 and $51; women's kapron stockings, $10; silver fork, $20; silver table spoon, $20; silver teaspoon, $9; metal tea spoon,

$3; a tea service with twelve cups and saucers, $102; teddy bear, $12; tricycle for three-year-old, $20; small drum, $3; toy motor boat, $3; toy metal auto about three inches long, $4. Outside the store a little street stand sold tomato juice at 50 cents a glass, apple juice for 75 cents and ice cream for 20 to 40 cents a scoop.

Next door a new bookstore advertised subscriptions to magazines on mechanics, astronomy, and mathematics for $5.60 a quarter, and a chemistry magazine sold for $18 per half-year. In this store I found a number of books in English and French. Galsworthy's *White Monkey*, Thackeray's *Vanity Fair*, Dreiser's *American Tragedy*, Dickens's *Oliver Twist*, *Hard Times*, and *American Notes*, Howard Fast's *Last Frontier*, Hugo's *Man Who Laughed*, Barbusse's *Le Feu*, Flaubert's *Madame Bovary*, Heym's *The Crusaders*, Voltaire's *Zadig ou la Destinée*, Romain Rolland's *Pierre et Luce*, Albert Maltz's *Short Stories*, and four plays by Bernard Shaw: *Major Barbara, Augustus Does His Bit, Heartbreak House*, and *Too True to Be Good*. Many Russian books are published in small editions of 2,000 to 5,000 copies, and then a few months later similar items by different authors, with only slight changes, frequently appear. The second-hand book market is quite extensive. Rumor has it that this is because of the housing shortage; books are stored under the bed, and when the space gets crowded, old ones are sold. Pamphlets are disbursed in the millions. Stalin's "Economic Problems of Socialism" was printed in an edition of 20,300,000 copies. Five million copies of Malenkov's speech to the Supreme Soviet of August 8, 1953, had been issued and they were sold out. Two more items: a publisher told me authors were paid by the page and not by the copies sold "because all our books sell well," and I met a magazine editor who told me poets were paid by the line; the going rate—$2 to $4 per line.

Next I went into a bread store where nineteen different kinds of bread were for sale. Business was so brisk that it required five clerks and two cashiers. On the walls were two signs which caught my attention. One said that the limit per person was 4.4 pounds of black bread and 1.1 pounds of white bread, but a cynical Russian informed us that it didn't mean anything. "All you have to do is just come back in the store and buy it a second time." The other sign encouraged informers. This is an old custom from czarist days. Chekhov once wrote a humorous story about it called *The Complaint Book*. The bread-store sign proclaimed: "To visitors; the complaint book is in the cashier's office and is given upon first demand, but you may also complain about wrong things by writing to . . ." I had heard of these complaint books in Moscow, where I learned that they were given serious consideration by the authorities.

Recently several restaurant managers had been changed as a result of complaints in their books, and I saw a vaudeville skit in which an irate customer demanded that the waiter bring the complaint book. "Sorry," said the waiter, "We have only one complaint book and many customers."

"Then bring me the manager."

"I can't; he's already been fired."

The signs in the post office—where all the clerks were women—also interested me: "You may send a letter without a stamp, but it will go more slowly. . . . Use telegraph and write in clear handwriting. . . . Show your passport to get your letters. . . . Your investments in this office will help restore people's industry in our country. . . . You may save money to buy valuable things by investing in this office. Here you may buy Government obligations."

Outside the post office I checked the pamphlets for sale at a near-by kiosk. Four were by Marx, twenty by Lenin, twelve by Stalin, one by Malenkov, and none by Khrushchev or Molotov.

Next I went through some free markets. One peasant woman told me the milk she was selling cost three rubles, but added, "If they don't give three rubles soon, it will go cheaper."

Another, when I asked the price of some scallions, replied, "Take them, nobody is buying them."

Russian salesmanship in the markets was ever thus. In another place one morning I asked an Uzbek farmer how much his cuts of lamb were, and he answered, "I don't know; it's too early."

Kiev Seven Years Later

The prices here in dollars and cents were: a glass of cranberries, $.25; of sunflower seeds, $.12; a quart of milk, $.75; a pound of butter, $3.75; cottage cheese, $1.50 per lb.; eggs, $.27 each; lamb chops, $2.00 per lb.; ham, $2.50 per lb.; apples, $1.25 per lb.; cabbages, $.25 to $.37 each; small hens, $2.50 each; glass of sauerkraut, $.25; macaroni, $.70 per lb.; and one dead chicken which weighed about 1½ lbs., $4.00. As we were leaving, I asked the price of one white hen and got the reply, "Fourteen to fifteen rubles, possibly even thirteen."

I listed all the items sold in the market. In addition to those priced above, I saw for sale: carrots, tomatoes, onions, radishes, horseradish, garlic, parsley, pumpkins, beets, potatoes, and one duck.

From the market I went to the best department store in town and found a mink coat priced at "20,004 rubles." When I asked, "Why the four added on?" I got the reply, "Women are strange." Russian women are still stranger, apparently. We would price it in the U.S. at $4,996. Maybe our State Department should ponder this example of Russian psychology. To add to the confusion, I can cite Maria Gortova, a milkmaid. A magazine wrote that she patriotically proposed a resolution that her brigade on a prize farm raise the average milk yield per 100 cows to exactly "12,669 pints." I heard one other example of Russian feminine mathematics in a comedy act. One woman said to another, "I'm thirty-eight now, and in five more years I'll be forty."

While we were looking at the minks and silver foxes in Kiev's best shop, three tiny and very ragged gypsy kids whisked through the store like a Kansas dust storm, dancing, singing, begging at a whirlwind pace. One child grabbed me. "Show me your hand, and I will tell you your fate," and she did a little gypsy dance, including a shoulder shimmy, while her four-year-old brother in a conical hat turned round and round in a circle, droning an inaudible tune.

Everyone smiled at them, a few gave them coins, and one man remarked to me, "They are the homeless people." This caused my one bad entanglement with a Russki citizen. I tried to take a picture of the oldest child, who had all the legendary charm of the gypsies though she was in rags, and an irate woman stepped in front of my camera. She was indignant, Victor fled, and I was unable to explain that I was not seeking to put her country in a bad light. But I did not see her give the children any money, though she was very well dressed.

This was one of the few times I was to see gypsies on this trip. Previously I had seen many bands of them wandering with their horse-drawn wagons on the roads of the Ukraine, Soviet or no Soviet government. Now I am told they travel about in trucks. The official line is different: at the circus, the last and most popular of three acts was given over to the gypsies. They entered in their traditional wagons, singing their traditional songs, and one woman shimmied just like the little girl in the store. The closing scene changed all this. The gypsies were depicted as happily settled and working on collective farms, and they sang Soviet songs about a good harvest; but Russians around me acknowledged what was obvious—more than half the cast were not truly gypsies. Soviet city life, even in a circus, seems not strong enough against their wanderlust.

Similarly, city life seemed not for Russian dogs. In three weeks in three cities I saw only seven dogs—four in Moscow, none in Minsk, and three in Kiev. (These little statistics on dog life illustrate the pitfalls awaiting tourist-travelers who make any generalizations about Russia. Later in Moscow on a Sunday morning I saw five dogs on leash within one city block.)

After our tour of the shops, Victor and I adjourned to one of the new champagne stores and tried a glass of the excellent sweet stuff, which comes from Georgia. There was an old moujik there who had apparently knocked off most of a bottle and was quite drunk. He was in an amiable mood, but a couple of younger men were disturbed that we saw him in such condition. "Be calm like those gentlemen," remarked one.

The old codger broke his glass and then tipsily asked the patient girl behind the counter, "Am I offending you?"

Kiev Seven Years Later

When she answered, "Not yet," he said, "Yet? Well then, I'd better go," and out he tottered, singing lustily. I would say he was about seventy-five, a real survivor of the Revolution.

From this walk about the town, several impressions were outstanding: its new construction, so extensive, so old-fashioned, so uniform; the cleanliness of the city and its streets, making Kiev, like Moscow, far ahead of New York City in this respect; and everywhere outside the main shops, long queues which seemed to have been standing there since last I saw the town. Outside a dairy, I counted a line of over 300 waiting to buy butter. At the main department store six policemen spent the day herding a line of people who were waiting to buy curtain cloth limited to nine yards per person.

After this day wandering about the city, I spent the following one quite a ways out in the country at another big collective farm with 12,000 acres, called the First of May Farm. I had asked to visit one of the farms I had seen before, but of course they took me to one that was new to me. We inspected the barns, the schools, the local club and a peasant's home—all of them exceptionally clean—accompanied by the chairman and the director of the school, both of whom were Communists, and by the chairman of the farm village, who, strangely, was not a member of the Party, and we were invited to lunch at the home of the chairman of the farm. There his "better half," as he called her, joined us at the table. She was one of the few wives I was to meet on the trip. In the next room the radio was playing, and suddenly I heard English words in unmistakable American accents saying, "This is the music of Stan Kenton and his band." That gave me a chance to ask about the Voice of America. All three men said they had heard it; the schoolmaster, who did the most talking, said they didn't believe such stuff, that they laughed at it; and another chimed in that the BBC was much better. (I had heard that the latter doesn't go in for propaganda to the U.S.S.R., but just puts out straight news. Later in Baku, hundreds of miles from Moscow, I turned on my hotel radio—most radios in the Soviet Union are short wave—one morning and heard a BBC transcript of a press conference given by Dulles in Washington the day before. The Voice and the BBC do penetrate the Soviet Union, though they are heavily jammed by the Soviets in the Moscow area. One Russian told me he heard the Voice clearly in Leningrad and in Kuibyshev, but he could not get it in Moscow because of a "lot of static." He told me dead-pan that he thought there must be a lot of electrical factories near his apartment.)

The conversation with the farmers went on in Russian and Ukrainian, one person speaking one language, another the second, and still a third man alternating between the two. Victor took all the interpreting in stride. During the meal they asked me: "Why is the United States surrounding the Soviet Union with military bases? . . . Why are you in Egypt? . . . Why are you in Ireland? . . . Why are you in the United Kingdom? . . . Against whom are you defending the United Kingdom? . . . Can't the United Kingdom defend itself? . . ."

When I retorted that the Soviet Union was threatening all the world with the possibility of war, they burst into laughter, which I was certain registered genuine disbelief. When I pressed my point and said some of my friends were afraid I might not get home from their country, they looked at me as if I were class idiot. I must admit that I certainly felt safe in the presence of those open, honest-faced Ukrainian farmers, so generous in their hospitality. They replied immediately, "When did we ever attack anybody? What have we done that caused this fear?"

And one Ukrainian added, "Why are you afraid? We drank spirits with the American soldiers in Germany, we met many of them. They know we don't want a war, and we know they don't want a war."

CHAPTER 12

Reunion

FROM OUR full day on the farm we drove straight to our scheduled "meeting with Khomyak," without rest or change. Only upon arrival did I learn that this was to be a formal dinner (which was to last for almost five hours), held at the ornately furnished house of the Society for Cultural Relations of the Ukraine. It was here that I first met Khrushchev, General Grechko, now the Soviet commander in Berlin, Manuilsky, the Ukrainian Foreign Minister, and many other well-known Soviet officials. This time, in addition to Victor, there were present: an official Government interpreter, who was excellent; Senin, the Deputy Chairman of the Council of Ministers of the Ukrainian Republic, still holding down the same job he had held under Khrushchev; Stefanek, another vice president, who had been an assistant to the mayor of Lvov in 1946; Rudnitsky, Ukrainian Minister of Agriculture, who had been a vice president at the time of my last trip; and Khomyak, who had been the head of the Ukrainian UNRRA Bureau and was now head of a technical advisory division in the Ukrainian Ministry of Food.

In 1946 the Russians had established an UNRRA bureau of some fifty Ukrainians under Khomyak, a former partisan colonel, to deal with our UNRRA Mission. This was an efficient method of operation for both the Ukrainians and UNRRA, but it also screened us off from the various ministries, which we could approach only through Khomyak. Khomyak was very able and a prodigious worker, and he was also a man of great personal charm. It is not customary to speak of proletarian Communists as gentlemen, and many are crude and rough, but Khomyak was an instinctive gentleman. He had the respect and liking of every member of the UNRRA Mission. While we did not know Senin as well, we had a healthy respect for him, a man who was deputy to Khrushchev at the age of forty-three. Because I had known all these men and felt that they were sure I had genuinely sought to help the Ukraine as a former ally and had been honest in my dealings, I now took the liberty of being extremely blunt with them in our talk. Most of the evening was sort of a debate between Senin and myself, with the others coming into the talk only now and then. Senin spoke some English; this, and the fact that he had once been in the U.S., added spice to the talk. He is an articulate and confident man. A few months after our meeting I read that he had made an important speech at a session in the Kremlin, lecturing local officials—like himself—for trotting too often to Moscow, where he delivered the lecture.

First they inquired about various members of our mission; it was clear they had heard nothing in seven years as to their activities. After that they asked me what my impressions were on this second trip. I told them honestly what impressed me and what I disliked.

When I criticized their press for exaggerating poor conditions in America and for great untruthfulness, chiefly in what was omitted, Senin attacked our press, saying that the Soviet people were not interested in personal matters but in events, and that the American press was too full of distortion, and sensationalism—stories of murders, divorces, robberies, and suicides, particularly suicides.

It was true that the Soviet press had not been reporting such crimes, but even as we spoke, things were changing. On December 13, 1953, *Pravda* carried what is now a fairly typical crime report. The article, loaded with the usual editorial comment, tells about three young comrades who "constantly got drunk, acted like hooligans, and caused uproars." One evening the "fine fellows, feeling their oats as usual, turned up in the canteen of the coke and gas factory, began to annoy the workers . . . and tried to pick a quarrel." The fight they started resulted in the death of one worker and injury to two others. The three troublemakers were sentenced to long terms in a corrective labor camp, and the story concludes: "The workers of the coke and gas factory present at the trial greeted the sentence with unanimous approval. The hooligan bandits received their just deserts!"

After Senin's remark about suicides, I could not resist telling him I understood Communist East Germany had the present record for suicides. This led to a discussion of the current political situation and their denial that there had been any major change in Soviet policy since the death of Stalin.

Then we turned to the United Nations. They were the only persons who ever discussed the operations of the U.N. during my entire trip, possibly only because I raised the subject. Generally I tried to let the Russians introduce subjects. They thought the U.N. had done well in some ways, but they criticized the failure to admit Communist China and complained about "the organizing of countries against the Soviet Union."

When I said there was a rumor in the West that Soviet officials were afraid to talk to foreigners unless another Russian was present, they said this was not true. Senin retorted, "As for suspicion, when I was in America in 1932, an American asked me if I carried a knife. I don't know whether or not he was joking."

This gave me an excuse to complain that Russians had never invited any of the mission to their homes in sixteen months, except on two occasions: some of our mission had been to Senin's apartment where he lived with his wife and daughter, and a couple had once visited Khomyak's country *dacha*. This broad hint perhaps deserved the treatment its crudity earned, for on this second visit of mine to Kiev, no such invitation was forthcoming. An American might have taken up such a challenge. I know I would have said, "All right, come to my house tomorrow and see for yourself."

Senin countered, however, that he had been in the United States for months and had not been invited to any home, and Khomyak spoke up, "When you were here before, you and the members of your mission were alone with many Russians at many times, on boats, on trains, in hotels."

I replied, "That is quite true, and in our offices and in yours, but *not* in your homes."

I went on to say I had also never seen the inside of one of their prisons or corrective-labor camps; and then I added, "I'd even like to go into the Lubyanka (the MVD headquarters in Moscow in whose cellars, legend has it, many men have been peremptorily executed)." When I added, "And come out again," one of the Russians guffawed, and the others could not but restrain a smile.

They told me I would have to ask the Government. I pointed out to them that this was like the satire I had seen in Minsk about the little guy shunted back and forth between bureaucratic departments. Here were three leading members of the Ukrainian Government telling me "to apply to the Government." Why couldn't I apply to them right now? Senin smiled suavely and replied, "But you see, ours is a *collective* government. You will have to submit the request to the Council of Ministers." I put them on notice that I would file a formal request the next day, and I did, but without results. Later I reiterated this request in Kharkov and in Moscow, to no avail.

Stefanek observed that when he had been in America—so I understood him—he had been refused permission to inspect our Sing Sing prison. I could not resist assuring him that when the Democrats were in control in Albany, we would be delighted to take him into Sing Sing. But this may never come about, for since our conversation Stefanek was removed from his high office.

Reunion

I asked them who originated all the slogans plastered everywhere, and how these were selected. A discursive reply claimed that the Government expressed the will of the people, and I countered, "What did Stalin know about the people? He sat up there in the Kremlin for nearly forty years. He was as remote from the people as he could be. He never traveled around."

All of them got very excited about this and cited frequent conferences Stalin held with persons from all walks of life, and I had to admit that Khomyak, who was only a middle-rank bureaucrat, had recounted to me in the past a number of conferences with Stalin which he had attended. Senin went on, "Take Comrade Khrushchev. Before this recent important speech of his on agriculture, he conferred with many people, and we can give you names and places in the Ukraine where he discussed these matters." (Certainly I did have the impression that the new rulers got around more and were more accessible.)

Stalin's name led me to say that we foreigners, while we understood their natural respect for their leaders, thought the cult of Lenin and Stalin, particularly of Stalin, was overdone, with pictures of them, for example, in every room. The government had hinted since Stalin's death that there should be no cult of the individual, but it had not explicitly referred to Stalin by name. Senin was notably direct. Said he, "You are probably right about the exaggeration of Stalin. He was greatly loved and he did a great deal for the country and the people, but there was possibly some exaggeration because of this love. Now, under Malenkov, the emphasis is on collective action." So I remember his words; the first and only Russian I ever heard of who used Stalin's very name in admission of exaggerated esteem, even while he justified it.

These remarks had a curious sequel. On my last night in Kiev, the chief of the Society for Cultural Relations invited me to a private dinner in this same building where I talked to Senin and the rest. It was all very cozy, and I had the distinct feeling that the purpose was to pump me as to my reactions thus far on the trip. After all, the same approach had been made in Moscow when Bruslov, who had met me once formally in Washington, suddenly phoned my hotel room. "Mr. MacDuffie, this is Bruslov, remember me? How's life?" and then had taken me out to a lavish dinner at a fancy Georgian restaurant, during which discreet questions as to my reactions slid forth.

In Kiev that last night—and I suspected a tap in the room—I launched into my standard criticism of the cult of Stalin. My host became indignant, said Stalin "was not a clown," that in the Patriotic War "Stalin became as a God and we worshiped him." Such a remark, if there was a tap on us, was O.K. for the old Soviet line, which had not been fully obliterated. I then quoted Senin's remarks that top Government men seemed to agree that adoration of Stalin was overdone. My host smiled and said, "Yes. Yes. Very good, very good."

I asked him, "Why do you say 'very good' to this criticism, when before you said he was worshiped as a God?" He smiled a little sheepishly and shrugged his shoulders, but remained silent. It was only later that I realized that if there had been a tap on us at that time, which he would have known about, it was best for him not to utter a word "for the record." He was not going to contradict Senin deliberately.

Then I shifted the talk to Beria, saying that we in the West thought it was just a power fight, that we had predicted one or more of the leaders would be liquidated after Stalin's death, and the Beria case proved our point. Senin did not seek to link Beria to a Western plot, but otherwise gave what was to become a stock answer two months later. "That's not true. He was a traitor, and we have the documents. He is undergoing questioning and he will be brought to trial." This was one of the few mentions of Beria I encountered till the public announcement of his trial. As in the case of Trotsky, once he was condemned, they claimed he had been evil all his life.

To my questions about their opinion of the American people, and the American people's fear of war, Senin responded: "The American people do not want war, and of course the Russian people do not want war. When did Russia ever attack? Where do you get such ideas?"

Stefanek then gibed at me about U.S. unemployment. I swung around and asked each of them to tell me how many people they thought were unemployed in America, thinking they were misinformed. One said, "three million," another said, "two million," and the third said, "a little over a million." Pretty good estimates, I thought, for I had expected a figure from them of five or ten million. I explained our figures, accused them of a lot of fake make-work jobs, like six doormen in a hotel where we would use one automatic elevator, and pointed out that a lot of their knowledge about America was from books fifty years out of date. One public school superintendent had asked me if teachers were still punished in America for teaching Darwinism. This remark about their ignorance touched somewhere, for frequently after that Senin would begin, a little ironically, "Perhaps you think this too is bookish."

When I enumerated all the beggars I had seen outside their churches (a record twenty-eight at a church in Kharkov was still ahead of me), Senin retorted that he had seen the equivalent in America—apple-sellers on each corner. "That's like all your figures," I answered. "You're talking about something over twenty years old; I'm talking about the present-day Soviet Union. Today, for example, the average American wears better clothes than you or I have on right now." This was pretty crude, but sometimes something so blunt makes a strong impression on a Russian. At least he respects such words more than flattery.

Next I cracked about their "full employment" of slave laborers, told them of Western estimates that there were as many as twenty million, and asked, "How many slave laborers do you really have in Siberia?"

Senin ducked it with a smile. "Would you like to go to Siberia and find out for yourself?"

"I'm afraid I'd never get out."

The conversation swung to foreign affairs and questions of peace and war. They admitted they had an atom and a hydrogen bomb and showed by their answers that they were fully cognizant of the power for destruction of such weapons. They put forth the standard line that American war profiteers were whipping up the current frenzy. They contended, as did many other Russians, that their military officers—though the ministers did not seem to know their exact pay—were no better off financially than Russian engineers. They also raised questions I was to hear with sickening repetition— Why didn't we let Paul Robeson come and collect their peace prize, and why did we throw impediments in the way of the visit to America of their chess players.

Stefanek intervened to say, "You have been free to take pictures on our farms, you have been free to go through our country and see things. See how free we are with you. Why are your people afraid of us?"

I let him have it. "If you'll pardon me, I think that's a lot of nonsense. What has my taking pictures on a farm got to do with atom-bomb warfare and your security?"

Naturally Stefanek was nettled. He switched the subject, retorting, "Our whole discussion reveals the fundamental decay in American education. Your failure to provide free education for all students who want it, your failure to provide free medicine, show that your government and your rulers do not really care for the welfare of your people."

I couldn't resist asking him if it was their solicitousness for their people which made them so reluctant to let anyone leave the country to tell about "its wonderful care of its citizens."

A couple of Senin's remarks surprised me. I twitted them some more for the barriers around their country and their unwillingness to let citizens freely leave their Utopia, and asked, "If a man wants to live somewhere else, why don't you let him go?"

He replied, "I would consider a man who left my country in such a way as one who would put a knife in my back."

When I charged that their method of publicly displaying leaders always in rigid and unvarying precedence appeared stilted to us, he replied, a little brutally, I thought, "This is to indicate the responsibilities of a man and what he does. Take Mr. Rudnitsky (who was sitting next to him). He used to be vice president; now he is a minister (a demotion). Any public announcement about him must accord with his duties." Rudnitsky said nothing. But in June of 1954 for the first time in years the Moscow papers began to list the rulers of the Kremlin in alphabetical order instead of according to prominence, and I wondered whether Senin would stick to his former statement.

Two or three random remarks also stuck vividly in my memory. Senin said, "I have seen advertisements in *The New York Times* asking for sixteen- and seventeen-year-old girls to work as secretaries. I don't think they wanted them for such purposes."

I was shocked. "That's the most fantastic statement I ever heard," I snapped.

He laughed. "Maybe they weren't sixteen or seventeen," he said. "Maybe they were eighteen."

And another: When I asked why they didn't let more people visit their country, he mentioned Allen Dulles by name and said that he had read of a secret appropriation for Dulles's Central Intelligence Agency. This put a few chills up my spine, for years before in a New York law firm I had worked intimately with Allen Dulles. How could I be sure as I went about this land, jotting notes and snapping photos everywhere, that the Russians would know I had not seen Allen Dulles in years and had never worked for him in any governmental job?

One final remark cheered me as they obligingly posed for some pictures. "There is a good possibility that you will see Mr. Khrushchev," said Senin, with a smile.

To me this had been a most unusual dinner. There had been an open arm's-length discussion, not without its humor and pleasantries. While there were sharp differences of opinion and philosophy, there was at the moment a seeming tolerance for the other's view. I left the dinner, on whose excellence I had been unable to concentrate (for once, thank goodness, the toasts had been very few), with respect for their abilities, appreciation for their unusual courtesy, and a feeling of frustration and annoyance at many of their views.

The next evening Khomyak came to the hotel as my guest for dinner. We talked alone in German for a while, then shifted to our own tongues when Victor arrived to interpret.

I had worked with Khomyak for many months. In all that time his conduct was of the highest character. He had, so far as we knew, never broken his word, nor had he ever lied to us. It was to his advantage to receive all the help we could give, but among the numerous bureaucratic differences which can arise over a relief program of about $180,000,000, there was never a real quarrel with him.

There had of course been differences. Once representatives of the American, British, and French press had been allowed to tour European Russia to report on UNRRA's activities. UNRRA matters in the Soviet Union were under the jurisdiction of the Ministry of Foreign Trade, which knew their business, but a Foreign Office lad had the press in tow. My Canadian agricultural adviser was upset. "Mac, this show-offy Russian Foreign Office dope takes them to the best farm I've seen in the Ukraine—artificial insemination, electric milking, and all that—and when the boys ask him if it's an average farm, he tells them, 'It's less than average.' Now they have the idea UNRRA has been duped into importing food and that tons of Russian meat from rich farms are flooding the free market, which I can swear is not so."

I went to Khomyak and insisted that the airplane for the press be delayed so that I could personally take them through the markets and thereby kill this wild story. I almost had to slug him to get him to co-operate. He could see no reason for my perturbation. His position was, "Mr. MacDuffie, *you* are the official American representative. *You* know it isn't true, and are so reporting, you tell me. What does it matter what these correspondents send home? Your word will be accepted." Finally we got the reporters, a disgusted group as they saw a story fade, into the markets, and in the whole city they found less than a pound of fresh meat.

(This was not the only time I had run into exaggeration by Foreign Office minions. When I was about to leave the country after my first visit, I had gone to the Ukrainians and said that since the Ukraine had representation at the U.N. and a Foreign Minister, the Ukrainian Foreign Office should give me my exit visa and not make me go to Moscow for it. This, I am sure, was the first exit visa ever requested from that newly established organization. Finally they complied—and they numbered that first Ukrainian exit visa 100,001!)

Khomyak and I had basic philosophies which were miles apart; it was even possible that our countries might become mortal enemies. But we were then two human beings, from countries which had been allies, who worked co-operatively with each other toward a common purpose, and each, I believe, with a respect for the worth of his fellow worker. I took delight in seeing him at dinner, for only the unusual circumstances of the relief work could have created such a situation between the two of us in this age when our countries are locked "like scorpions in a bottle."

He was concerned for my future and drank a toast to my marriage and to a big family, and I proposed a toast to his recent first grandchild. Then we exchanged information on the whereabouts and lives of the Americans and Russians who had worked with us. As I had noted in Moscow, all the officials I had known before were functioning still in responsible positions except two: old Manuilsky, they told me, was seriously ill, and the mayor of Lvov had died. I got the distinct impression that from 1946 until the death of Stalin the Soviet bureaucracy had had little infusion of new blood at the top. Khomyak told me Pourabayev, our old factotum, was away on vacation in Sochi. Pavel Petrovich, as we called him, is probably the only Russian private citizen who has been the hero of a full-length "Profile" in *The New Yorker*. I remembered how he had once gotten an American up to Minsk from Kiev on an urgent trip. First he reported that there were no planes scheduled on that date. Later he came back to me with a broad grin and said, "There's a plane flying from Sevastopol to Minsk which will pick up your man here at Kiev." I asked him how he managed it. "Why," said Pourabayev, "don't you say any American can become President? I just radio the pilot and say, 'We have an important American here. Someday he may be President of the United States.'"

I also recalled young Sophie, the pretty blonde Russian interpreter, who, when I asked her what Americanism she liked best, replied in English, "I've had a *hell* of a good time!" I don't know what she was referring to, but she said it with relish.

Khomyak related an incident involving one of our American secretaries, a strapping, handsome Virginian, who handled her liquor like an old Southern gentleman. He said that after I had left the Ukraine, he had been invited to a Fourth of July picnic given by the remaining Americans. Maudie filled two of those Russian half-tumblers full of vodka, told Khomyak he must drink to the Independence of the U.S.A., and bolted the full tumbler, in the style of some of the bulky Ukrainian farmers we had run into. Khomyak gritted his teeth and matched her. No American woman would outdo him, he thought. Thereupon, he related with a smile, Maudie filled two more tumblers, looked him in the eye, and said, "Now we will drink to peace." He admitted laughingly that this was one time an ex-partisan warrior threw in the towel. I could see it was a tale he must have repeated often to some unbelieving Russian pals.

It must have been at this point that Victor delivered himself of that immortal remark, "What man does not like women and vodka?" soon to be followed by "an old Russian proverb": "At first a man's wife seems perfect; but pretty soon only other men's wives seem perfect."

I countered this with the time Burinsky, the chief Russian in UNRRA in Washington, had suggested that I not prolong my bachelordom too far. "For," said he, "as a bachelor gets older, he gets too particular. He wants the perfect woman to bring up his children, the perfect woman to love, the perfect woman to

Reunion

cook, the perfect woman to entertain his friends . . . but, Mr. MacDuffie," he confided, "there is *no perfect woman*. Not even in the Soviet Union!"

Burinsky's views on America had been unique even for a Russian. After he had been in Washington some months, I said to him suddenly one day, "Tell me, quick, first thing in your mind, what do you like best about the United States?"

"Your traffic regulations," said he, blinking through his glasses; "they are excellent. I have been arrested three times!"

I had pressed him on one other aspect of American life. "You have seen our papers, tell me honestly now, can't you read the truth in our papers?"

"Yes, perhaps you can," said he, "but a person would have to read twenty papers daily, and I don't think your citizens have the time."

"Well, what about your papers?"

He looked at me with an absolutely serious face and responded, "Why, we have small-sized papers, usually only four pages, and, you see, we have a committee . . . It sees that the truth is put in." From the way he said it, it was clear he believed with all the faith of religious devotees who accept miracles.

Khomyak then spoke of the "good memory" they had of the work of UNRRA and said, "many differences had been worked out well," and he hoped that was the way the U.S.S.R. and the U.S.A. would be able to work in the future. From this the talk went over to the work each had been doing and on to a rehash of some of the previous night's discussion. We talked a bit about economics and the Russian organization of agriculture, and again Khomyak returned to my cracks about Stalin's not knowing the people. Khomyak gave some convincing arguments to illustrate how well-briefed Stalin was with regard to conditions in the Soviet Union.

For the most part the conversation was not serious, but rather a reminiscent evening between two friends, ending on a sad, nostalgic note. I asked him about Krupkova, a famous but aging actress in Lvov, who had reportedly had a tempestuous and romantic life, and with whom I had had some pleasant encounters. "She is still an honored artist," he said, "and she is still acting in Lvov . . . but it is better to see her on the stage."

That night at the Intourist restaurant I met another man whom I had seen a lot of in the past—a wonderful old waiter. He was constantly smiling, always bustling and eager to serve—a real pro in any land—and like pros everywhere, he loved his work and was proud of his skill. We used to call him "Mister Goodby," for he would repeat several times over in English the word "good-by" whenever he greeted us. This time Zavorodnik (which was his name) told me a little of his history, the history of a little man who went almost unscathed, and quite successfully, through the terrible vicissitudes of life in Russia these past five decades. He was sixty-eight years of age and had lived the past forty years in the same two-room flat (which had 320 square feet of living space plus a kitchen, toilet and bathroom, and "gas heating," which he emphasized). He had been a waiter all his life. He had served as a waiter in this same restaurant from 1916 to 1918 when it was part of the Continental Hotel; then he had worked at the railroad station's restaurant until 1932; and from that date on he had been at his present job, except for a brief interlude when the Germans occupied Kiev. During that time he worked in a tobacco plant. He told me that he averaged about 550 to 600 rubles a month basic pay, but that with percentages for being an old waiter and including a small pension, his total came to about 850. "Tips are not widely practiced, as before the Revolution." His daughter had graduated from a teachers' college and now taught French and English in a middle school. His son was "a sportsman," that is, a teacher of gymnastics, at Kirovograd. He said in Russian, "Life is very good now. All my family have good salaries. I am quite happy. Very good, very good." And then he added as always in English, "Good-by, good-by."

Next to seeing people I had known before, I enjoyed roaming about this city I had also known so well. Ancient Kiev on the high hills overlooking the Dnieper is a comfortable, sophisticated, pleasant city with a half-European air and something of the gaiety of old Vienna. I am inclined to think it is the happiest city in the Soviet Union. The milder weather, the more volatile Ukrainian temperament, and the long and proud history of the city all contribute to this effect. Or perhaps I just felt more at home there than in other Soviet towns.

At any rate, I was content just to idle about the place and appreciate the many architectural additions which had covered over the scars of invasion.

Unfortunately, what I encountered here that was new to me was a little depressing. For the first time I had an opportunity to see one of the much-touted Soviet resthouses, institutions of which the Russians are so proud that—from a Westerner's point of view, at least—they exaggerate their delights inordinately. "The resthouses," they told me everywhere, "are country retreats where people can enjoy inexpensive—even free—vacations." From all the talk, I thought they must be something like the exotic resorts of the Western world.

The Kiev Resthouse, run by the All Union Central Committee of Trade Unions, consists of fifteen or twenty little buildings scattered through the trees of a birch forest. There are ten houses for guests, a dining hall, a clubhouse, an infirmary, a library with about twenty-five shelves, and a concert hall. Among the guests, who came from all parts of the Ukraine, I saw workers, shop foremen, engineers, doctors, even an author. There seemed to be little for them to do but eat and sleep. There was a radio loud-speaker in each guesthouse, but the master radio set wasn't working. The guests could play a little volley ball or occasionally attend movies or a concert.

There were six or more narrow beds in each small room, crowded so closely together that there was only about two feet between beds. I saw no closet space; I suppose clothes were kept in suitcases beneath the beds. So far as I could tell, there was no provision for families; the drably decorated guesthouses were split up into men's and women's dormitories. Meals were served at fixed hours, and all lights, I was told, went out at 11:00 P.M.

For some people, the resthouses are indeed free, or low-priced. They are the workers whose vacation bill is paid in full or in part by trade unions or by the organizations for which they work. But there apparently are many thousands of Soviet citizens who don't get that kind of help; for some of them, I'd guess, a stay in a resthouse must be just a dream. The cost, I was told, ranges from about 100 to 150 rubles a week per person—a high price for the average Russian, who barely can support his entire family on a wage equivalent to about 160 rubles a week.

By Western standards, the Kiev Resthouse offers a vacation only in the sense that one gets away and has another place to sleep and has a little time to read—and doesn't have to work. It will *not* furnish any competition for the average American resort.

It was also saddening to have a sweet-faced kitchen girl ask me pathetically, with anxiety in her eyes, "Do the American people want to make war on us?"

At Kiev University I was further depressed after seeing the people honored by portraits and statues. Only enumeration can make one feel this wearisome repetition of their gods. In main assembly hall: paintings of Marx, Engels, Lenin, and Stalin, and statue of Stalin. Museum of stuffed animals: paintings of Michurin, Darwin, and Stalin. Botanical museum: several botanists and Stalin. Ichthyology department: Stalin and Khrushchev. Hallway: Stalin, Stalin and Lenin together, and statue of Joe. Next room: miracle! four scientists and no politicians. School of philosophy study hall: Marx, Engels, Lenin, and Stalin plus busts of Stalin and Lenin. Next room: Molotov wandering through spring fields. Classroom: big paintings of Lenin and Stalin, and 100-odd smaller ones of various people in academic world. Another classroom: Stalin, Lenin, and fifteen photos of Pavlov, Michurin, and other Russian scientists. Hallway: Kaganovich and Mikoyan (of present rulers). Physics lab: Stalin, Malenkov, and Shvernik (ex-President of Soviet Union). Library: Stalin all by himself. Next hallway: Stalin and Lenin on one side; on other, Malenkov, Khrushchev,

Reunion

Molotov, Bulganin, then a painting which was obliterated (Beria?), and then Shavchenko (the Ukraine's Shakespeare). Main lobby: Lenin and Stalin, Shavchenko, Stalin and Mao, Stalin and Lenin.

We went to another building, the main library. Lobby: statues of Stalin, Lenin, and Shavchenko. Down the hallway: Malenkov, bust of Lenin, bust of Stalin, statue of Stalin and Lenin sitting together, and then a couple of paintings and busts of writers and scientists. Reading room: Stalin and Lenin in front, Molotov and Khrushchev on one side (and presumably Malenkov on the other side, which I could not see), and statue of Stalin in rear. Another reading room: in front, Marx, Engels, Lenin, and Stalin, also bust of Stalin; in rear, Stalin, Lenin, and bust of Stalin and Lenin together. Next four rooms: No. 1—busts of Marx and Engels; No. 2—Lenin; No. 3—Stalin; No. 4 —Zhdanov (deceased Poltiburo member), and busts of Malenkov and Khrushchev.

Next floor, first room: over door, bas-relief of Stalin and Lenin. Study: statue of Lenin and Stalin. Room on right: all nine members of present Presidium, beginning with Malenkov. Room on left: Marx, Engels, and eight historians. Large hallway: huge portrait of Lenin. Another study: Marx, Engels, and Stalin in front, plus bust of Lenin; Malenkov and Molotov on one wall and Khrushchev and Bulganin on the other. And in one last hallway, three portraits: Malenkov, a portrait which had been obliterated with a cement covering, presumably Beria, and then Molotov. Such were the portraits displayed to the youth of the Ukraine in its leading halls of learning, the University of Kiev, which has over 6,000 students and more than 600 professors and teachers.

I have written this in detail to show what confronts the eye all over the Soviet Union. In most executive offices there was a portrait of Stalin over the boss's head; in nearly every schoolroom and every orphanage there were portraits of Stalin. Many statues of Stalin had little flower pots around the pedestal, as at a shrine. Next to Stalin, Lenin received by far the greatest attention. Among the living leaders, Malenkov had a slight lead.

During our tour of the university, we met only a couple of English-speaking students, who were rather shy. I asked one girl if she ever practiced English by listening to the BBC or the Voice of America, and she replied, "We don't have radios."

Seven years ago I had asked why so many Kiev students spoke English with a pronounced English accent, and they had explained, "Because we listen to the BBC."

This quick trip did not bring forth the pleasant occasions at the university such as I had experienced in the past. I had gone to "English-German evenings" and "English evenings," where the kids put on shows in the foreign languages. One night they sang Negro spirituals, put on a play called *The Busy Broker*, from a story by Jerome K. Jerome, and recited poetry, all in English. The high point in my memory was when a young Russian girl, swaying back and forth as she recited, rendered bits of *Hiawatha*, with a strong Russian accent: "Bye-ya thee shorres of Geeetcheeey Goooomieeee!"

It was late in the afternoon when we left the university. As darkness was falling, to the slight nervousness of my interpreter, we made a hurried exploration of the Baikov Cemetery, where Soviet heroes lie buried beside many Christian graves. The Communists usually have a marble obelisk with a red star on top. The Christian graves, most of them poorer and older, have the cross with two bars of the Greek Orthodox Church, many of them made of iron. Otherwise the little Christian and Communist plots were similar. Often a portrait under glass would be encased in the stone monuments.

I saw a newly made grave, covered with mounds of artificial flowers bearing white paper streamers, each with black printed messages: "To unforgettable Valentina Karovna from the Kvass Factory. . . . To Valentina Karovna from her sisters. . . . To beloved Valya from Katya, Tanya, Ala and Uncle and Aunt. . . . To dear Valya from relatives. . . . To dear Valya from friends. . . . To dear Valentina from neighbors. . . . To Valentina from House number 11. . . ."

Among other gravestones I found these inscriptions: "Vice General Director of Railways, hero of socialist toil, I. V. Kovalev, 1894-1952—from the South Eastern Railway Department. . . . Honored Professor of Kiev University 1858-1928, from the Kiev Surgeons Society to their unforgettable Chairman. . . . Kebrin, S. J., 1886-1949, from Kiev City Council."

On another white marble shaft with a red star on top was the portrait of a young man who died, according to the figures at the age of twenty. "To . . . First Lieutenant of the NKVD, who died tragically in Poland, from his ever-grieving and always-with-sorrow Mama and Papa." You have to remind yourself that when some underground patriot slit the throat of an NKVD agent (now MVD), there would be off in Kiev a human tragedy and a grieving "mama and papa," for the words are similar in Russian.

CHAPTER 13

The Pittsburgh of the Ukraine

FROM KIEV, the capital of the Ukraine, we headed south by plane to one of its major industrial centers, Zaporozhe, the seat of the largest steel plant in European Russia and the city whose great dam across the Dnieper (built with the help of American engineers) is one of the major symbols of the industrialization of the Soviet Union. I went there to examine the plant and the dam, both of which I had seen in ruins just after the war. The chief engineer in charge of reconstruction had shown me great rents in the giant dam, one made intentionally by the Russians before they retreated, and a second added to it by the Germans when they in turn retreated. In 1946 repairs had only just begun.

At the steel plant I had seen a mass of twisted girders, what seemed an empty shell, and I had guessed that the giant steel mill was about 90 per cent destroyed, only to hear hopeful Soviet engineers assert that it was no more than two-thirds ruined. In those days the phrase "only two-thirds ruined" was a sign of good luck, something to be glad about.

Last time there had been no hotels and no large buildings standing in this city of several hundred thousand people, and we had stayed in the little home of a local citizen, a Jewish woman, who had been given the "honor" of housing us because

The Pittsburgh of the Ukraine

she had lost three sons in battle. Now we were met at the airport by the assistant to the director of the steel plant, Maksienko, who, like most executives, was a member of the Communist Party. He carried us off in a big black seven-passenger car to the hostel of the steel plant, a hotel run by it for its business visitors.

On my last visit to Zaporozhe our mission was overwhelmed by two elaborate dinners given to us within a few hours, one by the old city, one by the new. After this hospitality, one of the two mayors had accompanied us to a steam bath, of which they were very proud. In a few minutes three Americans found themselves without any clothes, standing with the nude Russian mayor in the midst of a vast shower room, completely encircled with an array of shower stalls, from each of which water of varying extreme temperatures seemed to shoot forth in different and strange directions. We had no clothes on. We could speak no Russian. And the champagne of the banquets had made us carefree and careless. In one corner of the shower room, sitting behind a deskful of gadgets—it looked like the captain's deck on a steamship—stood a man who, when he smiled, or more often sneered, looked exactly like Boris Karloff, only worse. This gentleman proceeded to turn a hose upon us, driving us from stall to stall. When he forced us into one of these cabanas, he would turn a knob on his desk, and a needle burst would strike us at a tender angle. Around and around we ran and leapt, relentlessly hosed and showered and battered, yelling incoherently, naked and defenseless, unable to communicate with anybody. To add to our confusion, buxom Russian maids would stride in and out blithely, paying no attention to what little opportunity we had to be embarrassed. When we finally escaped from this Siberia, the memory of the two champagne parties was as remote as the first czar of Russia.

This time Victor and I went directly from the Zaporozhe hostel to the steel mill, where we spent four hours wandering through its variegated buildings, talking with workers all along the line. I did not bother with production figures, having heard how others had been put off, and meeting too-vague answers at the start of my questioning.

I do recall that Maksienko told me the lowest pay in the factory was 600 rubles a month. No sooner did we leave his office than we accosted three men, all of whom were getting a lower figure. I saw one of them standing in the middle of a yard, urinating, without attempt at concealment. Near by were two men loading some cans into an old horse-drawn cart. The three men, aged 45, 55, and 65, and all looking well over 60, were a driver and two loaders. They earned respectively, 460, 450, and 500 rubles a month. In front of the boss they complained to me, pointing to their ragged clothes. "It is cold. We do not have enough money. We do not consider this enough money."

I asked some more questions, and one replied, "This is the best an old man can do. I left the farm in 1931." As we had a long tour ahead of us and as we were just starting our inspection, I did not press the matter further, not wishing the assistant director to think I was looking only for dirt. Throughout my entire trip, I was to encounter such complaints on only two other occasions. I do not mean by this to imply that I innocently thought everybody was blissfully content. Under the circumstances of my tour of the Soviet Union, it would be very unusual when anyone complained to me. On my previous trip I had run into similar complaints only once, as a Russian-speaking American and I strolled through the fields near a Minsk farm which had been occupied by the Nazis. There some peasant women gathered about us, asked us who we were, what we were doing, and volunteered, "Maybe you will stop those Jewish crooks who run the city from stealing so much." Was this the old disease of anti-Semitism of czarist days, nourished perhaps under Soviet rule, or was it a new infection from the Nazis?

Since I am not a technician and one steel mill looks like another to me, I concentrated on striking up conversations with the laborers, shouting over the roar of engines and blast furnaces. I asked chiefly about monthly ruble earnings. A metal pourer got 1,300, a fitter, 800, two women railway workers

The Pittsburgh of the Ukraine

pushing a small car got 670 and 700, an engine driver on a small train, 760, and two loaders of ore, 1,450 to 1,500. Then I tripped over a couple of technicians earning 1,200 and 1,300. Near where they were pouring metal, I found myself in the usual ring of workers. "How much do your workers get? . . . How many hours a week do they work?" In the group were three Russians, two Ukrainians, and two Georgians who were earning between 1,200 and 1,500 each. Their shop superintendent was earning 2,000. More questions were fired at me, "What about the workers in your country? . . . Who are you? . . . Are there equal nationalities in America? . . . What about the Negro worker in America? . . . Does he have equal rights? . . . Do your workers have an opportunity to work for peace?" (Which I suspect was a planted question.)

To a group of nine about me, I stated that in the U.S. our people thought that the Soviet Government was aggressive. They all laughed at me, and one said, "Is it surely your working people that think so?" and as we walked away, the foreman added, "They laugh at you when you say that our Government wants war."

Just after this a man at the blast furnace asked me, "Can workers have meetings in America?"

A little farther on I came across a woman locomotive driver earning 1,500 rubles, and then two men who had an obviously dangerous job unloading ore, for which they got 2,000 each. Again they asked me, "What do your workers get paid for this work?"

After this we came to the steelmakers, where highly skilled and arduous labor is performed. In one building the Ukrainians claimed they had 800 people averaging 1,800 rubles, and here I heard of steelmakers averaging 3,000 rubles and metal pourers 2,500 rubles. The superintendent told me he could make up to 5,000 a month and averaged 4,000 last year—equivalent to the wage of a top executive in most big Soviet factories. He claimed some melters and pourers made more than he did, that in this building the workers owned more than twenty automobiles, an astronomical figure in the Soviet Union, and "we need a garage for them." Yet I heard later that the assistant director accompanying me went to work by bus, and his big car for us was a factory car.

As we went through this building, I met the "State inspector" from the Federal Government, all dressed up like a doorman in blue uniform with red piping and wearing a peaked military cap. He made a good amount too, 2,500 rubles monthly. Here I met a melter who boasted of making 3,000. Then I saw a young girl breezing along, obviously not dressed for heavy work, but clearly at home in the mill. I grabbed her and found out she was a time clerk earning 550. This led me to ask Maksienko and the shop superintendent about women workers in a steel mill. They said women did not do the "heavy work" close to the hot metal or where there were dangerous gases. But a little farther on I saw a crew of women dismantling a furnace with crowbars and sledges. It has to be man-killingly heavy before the women are excused, in my opinion. In this building I also elected to inspect a toilet, and of course there was no toilet paper.

In the factory I noticed engines bearing a General Electric label and other machinery marked Alliance and Morgan, bought, they said, during the second five-year plan.

Near the furnaces were little shacks from which a woman dispensed soda water. In the U.S. I recall automatic water coolers and salt pills. Just another example of Soviet "full employment."

Then I met the metal-heating master, a giant of a man, who was 69 years of age and had worked 52 years in steel plants. He didn't look over 50. In the roar of the mills he poured out a gush of Ukrainian, "so many technical words—like a foreign language," said my interpreter. I did learn that he made 1,800 rubles base pay with 1,000 additional for long service, and that he had 75 men under him who received between 1,400 and 1,700. Here I copied down the production figures which are often displayed prominently on walls of the shops. The explanation which they tried to give me was confused and baffling, but it is

The Pittsburgh of the Ukraine

a hint as to the meaning of publicized Soviet production figures. The chart read:

	I		II		III	
PLAN	DAY	MONTH	DAY	MONTH	DAY	MONTH
Shift 1	101.8%	102.3%	143.3%	123.9%	79.2%	83.6%
Shift 2	118	103.1	152.5	125	82.5	82.7
Shift 3	106.7	100.4	141.9	122.5	85.5	83.1
Average	108.8%	101.9%	145.9%	123.8%	82.4%	83.1%

The explanation shouted to me in the din of the mill through labored interpretation was that Column II represented the "norm" for that shop, and it was on this calculation that the workers in the shop were paid. Column I represented the "Plan" for this shop and related shops. Thus this shop might average 145.9 per cent for the day (Column II) and yet, because of poorer pace elsewhere, the fulfillment of the over-all "Plan" for their division might average only 108.8% (Column I). When I asked why Column III was so much lower than the other two, I received the impression that this referred to "perfect production." In other words, this shop with others might grind out 108.8 per cent (Column I) of ingots, but when the rejects came back, their average fell to 82.4 per cent (Column III).

Columns I and II are typical of those seen all over the country. It is the rare exception when somebody's figures in these charts are not over 100 per cent, which is why this particular Column III intrigued me so much. I have a theory—only a guess—that Soviet plant targets are set low so that continual progress may be more easily boasted about. In other words, they talk of I and II, but the figures in III are reality. For example, I read about a grinding-machine operator in Minsk who fulfilled in the first eight months of 1953 all his quotas for twenty-two months. This was hailed as "one of the countless new labor successes with which the Soviet people are welcoming in the Thirty-sixth Anniversary of the great October Socialist Revolution." I have a suspicion that in America this would have been hailed as a miscalculation made in some plant by some statisticians or budgeteers. There is too wide a margin.

The Zaporozhe chart supports my other theory that the Russians are "percentage-happy," for here were twenty-four different percentage figures for one small section of the plant. In almost every section of every factory I was to see similar boards with huge lists of tables, but I did not see the Column III table again. Shortly after leaving these figures, I saw four railroad cars, each with forty tons of smoking ingots which had been rejected.

(Knowing this Soviet penchant for percentage figures and their making a great to-do about "overfulfilling plans" by such and such a percentage, I pulled their leg a bit on my previous trip. Since UNRRA was doling out millions of dollars to the Ukraine, the Soviet Government was obligated to pay the local expenses of our mission. They asked me to submit a budget and monthly reports. I gave them a good fat budget, minuscule compared with the UNRRA largess. Every month we ran well under our estimated expenses, and I would file a solemn report weighted with elaborate computations showing how we had "overfulfilled our plan" by dazzling percentages, based on rubles not spent. The percentage by which I "overfulfilled my plan" for personal haircuts was astronomical. The Russians never batted an eye.)

Just before we left the steel mill, the old man got in his licks. He said conditions now were much better than under the czar, that then the buildings were low, dark, and dirty, and, "Now," he added, "we are not so rich as to build bad factories."

Outside the factory I spoke to three old women cleaning the sidewalks with twig brooms. They told me they were earning 360 rubles a month, about as low pay as I was to encounter in the whole country. The last sign I glimpsed read, "Our plan is 15.3 per cent more than 1952. Comrades, our country asks that we overfulfill by 5,000 tons." I assumed the figure was for that section.

As I departed, I had that same confused impression any layman might have leaving any steel factory. You have been in an inferno. Is the confusion, noise and terror and glare of one

The Pittsburgh of the Ukraine

inferno comparable to another? I don't know. It was just another steel mill, but to my imagination there seemed a bit more confusion, a little more disorderly debris, a little less precision of operation than at home. The men were working hard, and conduct and pace seemed no different from ours. A human being is a human being, and there are limits to what he can do physically.

These impressions were somewhat confirmed when I recently read expert analyses of Soviet steel industry statistics. The Russians have an annual output equal to about 40 per cent of American production. The analysts say that the productivity of the Soviet steel worker falls far short of ours, but that the Russians use larger furnaces and utilize them more intensively than we do, stressing quantity of steel output over quality.

During our tour of the factory, the jaunty Ukrainian assistant director stood close by my elbow, his eyes alert, his smile ever-present, listening with great curiosity to my conversations, and never interposing any comment of his own. As I grew to know him, I found him one of the most pleasant Russians, or rather Ukrainians, I was to meet. Perhaps I am prejudiced, for he and a court procurator in Moscow were the only two strangers who praised UNRRA's work. One other mentioned it. In answer to my criticism of Soviet cloth, a Kiev textile executive told me he had seen some UNRRA shirts and they were lousy—fell apart in no time.

Had I not heard Maksienko speak, I would have sworn he was an Italian, with his dark eyes, his swarthy complexion, his Latin mannerisms. That night at dinner in the hostel (hors d'oeuvres with vodka, Ukrainian borsch, steak, rice, carrots, and, as always, French fried potatoes) he said, "This afternoon as we went through the factory, you kept saying to the workers, 'Do you have any questions?'" He went on: "Lots of them didn't speak to you because they were a little shy in front of strangers. But they saw me with you, and tomorrow when I go through the factory, I'm going to get many questions from them that I'll have to answer."

He started in: "What about the four hundred American bases which are surrounding us? Everybody laughed when you said the Soviet Government was stirring up trouble in the world. The Soviet Government reflects the will of the people. The Soviet people don't want war and neither does the Government. Why should we be in such a hurry to build? Look at all our new buildings which are peaceful, our concert hall, our theaters, our museum . . ."

I countered with some remarks that the Soviet people were misinformed because the Government didn't tell the truth, and he shifted his attention to the Voice of America. He said, "I am offended by its lies and by its broadcasts, and I am offended by what it says." Maksienko took off his wrist watch and flung it on the table. "This watch was given to me at the end of the war by the Americans." I read the inscription which said, "To the Heroic Soviet People from the Russian War Relief Organization." "I almost feel I do not want to wear it because I am offended by the Voice of America. The Voice tells nothing but lies and everybody laughs at it."

I pressed him to give me some specific examples, but all he could think of was that the Voice allegedly had not given the Soviets proper credit for the capture of Berlin. "We did most of it; we did it with others, but we did most of it," said he.

The sequel to this interlude came on my return to America. I talked with the man who had been chief of the Russian War Relief Mission in Moscow. Yes, he knew about those watches. Certain medical men needed watches with second hands. All watches bearing such inscriptions had been given to the Soviet Union on the understanding that they were to go only to doctors and surgeons!

After Maksienko had calmed down, he shifted to questions about the chess players, a defense of the Communist press and Party and the inevitable subject of war and peace. I remember his saying that the Soviet people were not afraid of an atom or hydrogen bomb and they looked forward to the day when this power would be used for good purposes. To my mention of

Nikita Sergeyevich Khrushchev autographed this official postcard and inserted the date, November 14, 1953. Signature reads "Н. Хрущев 14-XI-53 г."

The author, at the start of his tour of the Soviet Union, stands behind the famed St. Basil's Cathedral on Red Square in Moscow. On left are the Kremlin wall and main tower, with ruby star on top.

Moscow University, built in 1953. It is only 32 stories high but Russians say it soars 787 feet, making it taller than any building in the United States except the six highest in Manhattan.

View from the author's rooms in the National Hotel, Moscow. On right are the red Kremlin wall and tower, the yellow Kremlin office building. The center street leads to Red Square, the tomb of Lenin and Stalin, and St. Basil's Cathedral.

The heart of Moscow. Left to right, new skyscraper, and—on Red Square—St. Basil's, the tomb of Lenin and Stalin, the Kremlin walls, the interior of the Kremlin.

The author was told not to take any photographs of bridges. He bought postcards at his hotel of six bridges, including this of Krimsky Bridge, Moscow.

In the yard of a Moscow nursery. Working mothers leave children here for twelve hours daily at a cost of $2.50 per month.

A class of eight-year-old girls in "Middle School number 1850 of the Sverdlov District" of Moscow. The sign in back says "Summer work, pupils of second grade."

A third-grade class in the same school. The little girls asked if American girls studied Russian, and sent messages: "Study hard. . . . Have good discipline." One blurted out, "America is practical," and sat down, blushing.

Boys rushing out of Moscow Middle School at the end of the day.

A typical street in Moscow, in the Sverdlov District. Note the giant construction crane on right.

Leningradsky Street, reputedly the broadest street in Moscow, over 100 yards from building line to building line.

Lubyanka prison and MVD headquarters. This photo is one of few to show the famed jail after completion of the new building at right.

Much Soviet urban housing has a worn, beat-up aspect like this building in Moscow.

A student's room at Moscow University. The man on right, formerly of the Soviet Foreign Office, is studying international law and writing a thesis on "The Definition of Aggression."

Moscow District Court. Left to right: the public procurator, an architect; juryman, a store clerk; jurywoman (acting as judge), an engineer; jurywoman; the clerk; the plaintiff (Mrs. Smirnova), a street painter.

The chief rabbis and elders of Moscow's only synagogue, where 230—all but one over fifty years of age—attended a Saturday service.

The salesgirl at the wine counter in a Moscow food store. The sign advertises cordials. Customers urged her to stop waiting on people and pose for the picture.

A fashion show in Moscow featured this unusually slim Russian model, unusually long skirt. The woman in the white fur hat is Zorya Novikova, Intourist interpreter.

The author hurriedly took this picture of two MVD men when they met at a station between Moscow and Minsk. The woman on left is a conductor.

Train passengers cadge some breakfast at a stand marked "Buffet." Note two officers; the man in pajamas also is an officer.

Some curious Byelorussians at a farm fair examine a 25-ton truck produced by the Minsk Automobile Plant.

In front of Minsk's leading department store on a Sunday morning. The woman in center is relatively well-to-do, according to the hat she wears, which costs approximately 112 rubles ($28).

Moscow's renowned Bolshoi Theater. Many other theaters in the U.S.S.R. are of almost comparable splendor.

A typical broad street in Minsk, showing part of the vast construction going on throughout European Russia.

New flats, for the workers of one factory, in Minsk. In front is a wooden snack bar.

The best waiter—"Mr. Goodbye"—in the best dining room of the best hotel in Kiev, capital of the Ukraine.

The doorman and the elevator operator in front of Kiev's Intourist Hotel.

Just before closing time, the same hotel's band obliged with "Smoke Gets in Your Eyes."

The author was arrested in Kharkov when he tried to take a picture of this sign advertising "grape wines."

The Kharkov police station, afterward, and from the outside.

The three cops in Kharkov who arrested the author.

A Ukrainian girl in the Rosa Luxemburg Clothing Factory in Kiev. She makes about 800 rubles ($200 at official rate of exchange) monthly, against the country average of approximately 750 rubles.

After the reunion dinner with Ukrainian officials. Left to right: Rudnitsky, Minister of Agriculture; Khomyak, Department of Agriculture; Senin, Vice President; the author; and Stefanek, Vice President.

Postwar buildings erected on Kiev's most famed street, the Kreshchatik, which was blasted down by the Germans. Lower floors are for stores, upper ones for apartments.

A statue of Lenin in front of Minsk city hall. The statue is typical of those throughout the country; the building is typical prewar "Russian modern." Police detained the author's guide because this photo was taken.

Women laborers working on the fifth floor of Kiev's new post office. Women do heavy manual labor such as this throughout the country.

Entrance to Zaporozhe market. Several signs carry Communist slogans seen throughout the U.S.S.R. Others announce "Precise mechanics . . . repair watches . . . cashier . . . photo shop." The center one says "You're Welcome."

Midday on the main road between Kharkov and Kiev, the fourth- and fifth-largest Soviet cities, traversing the Ukraine's famed black earth.

Main market in Poltava (population about 100,000) in midafternoon, when almost no meat was available, and just a handful of eggs and vegetables.

General knickknack booths like this are operated by co-operative organizations throughout the Soviet Union.

This tipsy-windowed house in Poltava is like the thatched-roof peasant homes seen all over the Ukraine. Cottages, usually smaller, are apparently erected free-style with no attempt to keep lines straight or corners even.

Soldiers hold the people in line as they parade toward Red Square. First banner shows Kaganovich of Soviet Presidium; second proclaims "Peace—Peace for the World."

Early in the morning at the Penza airport terminal: passengers, sheltered temporarily from the cold, wait to fly over the Urals.

In the airport waiting room for privileged guests at Alma-Ata, some Kazaks start up a game of dominoes (most popular after chess) with Lonya (second from left), the author's interpreter.

In the Alma-Ata free market, 150 miles from China, the author poses with two Kazaks and their donkey. The sign on the white building advertises "ice cream."

Some of the homes on the Alma-Ata "Rays of the East" Collective Farm, which had approximately ten thousand people living on it.

A broad empty street in Alma-Ata (population 500,000), capital city of Kazakstan, illustrates the scarcity of auto traffic in the Soviet Union. A girl traffic cop reprimanded the author for crossing against the light.

Secretaries outside the office of the Director of the Tashkent Textile Combine in Uzbekistan, one of the largest factories in Asiatic Russia.

Grammar-school children at a collective-farm school on the outskirts of Tashkent, Uzbekistan, about two thousand miles from Moscow.

Moscow papers complained about the feudal seclusion of women in the Soviet East, but in Tashkent girls like this willingly posed for pictures.

Gofar, my Uzbek interpreter, meets a girl friend in a Tashkent department store. He laughingly said publication of this picture would get him in trouble with his wife.

A Tashkent toy store. The clothing of the shoppers is fairly typical of the Soviet Union.

Three gentlemen of Samarkand. The man in the center wears an Uzbek skull cap which is hand embroidered.

The road in Samarkand leading to one of its famous fourteenth-century monuments—the tomb of an ancient king, with Arabic patterns and turquoise domes.

Tanktown on the route descending from the Caucasian mountains, north of Turkey, to Baku in Azerbaijan, just north of Iran.

Two Georgians. One gave the author his name and address, asking that pictures be sent him, later took it back saying he had given the wrong address.

An arcade in a Baku department store. The absence of soldiers is unusual, but the inevitable uniformed policeman is there.

The Baku court which decided a case of socialized medicine.

This doctor from Tashkent cured the author of grippe by administering Russian penicillin lozenges.

This lady, the best-dressed the author saw, was chief choreographer for the ballet in Baku (third-largest Soviet city).

The Azerbaijan University Rector, named Gadjiev, shown with his family, had the most sumptuous apartment the author saw during his trip. Gadjiev was among the highest paid men in the country—12,000 rubles monthly (officially $3,000).

A more typical flat belonged to Mamadov, an oil worker of Baku, who earned more than twice the average Soviet wage.

The family and apartment of Mamadov's neighbor, also an oil worker.

A peasant stands in front of her home near Kiev.

Interior of the same home, showing grandmother and two granddaughters. A religious icon and the picture of a relative are visible on the wall.

Interior of the church in Zaporozhe. The presence chiefly of older and poorer women is typical of scenes in other churches throughout the land.

A hotel room in Tiflis. The refrigerator is "for air-conditioning purposes." The walls are hand painted, not papered.

The inevitable chess game in a Georgian farm club.

The assembly hall of the club house on a farm in the Caucasus mountains.

A typical home of a Georgian peasant (about ten miles from the birthplace of Stalin).

Interior of the same home. The author with a Georgian mountaineer farm family.

Stalin's birthplace, now a public monument. His father, a cobbler, rented the small room on left.

The grave of Stalin's mother in a churchyard on the mountainside overlooking Tiflis. The stone says simply, "Ekaterina Djugashvili, 1856–1937."

A street in Gori, Stalin's home town. Buildings are low because of past earthquakes.

Georgians at a farm near Mejvriskhevi entertained the author with typical peasant hospitality.

The main square in the village of Mejvriskhevi in the Caucasus mountains, about sixty miles from Tiflis.

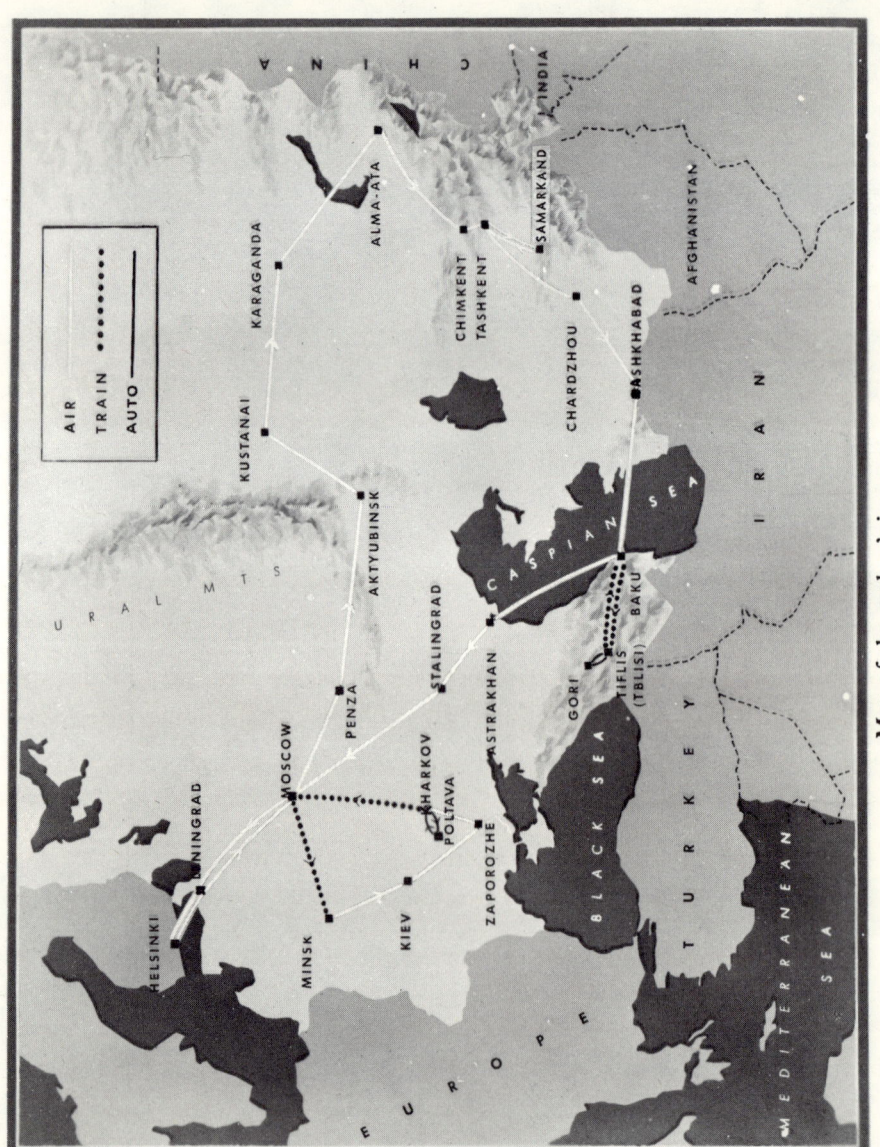

Map of the author's journey.

The Pittsburgh of the Ukraine

Soviet planes over Canada he replied, "Are you sure it isn't just rumors"—and I had to admit I was not certain.

The next day we went to see the famous Dnieprostroi Dam. Dams can be compared by height, volume, and length. The U.S. has nine of the world's ten highest, with a French dam in eighth place, and we have the ten largest. Anyway, Boulder Dam is 726 feet high with a volume of 4,400,000 cubic yards. Fort Peck, though much lower, has a volume of over 125 million cubic yards. The Dnieper dam is the eighth highest and eighth largest *foreign* dam—200 feet high and 291,800 cubic yards' volume. Nevertheless, it is the most powerful station in Russia and in Europe. The chief engineer informed me that it generated 650,000 kilowatts and that a new dam at Kuibyshev—reportedly the biggest construction then underway in the world, to be finished in 1955—would generate 2,200,000 kilowatts. He said that America's Boulder Dam and Grand Coulee Dam were a little larger than his dam and generated about 1,500,000 kilowatts. (Our *World Almanac* lists Boulder at 1,249,000 and Grand Coulee at 2,370,000.) When I asked him, "Is this generally known?" he answered, "You will find it in our newspapers."

Any great dam, like any great steel plant, is impressive to one small man, especially a layman. Its vast size made me appreciate the extent of Russian deification of its leaders, for I had seen many paintings of Stalin looking down upon this same dam, depicted in the posters as the size of Stalin's thumbnail.

First we went to the main office, where I met Ivanov, the director (a Communist Party man), and Jakovlev, the chief engineer (a non-Party man), who wore a new light blue uniform with three bronze insignia on his lapel. Later when I complimented him upon it and asked him why he wore it, he replied that the director, who was in civilian clothes, also had one, that a uniform shows the branch of service a man is in, and that it "serves to strengthen people and fix discipline and increases responsibility for work." He concluded lamely, "As you know, one must pay for his uniform while he is working." Certainly the proletarian Soviet Union is developing a passion for uniforms and marks of rank, which were so prevalent under the czars. In addition to the multitude of soldiers, many other branches of the Government wore uniforms if they chose. Foreign-Office employees had a gray one, railroad workers and bankers had blue ones, post-office men were garbed in green, and court prosecutors had brown ones with pink piping. Most all had shoulder epaulets or insignia on lapels, in this land of the common man. I began to believe that if Lysenko's theory is correct, that acquired characteristics may be inherited, then pretty soon a Russian baby is going to be born wearing epaulets.

At the main office of the dam they gave me some of the production figures I have already related. Reconstruction had begun at the end of the war and full-speed recovery was attained in June, 1950.

At the power station, six giant Soviet-made turbogenerators were humming away side by side with three turbogenerators made in the United States (generators from General Electric and turbines from Newport News) with no apparent difference in appearance or performance. Next to the nine large turbogenerators was a smaller one; the generator was American, the turbine Russian; I regret to report that they told me this combination did not work so well.

The chief engineer took out the original American chart diagraming the electric circuits that control the machinery. Then he showed me another chart, which the Russians had worked out. The circuits were now so simplified, he said, that the complexity and operating cost of the system had been reduced nearly tenfold.

In Kiev I had visited its brand-new TV station. There, too, its complicated new electronic equipment looked as good to me as any precision machinery made in the United States.

I am not an engineer, and of course it's impossible for me to draw any accurate conclusions from the sights I saw at the Dnieper dam, the TV station, and elsewhere. But to the untrained eye, at least, there is abundant evidence that the same country which can't seem to make such relatively simple

The Pittsburgh of the Ukraine

machines as elevators and tractors work properly can, on the other hand, do as well as any nation in the world with far more complicated machinery. The contrast was evident in the great control room at the dam. There, in the center of a roomful of elaborate electronic dials, was a table on which were a telephone and a master-control switchboard—and next to these, an old-fashioned abacus. In this roomful of the latest technical control equipment, the paint was chipping off the walls, a couple of floorboards were missing, the carpet was a worn old rag, and in the corners of the room were some ancient spittoons.

As I left Zaporozhe, I reflected on what all this meant in terms of Soviet war potential. As a layman in both engineering and warfare, I can give only the obvious answer. If the same hacks who repair tractors and build Russian elevators are turned loose on the equipment of modern war, the Soviet military machine will never be a match for the efficient armies of the West. But if—as we can probably assume from the verified atom and hydrogen explosions—the best scientific brains of the U.S.S.R. are at work on the tools of warfare, Soviet military devices should be among the best in the world. We must not deceive ourselves about this or let some Soviet crudities cause us to underestimate Russian potentialities.

CHAPTER 14

The MVD and I

In America people, when they hear I have been to the Soviet Union, always ask, "What about the police? What about the MVD? Could you move around freely? Weren't you ever stopped or arrested?" I have plenty to tell them.

Before I ever went to the Soviet Union, I had read some hair-raising tales about the activities of the secret police (the OGPU, the GPU, the NKVD, the MGB—now the MVD), and I had heard one or two first-hand accounts. Then on both trips I heard more tales from various Western diplomats and correspondents. I didn't know anybody who had been brutally treated or who had disappeared, but I knew of many who had been followed incessantly, impeded and harassed. Others had had harmless but amusing brushes with the Russian police.

I recall a story about Ambassador George Kennan, when he was an assistant in the embassy in Moscow, and Jimmy Byrnes, our Secretary of State, who was there for a conference. Kennan was sitting alone in the orchestra at the Bolshoi Theater the night of a gala performance. The theater was packed, but the curtain did not rise, for Jimmy Byrnes, the guest of honor, had not arrived. Everybody waited and waited. Molotov paced up and down the lobby, for once a little fluttered. Kennan unobtrusively went to a telephone booth to try to hurry the

The MVD and I

Secretary of State along. Just as he reached for the phone, a little man appeared from nowhere and said, "It's all right, Mr. Kennan, they just left the hotel . . ." and disappeared again.

In 1946 when our UNRRA Mission lived in Kiev, the members of the mission were not conscious of ever being followed about the streets of Kiev, and as one remarked, "On a couple of lonely streets at night, I wish I had had the reassurance of being followed." In Moscow there were some occasions at the theater when we were definitely tagged by flatfoots. Usually visiting delegates are given certain special boxes on the right side, lower level, of the famed Bolshoi Theater, and you can generally spot one detective in the back of the box. I have also been told that putting the foreigners in those boxes gives other police in the audience a good chance to identify them. But that may be just Moscow gossip. Until October, 1953, whenever the American ambassador traveled anywhere, a group of MVDers came close behind, ostensibly to "protect" him. Since that date the Russians stopped this practice of openly "protecting" Western ambassadors. One night, for example, Ambassador Bohlen and I ambled through the streets of Moscow from the center of the city to his residence, and this open surveillance was missing.

Once on my 1946 trip I was definitely "protected." I had written a letter to Khrushchev and signed it with my full name, "Marshall MacDuffie." My letter and his acknowledgment regarding their May 1 holiday were printed across all the front pages of the papers of the Ukraine. I had forgotten that the Russian custom was to sign with just initials, such as "J. V. Stalin," "N. S. Khrushchev." In the next town I went to, Zaporozhe, I believe, I noticed while I was inspecting a crowded department store that everywhere I moved, a solid phalanx or circle of men seemed to be moving with me; we formed a little solid ball of humanity rolling through the other customers. It suddenly dawned on me that I was completely surrounded by police. During the rest of the time I spent in that town, I noticed a heavy addition of detectives around me. When we got back on our train, I asked our principal Russian assistant why all the police. He replied, "In this area there are still many bad men left from the war, maybe even some German soldiers. You signed that letter; they think you are a marshal of the American Army; we did not want anything to happen to you!"

After I returned to the United States, I asked the American chief of the other UNRRA mission to Russia, which had been in Byelorussia, whether he had ever been tailed by the police. He thought awhile and said, "Only once. Ted, my assistant, and I once went into the big restaurant in the Moscow Hotel. There was a large line waiting. All of a sudden we were swept past everybody and given one of the best tables. I don't know, but I guess the MVD tipped off somebody that we had diplomatic standing, and they gave us a break. That's the only time I saw something like that in action." About a month later I met him again, and he said that in the interval he had seen his assistant and asked him if he thought the MVD had interposed its hand that day, and Ted had replied, "Hell no. Why, I gave that waiter twenty rubles!"

On my second trip to the Soviet Union I had several encounters with the uniformed police (called "militiamen," who are technically part of the MVD—which signifies Ministry of Internal Security) and with what we normally term the MVD—the secret police—who are not in uniform. It began with my attempts to take photographs. Apparently the taking of pictures by foreigners, now supposedly permitted, must be by individual permission, for many a cop is quite unaware of it. And I have seldom seen Russian citizens using cameras. I saw only a man photographing a family group in a Moscow park on a Sunday, a soldier in Poltava snapping his buddies, who were standing in full regalia in front of a Peace-for-the-World sign, and a little boy fiddling with a camera inside a Stalingrad theater. I have also seen cameras for sale in a few stores, but at prodigious prices.

When I arrived in the Soviet Union again, I was told I could take pictures—but not of bridges. I used to kid the officials about not snapping bridges, and told them they could buy photographs of our cities' bridges in any store. I ribbed them some more when I bought seven Russian postcards in my own hotel, all picturing important Soviet bridges.

They had told me I could photograph the Kremlin; so I started with one of the famous Kremlin towers. There was a cop directing traffic a few feet away. In my experience traffic cops seem to patrol their area too. I shot the picture of the Kremlin towers. A whistle blew, and the cop beckoned to me to come over to him in the middle of the street. I handed him the document I had composed in New York and which a friend had typed in Russian language and script.

This had the kitchen sink and Khrushchev in it too, for it was an all-purpose document. It said, "My name is . . . my passport number is . . . my visa number is . . . I was admitted to your country on the invitation of your Embassy in the United States, following my cabled request to the Kremlin to Nikita S. Khrushchev, Secretary of the Central Committee of the Communist Party." Russians like to repeat titles in all their lengthy syllables. I have seen the words "according to the September decisions of the plenum of the Central Committee of the Communist Party" repeated a dozen times in one short *Pravda* editorial. It's like an incantation, and I was not above self-serving mumbo-jumbo. The note went on: "I was told by your Embassy that I had full permission to take notes and photographs. I regret that my knowledge of the Russian language is limited. I should appreciate your assistance." Somewhere tucked into the note was the additional fact that I had been chief of the UNRRA Mission to the Ukraine in 1946. Somehow I neglected to insert the names of Stalin and Eisenhower.

The note stood up well on its first test. The cop read it. Then he blew his whistle, and I thought he was calling the wagon or riot squad. A policeman from the next corner of the Kremlin joined him and they both read the note. Meanwhile traffic was whirling around us, for I still was in the middle of the busy roadway. Finally they handed me the note and both saluted and bade me adieu.

There is an early limit to my courage; even though I had permission to snap the Kremlin, I started up the street away from it. About two blocks away five kids were playing behind a fence in a park. When I hauled out my camera, they all climbed on the fence and made a fetching picture, posing for me in assorted twisted figures, as only kids can do. I shot twice. The whistle blew. There was another cop in his handsome blue overcoat and cap. He saluted me and escorted me to another policeman on the corner, and I handed the two of them my note.

Just as they unfolded it, a citizen came bouncing along the street. I would take an oath the citizen was not an MVD man. He looked like the prize caricature of a professor. His fedora with a turned-up brim was battered, old, and too small, perched precariously on his head. He was carrying a brief case and he had on those doubly thick spectacles of a very nearsighted man. The kids had also gathered around us. The "professor" walked up to the cop holding my paper, stuck his head down over the cop's arm, for after all he was nearsighted, and joined the cops in reading the note. To my surprise, the policeman holding the note, instead of telling him to beat it, brought the note closer to Snoopy's eyes. Snoopy read faster than they did, snorted at them, made a mocking gesture with his hand as though to brush it all away, and, I would guess, said, "There's nothing to this." And off he tripped. The officers were more bureaucratic. They copied down my name and number from my very unofficial document, went to a wall telephone in the side of a building, made a call, and then motioned me on my way.

I went on a few blocks and came to a lovely view across a square. Just as I had my camera set, the traffic cop, whom I had not observed, far out in the middle of the square, blew his whistle and beckoned to me. I walked up to him, addressing him in English. Sometimes I have found sound and gestures work as well as anything. I said in some annoyance, "Look, it's perfectly all right. I've just been stopped down there and all my papers checked." He looked at me impatiently and motioned for me to go on about my business—he was whistling at somebody else and didn't give a damn about the big camera hanging from my neck.

A couple of days later, on my way to the Lenin Library, I noticed an unusual view of the Kremlin and promptly shot it. A near-by traffic cop blew his whistle and walked over to us this time. For once an interpreter was with me. The militiaman asked for her identification and for my papers. In trying to roll the camera to the next negative, I jammed it. I showed him the thing was now stuck, and he became so sympathetic that he didn't bother about our papers and motioned us on our way. A couple of minutes later I got it unjammed. That same day I ran into the two militiamen who had first stopped me near the Kremlin. I waved to them, and they gave me a snappy salute.

My cop-itis continued in other towns. In Minsk, the capital of Byelorussia, there is a thirty- or forty-foot statue of Lenin in front of the chief government building, about equivalent to a city hall. I snapped pictures of both. The inevitable uniformed policeman saluted us and began to ask questions. I was accompanied at that time by the local chief of the official tourist bureau, an official interpreter, the chief architect of the city, and the head of the Cultural Relations Society, a sort of local chamber of commerce. Nevertheless the militiaman hauled the Intourist chief into the government building, where they remained for nearly a half hour. Only the tourist official returned. It was O.K. for me to continue. But he was embarrassed, and good and annoyed. He muttered, "*malenki*," which I knew as "little." My interpreter said, "A little child . . . something inconsiderable . . . a very small thing."

My next Russian guide dealt with the police more summarily. In Kiev one day I was touring the public market, accompanied by Victor Ionkin, the able twenty-eight-year-old Kiev Intourist interpreter. Just as we were leaving the market, a policeman, seeing my camera, summoned me to step aside. He was with two other militiamen, all of whom had been openly shopping in the market. Unknown to them, I had already taken their picture. "Victor," said I, "that cop wants me . . . for the camera, I suppose."

"Don't pay any attention," said Victor, "come on." The officer gestured again. I was paralyzed between Victor's insistence on hurrying on and my normal upbringing under New York City's Irish cops. I couldn't imagine blithely disregarding that authority. "Come on," said Victor again.

"But . . ." said I, and I followed him to the car.

The three cops, moving swiftly, accosted us just as we reached the car. One saluted and addressed us. Victor shoved me into the auto and snapped at the officer, "Don't trouble my head with such nonsense." And he slammed the door of the car in the face of the three flabbergasted Russian policemen. Victor ordered the driver to start on. One man walked to the front of the car and looked at the license number, which seemed to give him no clue. The engine roared, and off we drove, the three militiamen standing one alongside of the other, each with his mouth agape. Only I was more shaken than they were.

About two days later we had a small similar incident. We were driving down Kiev's Kreshchatik, its Fifth Avenue. At a main crossing we stopped for a light, and I hopped out for a quick picture. Two traffic police were standing there. One saluted and asked, "Do you have permission?"

Victor shouted, "Permitted," slammed the door, and off we drove. The two cops looked like small boys hit in the face with a wet towel.

But Victor could lose his nerve, too. One day in Zaporozhe, we found a little church where a service was going on. I said, "Come on, let's stop just a minute. Let me take a quick picture from the back of the church." So we slid into the back; I let go with one quick flash photo, and out we ducked.

Later Victor said, "My heart was beating very fast that time —I did not know what such people would do."

The MVD and I

Such was my initiation with the police of Russia until I reached Kharkov. By good luck we finally had a sunny day on which I did not have any appointments. I went out of the hotel alone early in the morning, loaded with film. Since I had been traveling for many days, I had about thirty rolls of exposed film jammed in my pockets and all my scribbled notes of the trip, including one or two jottings about the number of soldiers in restaurants and other public places. I had not thought of it as "military" information; to me it was just illustrative of the life around me, but I was to realize belatedly how such data might be construed. I carried all my film and all my notes always on my person, for I had heard of too many others who lost them in their hotel to strange burglars. Some British diplomats had recently had their bags opened and their films spoiled deliberately. It was a burdensome precaution. My pockets were bulging. On trains I slept on my lumpy films. In hotels I never took a bath without my coat on a chair by the tub within reach. The incessant mindfulness of notes and film was trying in a minor way.

That morning in Kharkov I turned left from the hotel and crossed a bridge toward the center of town until I reached a department store, where there was a crowd of people waiting for the store to open. I took pictures of various buildings, of the store window-displays, and of people walking the street. As always, a few citizens struck up conversations and asked me about the camera. I could say little things in Russian like, "The camera is German, the film is American," and I showed them how it worked. I indicated partly by words, partly by gesture to one interesting-looking man that I wanted to take his picture. He pointed to his clothes as being too shabby. I drew my hand across my own throat and showed him I would take one only of his face, which to me was striking, and again he refused because he had not shaved. So I desisted. I shot pictures at random. Sure enough, up came the inevitable policeman, and I handed my inevitable note of explanation. He handed it back to me and left me unmolested. Immediately a crowd gathered around him asking him all about the note, and I think a couple seemed to be angry with him for not stopping me. This was one of the few times when I thought I detected some hostility among the Russians.

I stood my ground awhile, took some more pictures, and then started back to the hotel. On reaching the hotel, I continued down the street in the other direction, taking a couple of photographs of a perfume shop and a jeweler's. I came upon an interesting scene: on the side of a new apartment house was a big colored billboard advising the citizens to drink fancy wines. It was all very cheerful. Just below the sign was a long line of bedraggled citizens seeking to buy some lemons at about seventy-five cents apiece. I maneuvered to photograph the full scene, but before I could click the camera, there was a tap on my shoulder. When I turned, a uniformed policeman was saluting and addressing me. He escorted me a couple of blocks back in the direction of the hotel to a place where two other policemen were shepherding a large queue outside a dairy. He told me to wait on one corner while he cut across the street to confer with the other militiamen. While the three of them were talking, two men in civilian clothes slid out of the crowd on this busy street and joined in the conversation. The civilians had on as nondescript garb as I had seen in the U.S.S.R. One had on a cap, a padded coat, and a dusty pair of trousers. The other had on a padded winter hat, an old army coat, and a rather worn suit. Both civilians talked volubly and in very positive fashion to the cops, who seemed to listen deferentially.

(Meanwhile, on my little corner I had time to study a pitiful sight, which I had missed. At my corner were six "veterans' motorcycles," gifts of the Government to war cripples. They are low three-wheeled motorized bikes or cycles, with all steering done by a bar, as in our early electric autos. In each of the six vehicles was a man with both his legs cut off at the thighs—and two of them each had only one arm! While I stood there, still another legless man rolled up, using a board on wheels. Then the wife of one of the cripples came back, got in with

The MVD and I

him, and he drove her off. It was some sort of hangout while their wives shopped. None of the men were richly clothed, but neither were they in poverty. On a rough estimate I would say they were garbed in what I would term lower-lower middle class style. Out of any ten Ukrainians, I would say only two were poorer than one of these. They did not look downhearted or unhappy; but none were smiling or laughing. It hit me hard in the stomach to see them lumped all together, and it pointed up vividly how much that country suffered in the war, in its multiplication of damage. Later in that same city I noticed a touch of "Soviet realism," macabre practicality—I saw a legless man making his living as a bootblack. The pitifulness of the cripples took my mind momentarily off my own troubles.)

The three policemen and one of the civilians crossed to me and told me to accompany them in a direction away from my hotel. The cops spoke nothing but Russian, the civilian only a few words of German. By now it was clear to me that the two civilians had been following me. Their manner with the cops betrayed them. But most convincing, they had pointed in the direction of the department store, and I guessed they were describing my past activities; this was verified when one of them even made the same gesture—a cutting of the throat sort of business—that I had made when trying to photograph the civilian earlier in the morning.

I tried to get the police to take me to the Intourist hotel, which had now become for me a sanctuary where all could be explained. But they were firm. I thought they wanted to see what I had been snapping, so I went with them a couple of blocks. When we got to the scene of the "crime," they pressed on; that was not their objective. Somehow I got the idea from their vocabulary—the correct idea—that we were heading for the police station. In a crisis of life, all of one's past does not race by. But you can have almost simultaneously or in quick succession about four ideas, often conflicting. I thought of the Oatis warning; maybe I was about to be framed. Here I had gone through Byelorussia and the Ukraine. Perhaps I had learned too much, gone too far, and the Russians had changed their minds about my leaving their country. They certainly had all the "evidence" they wanted. I was loaded with notes and used films. The fact that the Russians were unwilling to let me go to Intourist for my interpreter weighted my fears this way. They were leading me off somewhere into the heart of one of the biggest cities of the Ukraine. I would be swallowed up. I even had an impulse to run, to cut and run for the hotel, thinking, "They won't dare shoot, and they won't catch me until I get there, and Victor and Intourist will explain it all; it would be harder for them then to take me off." I also had a strong feeling, "Well, they're mixed up; no real harm will come of it: it will all be a good story; so let's go." My curiosity was strong, but equally strong was the thought that it could be a long time in Siberia for a rash curiosity. I might have argued harder with them, but the result seemed inevitable.

Next we climbed aboard the last entrance of a double streetcar. The first lightness to ease the tension occurred when the conductress wanted my ticket. The cops teased her, snatched playfully at her roll of tickets, and finally pointed to me and told her I was one of the "militia." She thought that was a good joke too.

When we got off, we walked a half block into an attractive-looking two-story building, turned right, and entered a room which was straight out of Sidney Kingsley's play *Detective Story*. The room I entered was bare, dirty, beat-up. The walls hadn't been painted in years. The floorboards were worn and unpainted. Two long benches, a couple of stiff-back chairs, and one tiny hacked-up old desk comprised all the furniture. Behind the little desk was what must have been the "sergeant." There were three other uniformed policemen there and three civilians conversing with them. On one bench in the back of the room sat a man and woman who had the smell of stool pigeons a hundred miles away. A flock of other cops kept going back and forth across the back of the room to and from other rooms.

I sat down facing the sergeant, who took my papers but not

The MVD and I

my camera, and then he sent one cop out of the room with them. The men were quite friendly in manner, but nobody spoke English or German or French, except one officer who showed me the one English word he knew, which he repeated several times, I swear. The word was "good-by." Somewhere in the conversation I pointed to the one civilian who had accompanied me and to the three other civilians there—all of whom were talking intimately to the militiamen, picking up the phone and calling, and generally making themselves at home—and I asked each in turn if he was in the MVD. They smiled. All answered, "Yes" ("*Da*"—or even, "*Dada*").

When you are nervous and worried and waiting for the blow to fall, you snatch at any form of human communication. I showed my camera to the policemen, explained that it was German and the films were American, showed them how it focused, did anything to keep contact. Then I found a package of Pall Malls in my pocket. Though I don't smoke, I passed them around; all seven cops took one; for some strange reason the detectives refused. Then they tried to establish contact. They tried to pronounce the words on the Pall Mall—Famous Cigarettes package. "Paahhll Maahhll," "Pull Mull," "fah-muss," "fahmouse." But "cigarettes" was too tough.

The three policemen who had arrested me left. After about twenty minutes a new militiaman entered and signaled for me to follow him. This was the showdown. I had been hoping they had called the hotel (they had not). But maybe this was more trouble. I thought of the warning of our State Department. "They can be ruthless. . . . Remember . . . William Oatis." We climbed a barren stone stairs, as in any old public building in New York City. We went down a long dark cold hallway and entered a large office room, which at one glance was the chief's—revealed by the size, the furnishings, but most convincingly by the uniform and presence of the man at the head of the table. He looked and was dressed, it seemed, just like a British general I knew in Cairo. Sitting next to him was a handsome dark Russian in civilian clothes. Without being told, I knew immediately that one was the chief of police and the other the head detective. The chief addressed me. I did not understand. Then the plain-clothes boss spoke. Somehow I got the point when they handed me my papers. I pointed to my camera, and they both nodded. Whereupon they rose, we shook hands, and then the chief, with measured tread, walked out of his office with me, down the stairs, and to the door.

When I stepped out into the sunlight—and as I told this to a famous American expert on Russia, he winced—bango—I wheeled and snapped a picture of the police station!

To get home I followed the trolley tracks. First I came upon the scene of my crime, and carefully took the interrupted picture. Then, after I had gone a couple of blocks more, there were my three cops who had arrested me, conversing in the middle of the street, herding in the same line of people. They had left the lock-up before I had been released. I walked toward them gingerly, pointed to my camera, and indicated I wanted to take their picture. The cops were embarrassed and two turned away, though one was smiling. I was nervous, but I managed to take two hasty shots. A few minutes later I reached the hotel. Victor had just been about to go in search of me and would not believe that I had been pulled in.

In retrospect it was all so simple and harmless. What was I imagining or worrying about? But next time I'll let somebody else take that ride into Kharkov's depths with three sturdy Russian policemen and a helpful gent from the MVD.

CHAPTER 15

Town and Country

After my brush with the police, I had several encounters with Ukrainians in Kharkov that were more pleasant—at the famous tractor plant, at a gigantic publishing house, and on a State farm. And I managed to get in some diversions: some dancing with a pretty schoolteacher, an evening at the circus, and a day's motor trip to the little town of Poltava about sixty miles away. Even an argument with Victor, my interpreter, broadened my Russian-Ukrainian horizon.

I spent a couple of hours at the Kharkov tractor factory talking with the top four executives, whose basic salaries were fairly high—4,000, 4,000, 2,200, and 1,500 rubles monthly, with a chance to earn double that amount in overfulfilling production plans. All four of them were Communists. It was a big plant, extending over 420 acres and employing about 12,000 people, nearly half of whom were women. They said the plant was producing six types of tractors, of wheel and caterpillar variety. Their estimate of average pay in the factory seemed to me to match my estimates for the country: 700 to 800 rubles for the average workers and 1,100–1,200 for engineers.

When asked who decided on bonuses for executives, they declared it was in the hands of the Ministry of Heavy Industry and the Trade Union, which "played the strongest hand." They claimed the ministry recommended such payments, and then the Trade Union of the industry, and the All-Soviet Union Trade Union gave approval.

Following my questions, they immediately took up familiar themes, but with some slight variations: "What are the Democrats doing to stop the next war? . . . Is it true that the United States does not want war? . . . The Russian people suffered greatly from war. Why are you afraid of them? . . . You recall, for example, that our factory was totally destroyed. Surely you're not afraid of the fact that our tractors are picking up in production? . . . It is quite possible to use the atom and hydrogen bomb for civil purposes, to give the people a better living standard. We hope that there can be a great step for peaceful purposes. . . . Some of the U.S. broadcastings have many false things. It is difficult to say they are right. . . . We consider that the American people do not want war, but that certain warmongers do. Take, for example, recent speeches of John Foster Dulles. It would be great for the world if there were no men like him."

Their comments veered to a familiar line—the barring of the chess players, the failure of the U.S. to pass a law against warmongering, the rights of Paul Robeson (this time, in exasperation, I pointed out to them that, though the Soviet propaganda constantly deplored the status of Negroes in the United States, Paul Robeson had obtained a full college education in capitalist America at least twenty-five years ago—when the average European Russian couldn't get through grammar school, to say nothing of their eastern populations).

They repeated other remarks I had heard before: flat denials from all that the Soviet Union and Communists were stirring up trouble all over the world, complaints about the number of American military bases, and blame of the U.S. Government for scaring the American people. Said one, "We will show you our children, our children's gardens. You can see how our children are educated. If Americans and their children are frightened, your government must answer for that. . . . It is not correct breeding of children to let them read such stuff about war and atom-bomb dangers."

When I retorted, "But our children are educated. They hear what is discussed and read the papers and the magazines," a Russian countered, "But it is possible to say in your magazines that atomic energy and hydrogen can be used for the people's sake, and that it must be done more and more." He went on from this to a tirade about the complete falseness of the Voice of America and then he started to say something about the BBC.

I interrupted, "Is the BBC any better?" and they all laughed. "It's hard to say," they said; "it's hard to answer."

One continued, "It is hard to understand why both those countries say so many untruths about a country with which they have normal diplomatic relations. Our country is very big, east and west, north and south—very big. All around our country we are surrounded by American military bases. Why is this? Do you consider that the American frontier is next door to Russia? How would you like it if we had bases in Canada?"

Another followed, "I was in the United States a long while. I worked with the workers, and I know them, and my impression is that they are simple American people and that the simple American people are good fellows. They are energetic; they are truthful; they are people whom it is pleasant to work with, and their character is good; they have an honorable character."

The director picked up the peace theme. "We don't say the American people are bad. The American people are a peaceful nation. . . . But with two such social systems it is quite possible to live in peace. Your system is fit for you; you are satisfied whether your country is ruled by Republicans or Democrats."

I asked them to explain how the Communist doctrine, taught by Lenin and Stalin, of an inevitable conflict between capitalism and Communism could be reconciled with their statements. There was a long silence. At length the director replied, "You recall several expressions of Stalin and Malenkov about peaceful existence between the two systems." After I said that these statements were in contradiction with the inevitable conflict doctrine, there came from all of them the Russian word for "no" repeated a couple of times each.

The director went on: "It's all logical. What we said is truth."

"But don't you teach in your country that there is an inevitable conflict?" I asked.

"We do not teach that," replied the boss. The director went into a long speech. "We Russians are also afraid of war because we have suffered so greatly during the last war. We cannot want war. We are against war. The U.S.A. did not suffer anything like this. . . . We are offended that the American people are afraid of us."

"Did you say offended?"

"Yes, offended."

Whereupon I described what the Soviet Government and Communists were doing throughout the world, and they responded that this was not so. Said one, "If we tried to establish bases in Canada, how would you like that? Your bases are much closer to us than anything we have of ours."

We went through the inevitable contradictions until finally the director put an end to it, remarking, "We're glad to have had such a frank talk. You must come more often."

I went through one or two buildings which were quite neat and orderly, and in one I counted forty-four tractors coming down the production line. I also noticed a considerable amount of British and American machinery, including one with a War Production Board license on it.

My talks with the workers only confirmed figures I had gathered elsewhere as to wages, rents, and years of education. I remember one little girl who gave me a good peasant answer. When I asked her whether she didn't think the piece-rate system was tiring, she replied she had a chair on which she could sit. I found another girl studying at night school sixteen hours weekly in addition to her forty-eight-hour work-week. She asked me, "Do girls who work fast in America have the possibility to study at night?" Again, everyone asking about people

Town and Country

like themselves, and this little one possibly implying that slow workers there did not get additional educational opportunities.

I also ran into a foreman who assured me that they didn't fire anybody. (I report all this dead-pan.) Said he, "Impossible. We want hands. If they're bad, then we educate them." I asked if anybody could quit, and he replied, "One may go at any time."

After I spotted a very young boy at a lathe and remarked to the director that he looked under age, the director responded, "Ask him. Go talk to him yourself." It turned out the lad was eighteen and had finished elementary school and was going to night school. When I asked him what he wanted to be, he hung his head in embarrassment, finally muttered, "A good foreman," and shyly turned away to his lathe.

Then I met an elderly lathe operator and carried on a conversation with him that was both illuminating and comical. His name was Dekunin, and he was an elected member of the Supreme Soviet—something like a U.S. Congressman, though I don't suppose he had anything like the authority of an American legislator. Either Dekunin was an extremely conscientious worker or he didn't particularly want to talk to me, or maybe both. He kept his machine roaring all during our talk, with the result that all three of us—Dekunin, the interpreter, and I—had to shout to make ourselves heard. The discussion went something like this:

MacDuffie: "What's your pay?"
Dekunin: "Two thousand rubles a month."
M.: "What are your taxes?"
D.: "Don't know. Don't care about taxes."
M.: "How were you elected?"
D.: "Not by accident. The better man gets elected."
M.: "Do you think conditions are better now that Stalin is dead?"
D.: "From year to year we improve our life."
He asked me some questions, shouting, his eyes on his work.
D.: "All the world wants peace. What is your opinion?"

M.: "I think your government is causing an unpeaceful world."

D.: "The Communist Party is for peace."

M.: "The U.S. doesn't think so."

D.: "In your country, the government is run by capitalists."

M.: "Nobody controls our government. We can change it every four years if we want. You never change yours."

D.: "We are not fanatics. We see no reason for drastic change."

Dekunin switched his tack: "If your workers make as much as some people say, they're all small capitalists?"

M.: "That's right."

D.: "If they're all capitalists, how much money have you?"

I chose an arbitrary figure. "About eighty thousand rubles."

Dekunin's back stiffened. "*No more questions!*" he shouted. We didn't shake hands. I don't know whether he was just tired of talking, or didn't believe that I owned $20,000—or suddenly decided that such assets made me a big capitalist, not a small one, and therefore an enemy of all right-thinking Communists.

The chief engineer of the plant said he'd seen the Ford tractor plant in the United States. He said the Ford assembly line was much faster than his own (his produced fifty-five to sixty tractors a day), but he insisted that it was too fast for the good of the workers—that in Russia a man didn't have to pay unceasing attention to his work, but could relax. Maybe he hadn't met Dekunin.

On the way home from the factory Victor and I got in a slight argument. I groaned, "They talk about criticism, but you fellows never dare criticize your government." He replied that from 1925 to 1930 Stalin had been criticized, that the recent speeches of Khrushchev and Malenkov were critical of Soviet policies in the past, and that criticism of a ministry of the Government constituted criticism of a minister. Defensively he took up an old bromide, one I had not heard on this trip— Why had America failed to provide a second front? (I used to hear jokes at home about the American who found a slight defect in the magnificent Moscow subway and the Russian who immediately retorted, "What about Negro discrimination?" I have literally heard that reply introduced irrelevantly on more than one occasion, and now and then, "Why the delay on the second front?") He continued that he had been in Budapest and that Allied bombers had bombed workers' flats, but not the factories.

I brought up my "irrelevant" question— What about slave-labor camps? He replied with a story that an American church mission had come to Kiev with a map of purported camps, that they had flown around Kiev and not found one. (Something I could not trace in the U.S.) On my pressing him to tell whether he had ever known anybody who had been in Siberia, he told me of a young man who had been sent away for embezzlement, who had been paid while he worked in prison, and who returned with quite a bit of money in his pockets. Victor then retorted, "When I was interpreting for you, you said American workers were exhausted by the piece-rate system. Now this proves how bad capitalism is." Needless to add, this had not been my argument. He recounted how an American newspaper had shocked him; he had seen one telling about a man named Flynn on a boat with a woman who was not his wife. Victor made some cracks about the Rosenberg case and I jibed at him about Beria, to which he gave me a stock answer, "He will be brought to trial; the Government reflects the will of the people."

Most conversations do not proceed in orderly fashion. Ours wandered all over the lot. Victor told of being saddened by little children's shoes he had seen at Dachau and Auschwitz, and following that he spoke of the bombing of Berlin and sneered at U.S. efforts, saying they had not amounted to much. We started talking about my "arrest," which still nettled him. He said I couldn't have been taking just a picture of a wall, I "must have been taking a picture of people"—which was a little revealing to me, since I had not been prohibited from the latter —and then he asserted I should have resisted arrest. I could see myself telling the MVD to go to hell.

I remember, too, that he again brought up the Rosenbergs

and the fact that an American judge seemed to think they were not guilty. The Communists are like that; if eight judges vote one way and one dissents in a way they approve, they will completely disregard the existence of the majority opinion, and not even discuss it. I don't mind people differing in a fair and honest argument, but some of Victor's arguments like this one used to infuriate me.

He spoke of the German General von Paulus, saying that von Paulus had been captured and released and spoke well of the U.S.S.R. When I said von Paulus had become a puppet of the Soviets, he retorted that that was just American propaganda.

This was about the way all arguments went with any Russian I knew fairly well; never with any rancor, but never with any meeting of the minds. I heard of the wife of an American official who was delayed in a small city all one day waiting for a plane, and fell into one such prolonged discussion with an ardent Russian. Finally in desperation she said, "Well, anyway, I'm glad *you* have to live with all of it."

I must, however, give Victor his due. He knew much more about American and English literature than many Americans I know. He claimed to own at least a thousand books, and he showed clear familiarity with: Shakespeare, Dickens, Thackeray, Shaw, Twain, Thomas Hardy, Jack London, and the three Americans who have current Soviet acclaim, Howard Fast, Albert Maltz, and Langston Hughes. But he had never heard of Hemingway, Faulkner, Thomas Wolfe, or Scott Fitzgerald. Later I met various people in the Soviet literary world who revealed about the same range of knowledge and the same limitations, though I did meet a *Tass* correspondent in Tashkent who had read Hemingway's "Fiesta" (from *The Sun Also Rises*).

In a Moscow public school I had a chance to check what Western literature average Russians were exposed to. In a high-school reader I found selections from: Chaucer, Shakespeare, Swift, Fielding, Sheridan, Burns, Scott, Byron, Shelley, Dickens, Thackeray, Elizabeth Gaskell, Longfellow, Whittier, Twain, Galsworthy, Harriet Beecher Stowe, London, Dreiser, James

Town and Country

F. Cooper, Albert Maltz, and Howard Fast. The librarian informed me that an exceedingly popular book was Mitchell Wilson's *Life with Lightning* published in Boston in 1949. I had never heard of him.

The next day we paid a visit to a book-publishing house. It was called the Frunze Book Publishing Factory, run by a Ukrainian named Byelorus. He told me that they would soon be putting out "twenty million books and brochures" a year, having put out 13,000,000 by mid-November of 1953, 14,500,000 the year before, and 9,000,000 in 1951. To add to the confusion, he told me they put out 45,000,000 paint-posters, which, when analyzed, proved to be the numbers of colors multiplied by posters, most of which were five-color jobs; if accurate, then they put out about 9,000,000 posters. He said the material issued consisted of literature, textbooks, maps, posters, signs, and some books in braille.

Pay here was not so high, making publishing unenviable in one more country. He himself got between 1,300 and 2,500 rubles monthly, and the average for the plant's 1,200 employees, about 60 per cent of whom were women, was only 700, below the national average. Even the secretary of the plant's Communist Party group, a skilled worker who accompanied us on our inspection, only got 880 rubles.

I tried to find out how decisions were made on what to print and in what amounts. The story I got was that the Minister of Culture appoints the director of the factory, that the ministry and the director, on advice of an industry art council, make the decision. The industry art council is composed of representatives from various factories. In addition, an art council elected by the workers gives the boss the benefit of its advice—or so they told me.

The director, a young man of about thirty-five, was about the most dogmatic Communist I was to meet and also the busiest. He was the only executive I met who worked on other matters while he talked to me, signing papers furiously. He repeated the stock statements on war and peace and put forth some Soviet economic views. I noted his remarks as he made them in this order: "Are you acquainted with the publishing trade? . . . Why doesn't America speak for peace? . . . How can the Soviet Government threaten the world? . . . Do we surround you with bases? . . . Our income goes for the people, for a better living standard, for education, for resthouses, for flats of workers and engineers. Under the capitalist system and in America, this income is taken by private persons, by one person for his own good. He is rich and well-to-do. He exploits the workers (Khrushchev was to make an almost identical statement) . . . Is that right? In the second part of the twentieth century people must be equal to each other. . . . In America the big companies take all the money; in the Soviet Union they are state-owned. Are any of yours state-owned? . . . What is your personal opinion about the Soviet Union? . . . Our thoughts and deeds are inseparable. What is in our newspapers is true, without doubt. . . . Our people work by our budget, which is settled by the Supreme Soviet Session. We cannot conceal what we publish, the types of books, and how much we spend. . . . You mustn't think our people and government are separated. We want peace. We struggle for it. . . . What does the average American think about the release of the German war criminals, especially General Guderian? . . . I read the translation of the speech of the American prosecutor at Nürnberg and facts like that can never be forgiven. . . . How can you say our Army is increasing? We two (pointing to the Communist secretary) were in the Army, but we are not in it now. We are reducing. In 1949 I know the American Army increased immensely. . . . In this factory eighty per cent of the men were in the Army, and now they're back here; they're not in the Army. . . . We think the American people are not threatening us, but the American Government does not have the interests of peace at heart, and it defends only the capitalists. . . . Why didn't you let Paul Robeson come and get the Peace Prize. . . . Why did you keep the chess players confined to New York? . . . How did you like our talk?"

Here are the questions put to me by various workers as I walked through this plant: "How do young people without parents grow up in your country? (This was from an orphan girl who did not know I knew she was an orphan.) . . . Do you have women shop supervisors in America? . . . How much education is required to be an engineer? . . . How many years' education in other countries is needed to be an engineer? Do men and women do the same work in America? . . . Are they paid by the piece rate? . . . We teach our children with pictures of machines and cranes and not of pistols. . . . We are interested in peace all over the world. We do not think the American Government wants peace. Why do the Americans not agree with our proposals at the United Nations? . . . We build people's lives. We want peace all over the world. . . . We Soviet people are engaged in peaceful work, because the reason is that we suffered great damage in the war. . . . We are growing all the time. Why doesn't the United States still want an alliance with us as before? . . . But the Soviet Government doesn't build bases around your country. . . . We have been reducing our Army and our armaments. . . . Who started the war in Korea? . . . Why don't you leave Germany? . . . Why don't you admit the Chinese Government into the United Nations? . . . If we wanted war, would we be manufacturing things like this in our publishing house? What's happening in your country? . . . We help all who want peace and friendship, but in your country that's not so. . . . Soviet people have only a kind attitude toward the American people. We are interested in peace all over the world . . ."

The bulk of those statements or questions came at me on occasions when a number of people would gather about me, and I would scribble and answer as fast as I could.

Some items from the factory: There was a great deal of German machinery and one or two machines with French names which might have come from Strasbourg. The photographic room had cameras from Hahne of Germany, but of course the Russians assured me they made better ones. It made me think of one of my earliest encounters with a Russian citizen. I was inspecting a destroyed village when a stranger rushed up to me and tugged at my arm. He pointed to a long line of American lend-lease trucks. "See those trucks?" he said. "They are yours. They are very good trucks. But *Russians* are the best drivers!"

In one shop where girls were pasting pictures on book covers, with a squad keeping up with a moving belt, I saw the one case in the country where I thought I observed an extreme speed-up —and the kids were among the lowest paid, 450–500 rubles monthly.

The little orphan girl was a Stakhanovite (crack) worker, earning 900 rubles. In addition to her forty-eight-hour work-week operating a stamping machine by hand, she was attending nineteen hours of classes at night school. My questions about her earnings, rent, and expenses got the reply, "I am rich enough."

I ran into two grizzled typesetters who could be dropped right down into our plants. Typical of typesetters, untypical of Russians, they couldn't be bothered talking to me or asking me questions.

In one noisy, clattery roomful of 1927 monotypes, operators (one for two machines) worked only seven hours a day and got a special ration of milk or butter; and their pay ran 1,200–1,800 rubles a month. This was one of the rare exceptions to the universal forty-eight-hour week.

In the laboratory were pictures of Stalin and Malenkov, one of the few occasions when Malenkov got such a play. The director was more traditional; just Stalin and Lenin in his office.

I listed the subjects of their main posters which were being printed in the millions: women milking; Stalin re-establishing the mines of the Donbas; the excellent pupil at school; Young Communists rebuking a boy who got bad marks; some historic battle scenes at the Kremlin walls; a family receiving a letter from the front; the soldier returning to his family; golden autumn; home for vacation; Kiev autumn; the Carpathians; the Dnieper—all standard "Soviet realism." But there were also some excellent posters of the mosaics of the church of Saint Sophia.

The elevator operator was an old man of seventy-two, who earned only 360 rubles monthly, but who had 160 more in pension. A publishing house, even in Communist Russia, would have an elevator operator with waxed mustaches, a goatee, and a pince-nez!

After all this talk Victor and I were glad to escape to the country. We arranged for a one-day automobile trip to Poltava and back which would give me an opportunity to see the famous Ukrainian countryside again and get some rest from the constant "inspecting" of farm, factory, and institution.

I had been to Poltava twice before. It is a typical Ukrainian city of about 130,000 people, about sixty miles southwest of Kharkov on the main road between that city and Kiev, the capital of the Ukraine.

In one of the stranger incidents of the war, the Russians had gone so far as to allow the Americans to use this town as an air base for shuttle bombing. I do not know the full story, but I recall that the base was heavily hit by the Germans in a surprise raid, that many Americans and Russians were killed, that the Americans blamed the Russians for not maintaining adequate patrols, and that finally the project was abandoned. When I was there in 1946, the mayor reminisced about the habits of the GI's, who used to give the Ukrainian kids candy, who would come out and just sit on the fence of the main square and dawdle an evening through, and who almost broke up a local show when they whistled wildly at some really fast Ukrainian dancing. The poor girls took the whistling to mean disapproval, which it signified in that locality. He had a couple of special stories about a hunting trip he took with one American colonel. It was good to hear his remarks, to hear a man from the country we distrust and fear speaking so pleasantly of people whom he had liked and who had been his friends.

Just as we were leaving to catch our train, the Russians had informed our UNRRA Mission that there was a special American cemetery outside the town where American soldiers were buried, and that it was kept up "in the American fashion." It was then too late for us to visit the graves. Instead, on our Memorial Day, I arranged for the Americans in the UNRRA Mission to go to Poltava. It turned into quite a procession. The Russians sent busloads of people and officials to the cemetery some miles out of town. Not only that, but they had obtained three huge wreaths, one for UNRRA to put on the graves, one from the city Soviet, and one from the regional Soviet. There were, as I recall, five or six graves at least, a flagpole, and on a little monument one American airplane prop, which had been gilded. Most Russian graves are in mound fashion, but these were flatter, like ours at home. The colonel in charge of policing the area asked me for an American flag which he might fly there on special holidays.

Later, in America, I met the Quartermaster General of the U. S. Army, and I urged him not to transplant the bodies to the U. S., but to seek to persuade the relatives of the deceased that they should let the graves remain in the Soviet Union. I saw this graveyard as a permanent symbol, and also as an excuse for requests on memorial days and similar occasions that American delegations be allowed to go there. I told the same story to "Beedle" Smith, then our ambassador in Moscow. I had done all I could by notifying the American ambassador and by presenting the case to the general whose men would be charged with any removal of the bodies.

When I got to the Soviet Union this second time, nobody could seem to give me any information about the graves. I planned the side trip from Kharkov to see what shape the graves were in, and also in order to obtain one of the rare sights I could manage of the Russian countryside other than along the railroad. Under the present exchange rate, hiring of cars was extremely expensive, but I thought it important to get this brief glimpse at least.

Just before we set out for Poltava, our main purpose was exploded with the news that the bodies of the American soldiers buried there had been disinterred December 16, 1950, "at the request of the American Army," and had been delivered to the American authorities in Berlin. I think this was an error in judgment.

Since my latest trip to the U.S.S.R., however, a British diplomatic mission has pursued much the same aim. One of their chaplains conducted memorial services in 1954 near Murmansk at "Allied graves" of British and American seamen killed by German bombs.

Victor and I went ahead with our plans for the Poltava trip anyhow. The journey was uneventful. Except for the lack of traffic and the style of the homes, we might have been motoring through mid-Kansas on a fall day. As far as we could see around us lay the great flat grainfields and famous black earth of the Ukraine. It may be the richest, most fertile land in Europe; the earth is so deeply black, you feel that you want to scoop it up and eat it, or roll in its mellow softness.

The land was absolutely flat, and the horizon was broken only by patches of green or brown or black, and rarely some of the new tree belts, which stretched as far as one could see. The peasant homes of the Ukraine are little plaster jobs with thatched roofs and whitewashed exteriors, rather tiny one-story homes with, I would guess, no more than two small rooms in most cases. Now and then a wall would be painted blue or even pink, and occasionally I saw a tin roof. Winter was coming, and for warmth the peasants were lacing the houses with thick stalks of tall grass.

As we drove along, we would pass groups of peasants waiting for a ride. It is a custom, possibly even a law, that empty trucks must pick up "thumbers." It is not an unusual sight to see peasants asleep in the back of trucks, even on top of whatever goods are being transported. I recalled to a friend satirical cartoons in Soviet magazines about men lying with their dirty clothes and shoes on top of brand-new shirting materials, only to have her tell me that when she lived in Russia before the Revolution, she had seen peasants asleep in carts on top of carcasses of meat. Now and then we saw a man wheeling along on a bicycle, and once in the dead center of this farming land far from any port, I came across a sailor pedaling away. Others have written that you will find Russian sailors in the oddest places, which may account for the fact that some of the most famous battles they have won have been land battles. I even saw a fat peasant woman riding astride a dray horse, revealing some yellow bloomers with ruffles. There were old-fashioned horse carts trundling all sorts of materials, little boys tending cows, little boys herding sheep, little boys madly chasing goats off the road, and the inevitable brush with stray chickens and ducks, which still think highways are where they hang their hats. On this lonely road we passed smartly dressed traffic policemen, complete with batons, serving chiefly to check trucks as to licenses and destinations, I was told.

Now and then we would see wonderful old churches, and here and there new brick constructions of factories and machine-tractor stations, and once in a while a group of giant combines working through the fields. The Ukrainians, and most Russians for that matter, have clustered historically in villages. What astounded me was the sharp contrast within a few miles as to the quality or richness of these villages, some all neat and fresh and prosperous, and others, a few miles farther on, slatternly and patched, wheezing with poverty. Very few peasants were to be seen in these towns, though now and then an old grandmother would be sunning herself at the door in the crisp autumn weather.

The little town of Poltava seemed to be boarding itself up for the winter. It had been one of the most devastated cities I had ever seen, and now, while greatly built up, it still had a few houses which were just burnt-out shells, as yet unrecovered from the war. There was a bareness about the town exemplified by the absence of goods in the stores. In three food stores I found no meat except one small piece of pork. Then I went to the free market at about three o'clock in the afternoon. While the Russians with me tried to justify the lack of food by the

Town and Country

lateness of the day, I do not on reflection think this was an adequate excuse, for I was to see many other markets of larger cities at this or later hours, and they were comparatively abundant.

I have heard that Russian cities are classified in various categories, and I know travelers, such as I, see mostly the larger ones which have priorities as to workers and supplies. If my glance at conditions in Poltava is an accurate one, life in the smaller towns must indeed be bleak. This is what I found at the market: a woman with about three pieces of pork fat for sale; a woman with about a dozen eggs; a man with three or four tomatoes and a similar number of eggs; a woman with two bunches of onions; a truck with five or six chickens in it; and a truckful of cabbages. Furthermore, in the three food stores I found no fruits or vegetables, but I did find a woman dispensing tomato juice. All over the country this is sold from similar stands. The vendor has three or four glasses, usually chipped, which she washes in a cold water spray before dealing with the next customer. I never knew whether I was saving my life by getting the balancing vitamins or destroying it by getting unbalancing germs.

We went into a restaurant where we were able to purchase some borsch and mutton. In this little town in middle Ukraine I found that out of 39 people in the restaurant, 11 were in military uniform, 6 of them officers. Among the civilians, the men outnumbered the women 19 to 9. None of the women in the restaurant wore lipstick or jewelry. The stout maid (MacDuffie's Law—all waitresses in the Ukraine weigh more than 160 pounds) startled me by estimating our bill on a tiny abacus which she whipped out from a pocket of her apron. Still more startling was to see the hand and arm that rocked the ancient abacus displaying a brand-new wrist watch.

After taking a few pictures and wandering about this forlorn town, we drove slowly back through the twilight to Kharkov.

What surprised me most about this excursion was the backwardness, apparently, of Soviet motor transportation. This was the main highway between the Soviet's fourth and fifth largest cities (ardent Ukrainian nationalists in America insist in letters to me that Kiev and Kharkov are the first and second *Ukrainian* cities), with a combined population of about 1,700,000. For an hour and a half I counted everything moving in both directions —41 trucks, 5 automobiles, 2 busses, 1 jeep, 1 motorcycle, 22 bicycles, and 22 wagons—an average of less than one motor vehicle to the mile (on a fifty-eight-mile stretch). The best comparison would be the traffic between Washington and Baltimore, two American cities of similar size. Naturally, traffic within the large cities is much heavier. On one of the most crowded boulevards in Moscow, eight lanes wide, I have estimated traffic in both directions at the rate of 2,400 vehicles per hour, about equivalent to the pace through New York's Lincoln tunnel; and at the main intersection in Kiev, at nine one morning, I made a fifteen-minute check; rate: 700 vehicles per hour on one street, 500 per hour on the other. In Kharkov I never could determine where the main intersection was, the traffic was so thin; and in some of the Asiatic cities there was practically no motor traffic at all.

We reached Kharkov that night dog-tired, and prepared for our return train trip to Moscow. I went to bed in good spirits, remembering the desperate argument of the Kharkov engineer. When I said Russian newspapers only printed half the truth, he quickly retorted that American papers were only read half as well.

CHAPTER 16

Interview with "Mister Communist"

When I embarked upon my second trip to the Soviet Union, one of my major objectives and hopes was to obtain an interview with Nikita Sergeyevich Khrushchev, who now held Stalin's old job as boss of the Communist Party. As I journeyed back to Moscow from the Ukraine, my thoughts were concentrated on this. It was now or never, for my permit to remain in the country was to run out in about ten days.

As the train rumbled through the countryside—its speed had increased in seven years from twenty-five to twenty-seven miles per hour—I got to thinking of how I first met this powerful and interesting man. I became conscious of N. S. Khrushchev's importance shortly after reaching the Ukraine in early 1946. In the front windows of Kiev's leading art store there were two plaster busts, one of Stalin, the other of the bald, pug-nosed Khrushchev. On many buildings I saw large photographs of the Soviet Union's leaders, but often there were only those two, Stalin and Khrushchev. Obviously Khrushchev, a man almost unknown in the West, was one of the real powers of the Soviet Union. We found out that he was a member of the Soviet Politburo and headed the Government of the Ukraine, which made him the chief official of a republic of 40,000,000 people—

almost as many as live in England. I set about learning more of his background.

As with many Soviet rulers, Khrushchev's early years were shrouded in mystery. No one seemed to know where he had been born (I know now, from Khrushchev himself, that it was near the town of Kursk, just outside the Ukraine). His father was a miner, and Khrushchev also worked in the pits as a youth, which may help account for his powerful wrestler's physique. It was said that he received little education as a boy, but that after he was a grown man, the Communists sent him to elementary and industrial schools. Soon afterward he began to appear in a variety of official capacities.

In the early thirties he was named to a high post in the Communist Party of Moscow. For his part in the construction of the world-famed Moscow subway, he was awarded the Order of Lenin. When "bourgeois nationalism" erupted in the Ukraine before World War II, it was Khrushchev who was sent to eradicate it. Much of the industrial and agricultural progress of the Ukraine was credited to him.

During World War II, when the Soviets needed an inspirational leader to command a big guerrilla army behind the German lines in the overrun Ukraine, the job went to Khrushchev, now political commissar with the rank of lieutenant general. Later, when the Red Armies fought their way back to the German border, Khrushchev, a hero of the defense of Stalingrad, reportedly had the task of punishing collaborators in each recaptured town.

When I arrived in Russia as head of the UNRRA Mission just after the war, Khrushchev was back in the Ukraine—the undisputed boss of that vital breadbasket region—and I was invited to meet him. The meeting was little more than an exchange of amenities, but I was impressed with the dynamic personality of the man.

Khrushchev is a stocky five feet five inches, with a mobile face, jug ears, and humorous dark eyes. He talks animatedly with his hands. He reminded me of a New York political boss,

Interview with "Mister Communist"

and I later learned that he has the good politician's ability to recall names and faces; when he visits a factory or a collective farm, he surprises slight acquaintances by calling them by name and asking after young Nikolai and sweet little Tatyana, their children. It is rumored that he bones up on personal details before each visit—a method not unknown to American politicians. Whatever the secret, the technique apparently pays off. I learned that Ukrainians often called him by his first and middle names—Nikita Sergeyevich—with the same familiarity shown by people in the United States when they refer to President Eisenhower as "Ike."

At that first brief meeting of ours in 1946, I received two strong impressions: first, that Khrushchev apparently wasn't used to meeting foreigners (he stared at me quizzically and with great curiosity, like a man studying a bug on a rock), and second, that here was a man with a sense of humor—in marked contrast to the many dour Russians who represent the Soviet Union abroad. At one point I said I was "needling" UNRRA to keep Ukrainian supplies flowing, and the interpreter translated the word as something that sounded like "steeskeevat." Khrushchev laughed, almost as if he could see the needle going in.

The sense of humor became apparent again at a formal dinner to which he invited me and my staff. I sat alongside him at the head of the table, and soon we were tossing off cognac and vodka toasts and exchanging jokes. He suddenly pointed to one of his agricultural specialists—a man named Starchenko who was about five feet four inches tall and must have weighed 250 or 300 pounds—and said, "I must have been crazy to send *him* to the United States to ask for more food for the Ukrainians!"

On the eve of the Soviet Union's May Day celebration, I sent Khrushchev a polite little note on behalf of the UNRRA Mission, wishing his country well on one of its major holidays. A few hours later, a young girl arrived from his office to say that Khrushchev, having read my innocuous message "with tears in his eyes," begged permission to print it in the newspapers. The next day, the newspapers in the Ukraine ran it prominently on page one, alongside Khrushchev's expression of thanks.

Perhaps the most unexpected act of this unusual Communist occurred on the night before our mission left the Ukraine (I had already returned to Western Europe). Khrushchev gave a party at a country villa for the mission members and their wives —and when it was over, sat on the porch with them until long past midnight, discussing their personal lives and plans. I can't think of another instance where a leading Soviet personage ever met non-Communist foreigners on such an easy-going, suspicion-free basis.

And he *was* a top official, even then. He demonstrated his standing in the Soviet hierarchy once when a visiting UNRRA official expressed, almost casually, a desire to see Stalin before leaving the country.

Khrushchev walked away and returned a few minutes later. "I just spoke to Comrade Stalin on the phone," he said. "He'll see you tomorrow at two P.M."

But in 1946, Soviet-American relations already were beginning to strain. By the time the cold war was in full swing, I was back in the U.S. at the private practice of law. For years I thought only rarely about the chunky little man in Kiev.

Then Stalin died, and the stories of the funeral reported that Khrushchev was given the honor of introducing Malenkov, who was one of the three funeral orators. This and other reasons I have related led me to send my cable to the Kremlin. Then came the visit of the Soviet officials offering me a visa, and now, nine weeks later, I awaited my chance to see him.

The freedom with which I had been allowed to go about the country talking to people and photographing at will, the interviews and tours which were arranged, all made it clear that I was getting special treatment.

Furthermore, all outward signs revealed that Khrushchev was still rising in the Soviet hierarchy, reaching toward the very top. During the holidays pictures of the leaders had been placarded about Moscow. In these picture arrangements Khrushchev

Interview with "Mister Communist"

ranked third in Moscow, behind Malenkov and Molotov. Elsewhere in the country he ranked second, with only Malenkov ahead of him. Even then some experts believed that Khrushchev and Malenkov were equal, and that Khrushchev might have the most power in the country because of his position as boss of the Communist Party.

Shortly after I returned to Moscow from Kharkov, the big Anniversary of the Revolution parade was held in Red Square. I was invited to sit in the reviewing stand. The only other Americans so honored were the ambassador, military attachés, and the ambassador's guests (about twenty less privileged American, British, and Australian embassy people watched from my hotel room, not far from Red Square).

But though the signs of Khrushchev's influence were all about me, I still hadn't met him. Before leaving New York, I had cabled him again, asking to see him. As soon as I reached the U.S.S.R., I sent him a letter repeating the request. Then I spoke to the head of the Soviet tourist service. "Be patient," he told me. "Mr. Khrushchev is on his vacation." Finally, after my return to Moscow from the Ukraine, I wrote him this simple note:

> Hon. N. S. Khrushchev
> The Kremlin
> Dear Mr. Khrushchev:
> I have had a very good trip in the Ukraine, and next Monday I hope to go for two weeks to Central Asia.
> If it is convenient for you, I would like to see you this week and tell you what I have observed.

I waited nervously for some response to this note, for my permit to stay in the country was expiring and the Chief of Police (to whom I had applied for extension) was "ill." Two days after I sent the note I was told to stand by, that it was possible I would see Khrushchev by the end of the week.

On Saturday afternoon—November 14—a car picked me up at the tourist agency. With me was Zorya Novikova, one of the agency's best interpreters, dressed in her finest for what was obviously one of the biggest days of her life. The car swung toward the Kremlin, then turned left, by-passing the old fortress, and sped to a square a few blocks beyond. We stopped in front of an old six-story Moscow office building—Communist Party headquarters. (One evening outside this building at about 6 P.M. I counted fifty-five cars waiting; forty-eight had chauffeurs.) We hurried into the building, past two armed MVD guards, up an elevator, past another MVD guard, past a male secretary in an anteroom, through two leather-covered doors—and there, sitting at a table at the far end of a huge empty room, was Khrushchev.

His head was down, and he was studying some papers with great concentration. Other papers were to his right on the table, and the desk behind him was piled high with them. The walls of the big 30-by-50-foot room were half paneled, and the only decorations on them were a couple of good-sized maps, one of the Soviet Union and one of the world, and a picture of Stalin as a young man.

The room was comparatively bare, except for a wall clock, the long green cloth-covered conference table at which he sat, and his desk. He had a black phone and a green phone alongside him at the table, and three more on his desk—one black, one green, and one red. Various diplomats to whom I later described the scene surmised that the black phones may have been for ordinary business, the green phones a special connection to Communist Party offices, and the red phone undoubtedly a direct line to the Kremlin. Also on the table was a jar containing eight knife-sharpened pencils and two fountain pens.

Khrushchev got up to greet me. He hadn't changed at all in seven years. He was about fifty-nine now, but he had the same hard physique, round, animated face, and lively, humorous features. His eyes were dark, and I noticed for the first time that he had three moles on his cheeks and a tiny slit scar under his nose. His smile revealed two gold bicuspids.

Although I had been told that even top Soviet officials make

Interview with "Mister Communist"

no more than 5,000 rubles ($1,250) a month, Khrushchev was one of the best-dressed men I met in the U.S.S.R. His clothing was simple but expensive. His suit was of a blue serge similar to some I'd priced in Kiev at the equivalent of about $110 a square yard. He wore one of the few white shirts I saw in the Soviet Union. It may have been silk; if so, it cost about $50. I recall seeing only three other men wearing white shirts: a banker in Baku, a building engineer in Kiev, and a restaurant manager in Moscow. He had cuff links, also a rarity in Russia, set with red stones.

There was no one else in the room. Khrushchev asked me to sit beside him, with my interpreter at my left. I was so close to him that he often touched my arm for emphasis during our talk.

He began by saying, "I appreciate all that UNRRA did for us in the Ukraine. I remember particularly the help of Fiorello La Guardia (La Guardia had succeeded Herbert H. Lehman as director-general of UNRRA) in obtaining special articles for us against certain obstacles." That was a gentle dig—an implication that anti-Soviet Westerners had tried to block the relief supplies—but he said it with a friendly smile. In fact, all through the interview he never showed irritation or bitterness, no matter how controversial our exchanges. He constantly smiled and chuckled—and gestured broadly as he talked, more like a volatile Italian than a stolid Russian.

After some additional words of praise for UNRRA, Khrushchev got in a few more jabs. He attacked John Fischer, one of the members of my mission, who had written a best-selling book called *Why They Behave Like Russians* after spending two months in the Ukraine. Khrushchev shrugged his shoulders. "Oh, well," he said, "he wanted to make money, and he got his money. Anyhow, he probably was not working so much for UNRRA as for intelligence purposes—and he wrote what he was told to write." Khrushchev spoke without rancor, as if he were merely discussing an unfortunate fact of life.

I said, "I am as certain as I can be that he was not a representative of intelligence—I picked him for the UNRRA job myself—and that no one told him what to write. Though I disagreed with him on many observations, I believe he simply put down his own impressions, which is the way men in America write books."

Again there was that friendly shrug of the shoulders from Khrushchev.

At that point I decided I'd better make it perfectly clear to him that I intended to criticize strongly some aspects of the U.S.S.R., too. He listened, then replied, "It is all a question of proportion. Some people are too busy catching flies to see the main points. They concentrate on small drawbacks and make them very large ones, and they do not notice the big accomplishments of the Soviet Union."

I assured him that I would try to be objective, since (and I tried to emphasize the point) so few Americans had been allowed to enter the Soviet Union in recent years that I felt a great responsibility. Then I spoke of the trip I wanted to make to Central Asia and the Caucasus. "I still haven't received permission for the trip," I said. "The Chief of Police must renew my residence permit and the tourist officials keep telling me he's ill." (Khrushchev let that pass—but two days later the Chief of Police miraculously recovered, and I was given a new permit and cleared for the trip.)

"I wish I could go with you," Khrushchev said. "I've never been to Tashkent in Central Asia, and I haven't been to Stalingrad since I participated in the defense of the city during the war."

The mention of Stalingrad set him off on the first of a series of digressions—this one about how Hitler (he called him "Gitler") lost Stalingrad by overruling his generals in the matter of tactics. Hitler had refused to let von Paulus (he called him "Paulus") retreat, he said; as a result, von Paulus was surrounded and lost the bulk of his army.

Our whole conversation was full of digressions. I had come with a series of set questions, but I soon realized that the dis-

Interview with "Mister Communist"

cussion was going to go the way Khrushchev wanted it. He spouted Russian for minutes at a time, talking directly at me as if I understood, while my interpreter scribbled frantic notes. During the long intervals when Zorya translated, he stared into space with a bored expression and fiddled impatiently with his pencil, as if he wasn't used to such blank spots in his life.

Our discussion of the Battle of Stalingrad gave me a chance to mention the disconcerting number of troops I had seen in some parts of the country. "In Moscow and Minsk I have felt that the Soviet Union must be a vast armed camp," I told him.

He said, "Moscow is the center of transportation, and you have seen the many soldiers and officers who must go through Moscow to get to their bases. And there are military-training centers near Minsk. You will see fewer troops elsewhere." In typical Russian fashion he added, "You were lucky to see so many of our soldiers and officers." Whenever I complained about anything in the Soviet Union, I was told I was lucky to see the bad—as if it were very rare to see unpleasant sights in the U.S.S.R.

"I have been struck also," I said, "by the fact that there are three groups in the Soviet Union which seem to me to be the privileged classes—professors, members of the Communist Party, and Army officers. They get so much more money than most other people."

"If our scientists and professors receive high pay," he said, "that's not bad. We must create good conditions for them. Our country needs many specialists in order to build Communism. If our scientific worker is paid more than others, he works better—because our country is not like the capitalist countries." Then came the Marxist dogma.

"In capitalist countries, when a man gets better pay, he buys a factory and then exploits the workers. In our country, when a man gets more money, he buys more and he has a better cultural life, and he works better. That makes our state stronger."

He continued, "It is not true that members of the Communist Party get more money than others. Our people are paid according to their ability and according to the work they do." He cited an example which always was cited to me: "For example, academician Petrovsky, the rector of Moscow University, is not a Communist, yet he earns as much money as the rector of Kiev University, who *is* a Communist.

"Furthermore, Communist Party members have less chance to earn extra money; they spend all their spare time doing work for the country, for which they are not paid."

I showed disbelief, which he brushed off—again smiling. Then he resumed: "Our Army officers get good salaries, true. We must have the best people seeking careers in our Army, so we create good conditions for them. But they really earn only about the same as qualified people in civilian work. In war they are the first to suffer, the first to die."

Then Khrushchev permitted himself an intimacy extremely unusual for any ruler of the Soviet Union. "I had two sons," he said. "The eldest was a pilot and he was killed in the war. My second son is now studying in an institute because he wants to be an engineer. In the end he will earn about what he would make if he were to become an officer like my first son. Youths choose their careers; the prospects are about the same."

I took advantage of the opening to ask him some more personal questions. "Speaking of your family," I said, "is Premier Malenkov really married to your sister, as has been reported?"

"No," he replied, laughing, "that's just some more of your American newspaper nonsense. I read also that your papers said Stalin was married to Kaganovich's sister. That, too, is not true."

"And do you have any other children besides the two sons you mentioned?"

"Yes, I have many daughters."

I asked, "How many?"

He chuckled and said, "Enough so that I do not have to pay taxes for not having a large family."

Interview with "Mister Communist"

The most serious subject we discussed was, of course, the possibility of war. Khrushchev said, "In your travels you will not see anything that will give you any idea that our people want war."

That was true as far as it went, and I agreed. But while Soviet leaders have been hammering "peace" propaganda into the Russians, Soviet actions outside the U.S.S.R. have sown fear and distrust. I said as much to Khrushchev, pointing out in particular the world-wide inflammatory actions of the various Communist parties and the Cominform.

"As a result," I told him, "many people in the United States are afraid that the U.S.S.R. will make war on us—so much so that I know people whose children have nightmares, fearing an atom bomb might be dropped on them by the Russians."

"All that is done on purpose," retorted Khrushchev, "by the group which controls U.S. policy. They fire the passions of the people against the Soviet Union to prove they are justified in spending so much money for military armaments, for building bases abroad, for making atom bombs and hydrogen bombs. Those people who control the United States don't really believe the Soviet Union wants a war, but they want their people to *think* that the Soviet Union wants a war. Behind them are the magnates and capitalists who are interested only in profits and armaments. They just frighten people in order to show that Eisenhower is saving the nation, and to justify Eisenhower's policy."

I broke in to say that I am a Democrat and that most Democrats support Eisenhower's foreign policy. "Not only that," I said, "but our American industries are so heavily taxed in war that most of them make far more money during peacetime."

"Capitalists," said Khrushchev, gesturing, "don't care whether they make buttons or tanks. They're just interested in profits."

Then he grew solemn. "It is my opinion," he said, "that the American people do not think badly of the Soviet people and want nothing from them. As for our people, I know they understand war. War does not bring anything good. War only destroys. It brings only destruction and victims. Even a successful war leaves nothing but victims. That's why our policy now is dedicated to improving the living conditions of our people."

These words of Khrushchev made me think of a Russian painting I had just seen in the Tretyakov Gallery—Vereshchagin's "Apotheosis of War." This depicted a pyramid pile of human skulls, and in the background were the ruins of destroyed cities, with black deathlike crows hovering above. The painting had the legend, "This picture is devoted to all the conquerors, in the past, in the present, and in the future." Date: 1871.

A few minutes later Khrushchev was on the offensive again. He said, "I suppose that when you return to the United States, Senator McCarthy will summon you before him for being in the Soviet Union. Apparently there is no freedom in America."

I replied quickly, "On the contrary, McCarthy only proves that it is a free America. If Senator McCarthy has the full power to investigate me, I also have the freedom to write about McCarthy, as critically as I please, and he cannot stop me." In two trips to the U.S.S.R., I had encountered virtually no criticism of the Government by Soviet citizens. I hope Khrushchev got the point.

"Yet," said Khrushchev, "the Republicans control most of the press in the United States. How does that serve freedom? The capitalists have such power over the minds of the people through the press that they have created an air of hysteria in the United States. If someone says something good about the Soviet Union, he is called a Communist. If he writes something bad, the newspapers hail him and say, 'Here is a real American.' That is a tragedy for humanity."

"The American press can hardly be said to control the minds of the people," I said. "It's true that not many newspapers supported the Democrats in the last few presidential campaigns —yet Roosevelt and Truman won, and Adlai Stevenson received more than twenty-seven million votes.

"Furthermore, I have noticed more than distortion in the

Interview with "Mister Communist"

Soviet press. I think your newspapers are full of inaccuracies and deliberate bias."

He spread his hands deprecatingly and replied, "The Soviet newspapers give the news which serves the interests of the people. They report the news from the workers' point of view. Why should we print what your Republican newspapers want us to print? If your country builds bases around the world, for example, we explain to our people America's purpose in building them. If we say we want to do away with hydrogen and atomic bombs and the United States will not agree, we can only explain what it means—that you want to use the bombs against us." Then he grinned and said: "But of course, this is just 'some more propaganda'—or so you will say."

I tried a new tack: "You mention the American bases. They are a symbol to me of the conformity your newspapers have imposed on the minds of all Soviet citizens. Everyone I have spoken to so far has asked me the same three questions: Why is America surrounding the Soviet Union with military bases? Why are we persecuting Paul Robeson? And why didn't the United States welcome the Soviet chess team to play in a tournament?"

"Ah," he said, twinkling, "but *I* didn't ask you those questions. However, as long as you brought the subject up, the chess players indicate how the capitalists have whipped up war hysteria in the United States. Did your people think our chess players had atom bombs in their pockets? It reminds me of an old Russian proverb: 'If God wants to punish a person, he first takes his brain away.' "

(It took me a while to figure out why that old Russian proverb was so familiar. I finally recognized it as the ancient Latin saying which we know as, "Whom the gods would destroy they first make mad." All over Russia I kept hearing old Russian proverbs like, "Do unto others as you would have them do unto you." Many of the old Russian proverbs seem to come from such sources as the Bible or Aesop.)

Khrushchev launched into a discussion of Soviet economic

and agricultural problems, a topic of great importance to him. In addition to his other duties, he is in charge of the new Soviet campaign to increase the production of foodstuffs.

"It seems to me," I said, "that the people of the Soviet Union undoubtedly are better off than they were before, but are still poorer than the people of Western Europe."

To my astonishment, he agreed. It must have been one of the few times a Communist leader has ever admitted to a foreigner that the Soviet Union is not the best of all possible worlds.

"We were terribly damaged by the war," he said, "and we could not get back to the proper level because there was so much to be done. But if you return to the Soviet Union in two or three years, you will be surprised."

He continued with almost fierce pride. "When we started our first Five-Year Plan for heavy industry, they laughed at us in America and said it was nonsense—but we showed the whole world that we can accomplish what we set out to do. Now we are beginning to develop our agriculture and light industry, and already the people of the West see danger from our products. On the one hand they complain because we have built up our heavy industry and military might—and now that we want to build up our economic power and are prepared to compete with them in trade, they again say that it is bad."

He held up both hands. "Whatever we do," he said wryly, gesturing with one hand to indicate the military and with the other to represent economic development, "they think it's bad."

Then he made another significant statement. "We most certainly want better trade relations with the United States. It was the United States that interrupted the trade between us. It is strange that you do not want to exchange goods with us, because after all, trade is just a question of profits."

He spoke again on his favorite subject, the economic development of his country. A few weeks before, he had made an unprecedented speech disclosing glaring inadequacies in Soviet agriculture. "When I made that speech, the reactionaries said,

Interview with "Mister Communist"

'Now the Soviet Union is finished; there is so much wrong.'"
He laughed. "Since the new agricultural program went into effect this year, we already have set records. By October of 1953, we had exceeded the plan for pigs by thirteen to fifteen million."

He spoke further about agriculture. After a while I said, "I'm afraid I'm really not qualified to discuss farm problems with you because I am a born-and-bred city dweller."

He smiled and replied, "Anyone can learn. After all, I was brought up in the mines."

Then he changed the subject again, and I began to be aware that, whether by design or not, he had steered me several times to the matter of Soviet-American co-operation. "If people can only get to know one another," he said, "there will be understanding. During the war when we had a common enemy, we co-operated well against Hitler. If you remember, the Americans had an air base at Poltava in the Ukraine during the war, and on June 21, 1944, the German planes attacked it and many Americans and Russians died together.

"We have shared many pages of history in battle against the enemy," Khrushchev said. "We Russians have no pretensions against the United States. There is no reason for hostility. When Roosevelt was alive, the relations between our countries were good. But Truman did much to destroy that relationship. I have fond memories of Americans who worked with us and worked well." He mentioned a few—engineers who had visited Russia before World War II, La Guardia, Paul White, and other UNRRA officials who had worked in the Ukraine. His voice trailed away for a moment. Then he said, "Such examples prove that Russians and Americans can understand one another. If people come together with open hearts, they will succeed."

We reminisced for a while about the Ukraine, and then I saw that the interview was winding to an obvious close. I pulled out two official photographs of Khrushchev and I asked him to autograph them for me. As he wrote, I said, "You look so stern in these Government photographs. You ought to have a new one made, something closer to your character." He laughed and said, "That is the fault of the photographer."

"I have one last request," I told him. "I have a camera with me. Would it be possible for my interpreter to take a picture of the two of us together, so that I can show it when I return to America?"

He roared with laughter. "Mr. MacDuffie," he said, "I'm afraid you would be in trouble with Senator McCarthy if you were seen in such close association with me."

When I got up to go, Khrushchev said, "I have a little story to tell you. Once a man in one of the offices of the Soviet Union was asked whether he was religious. He replied, 'In this office, I have no religion—but at home, I believe.' I hope, Mr. Mac-Duffie, that it will not be the same way with you if you choose to write about your trip. So many people have visited the Soviet Union and have told us one thing and then have written the opposite when they returned home."

"That," I said, "is why I have tried to be as blunt as possible in my criticisms throughout our talk. I intend to be equally honest when I get home."

He smiled and shook hands with me. As I walked past the clock on his wall, I saw that it was 7:30 P.M. I had spent a full four hours there. I caught a last look at him as I opened the door. He was back at the table, already deeply engrossed in the paper he had been studying when we came in.

I have thought about my interview with Khrushchev many times since I left his office, and I'm still trying to weigh its significance. He emerged as a man with a great deal of warmth and charm—confident, relaxed, and fairly reasonable. But he showed a shocking rigidity in his thinking about the West—an apparent willingness to swallow the propaganda he himself has helped create. Furthermore, I couldn't forget for a moment that a man has to be very tough and very ruthless to climb as high in the Soviet Union as Khrushchev has.

Yet, on the whole, his attitude toward the non-Communist

Interview with "Mister Communist"

world seemed to me surprisingly far removed from the shrill, unyielding antagonism we have come to expect from Russian leaders. But Khrushchev, for all his power, is just one Soviet official—and my talk with him, for all its length, was just one conversation. At best, our discussion may have been a tip-off to a remarkable change in Soviet tactics. At worst, it may have been, in Nikita Khrushchev's own words, "just some more propaganda . . ."

Zorya, my interpreter, had been through a grueling four hours. I can imagine that any young American girl who had spent four hours interpreting for an American Cabinet member and a visiting Russian would also be exhausted. Despite that, I hoped to persuade her to review the conversation with me immediately. I had decided not to take any notes while talking, lest such activity take any steam out of the interview. Khrushchev started speaking in such long bursts that early in the interview Zorya began making lengthy notes as each of us talked. Near the end of the conversation I asked Khrushchev if Zorya and I could take her notes with us, and he replied with a smile, "Certainly."

As we put on our coats in the anteroom, Zorya placed the notebook on a table. I reached for it to put in my pocket, but she snatched it away, with a jerky laugh. In the auto I asked her to come back to the hotel and review the notes while they were fresh. This was the first interview with any Soviet ruler since the death of Stalin, and I wanted to be as accurate as possible. She pleaded that she was tired and her baby was ill. I in turn pleaded with her that this interview was so unusual an event that for the sake of accuracy we should go over our notes and memory immediately. She was, however, adamant. I started a new tack: "Well, let me keep the notebook—you might lose it." She refused, replying that this was absurd. I told her the notes were worth a great deal to me, but again she was unyielding. This was Saturday night. She promised to review them on Sunday. That night I wrote my own notes from memory. Sunday, no Zorya—her baby was ill. Monday, no Zorya; Tuesday, no Zorya, and I complained to her boss, who professed concern and said he had made inquiries. She finally showed up with the notes on Thursday evening. They seemed intact, and she went over them painstakingly for hours while we reviewed her notes and mine and her memory and mine, sharpening the accuracy of it all.

What went on in that interval? It's quite possible the baby was really ill. Zorya had that sort of Russian temperament that would brush all aside where her baby was concerned. A good student of the Soviet Union here has given me what I think is the real answer. He said, "Khrushchev accorded you the interview. He was certainly willing to let you have her notes and never requested her to check them. But she was protecting herself from the little bureaucrats between her and him. There was no witness that knew she had permission to give them to you. If later they pounced on her for turning them over to you, she might never have been able to get back to Khrushchev to absolve herself. So what she did was this: She went to the MVD and got a clearance. It probably took all that time for them to get back to Mr. Big, and when they got to him, no doubt he said, 'Why, certainly, I said she could turn them over to Mr. MacDuffie. What are you bothering me about?' But this way she protected herself."

CHAPTER 17

Ceremony in Red Square

I LEFT Khrushchev's office Saturday evening at seven-thirty. Early Monday morning the Intourist chief, rubbing his palms with pleasure, greeted me with: "Would you like to go to Central Asia?" Then, as though it had never happened before, we sat down and discussed my proposed itinerary, all of which I had discussed with him exactly one week earlier. The following Friday in the early dawn, I started out on the long trek to Central Asia which was to last twenty-three days. Leonide "Lonya" Hodorkov, a pleasant, intelligent young man who was an official Intourist interpreter, accompanied me.

Our first destination was to be Alma-Ata, the capital of Kazakstan, about 2,500 miles from Moscow and just 150 miles across the mountains from China. I chose this trip to the central and southern Asiatic area of the Soviet Union because it is the eastern area least traveled by Westerners, and because I thought the other main routes to the Soviet East, the northern routes to Siberia and Vladivostok, were going to be much colder, snowed-in, and therefore duller. It was now mid-November and Moscow already had had its first light flurries of mother snow.

My trip called for fairly lengthy stops at Alma-Ata, the capital of Kazakstan, Tashkent and Samarkand in Uzbekistan,

Baku in Azerbaijan, and Tiflis in Georgia. Kazakstan and Uzbekistan are part of the two great continental basins originally known as Russian Turkistan and Chinese Turkistan, ringed by some of the highest mountains known. The Kazaks and Uzbeks are chiefly of Turkish stock, though the Kazaks have quite a touch of Chinese, and the Uzbeks, of Afghan and Persian. I wanted particularly to go to Samarkand, the home of Tamerlane, which few Europeans had ever seen in all its history.

From there I planned to fly across the Caspian Sea to Baku, the Soviet's oil center, in Azerbaijan near Iran, and then to Tiflis in the Caucasus mountains of Georgia a little above Turkey, and after that back to Moscow, stopping on the way at Stalingrad.

We were awakened for our start at exactly 4:00 A.M. by the waiter bringing hot tea (the rest of the cold breakfast—caviar and bread—had been delivered the night before), in order to make the long journey out to the airport in the dark to catch the plane, which left exactly at 5:40 A.M. Just before leaving the United States, I had seen an article by Crankshaw, a well-known British expert on the Russians, scoffing at new Russian exhortations to the populace to be on time. My surprised experience was that they always started on the dot as scheduled, and generally finished on time too. My other surprise was to have my baggage weighed on each plane trip, something unheard of in 1946.

There were a dozen other men and one woman boarding the little two-engined plane, and the woman carried a baby. There was also a fat stewardess wearing a plain blue cloth skirt and a gray shawl. It was November 20, and everybody was huddled in heavy winter clothes. With the coming of snow, Russians seem to bloom. The variety of hats worn by Russian men in winter is much greater than in America. There were four fedoras—two gray, one purple, one green. One man wore a beige beret. Two men had on caps—one gray, one blue—such as we wear mostly at sea or on golf courses. The rest wore winter fur hats: a gray caracul; a black caracul; a black fur hat

Ceremony in Red Square

with fur earflaps; a black one with leather earflaps; a brown fur one with brown fur earflaps.

As we entered the plane, I noticed a man standing on the wing with a hoe, chipping off the ice. The plane itself was freezing cold, not being warmed up till we were aloft, as is the custom there. There were eighteen seats and a little storeroom for bags and coats between the passengers and the pilots. In the passengers' compartment was an altimeter. On every take-off the stewardess stood in the doorway to the storage room, facing the passengers, her head inches from the archway above her as the plane trundled down the runway. On one take-off, however, she varied this by holding the baby for its mother, this time holding the baby's head about three inches from the shelf above its mother. I trembled to think what the slightest lurch might do. On another occasion, she and a sailor, while the plane was trembling jerkily down the runway, poured milk down a funnel into the baby's mouth.

This was to be a dull trip, except for the ever-scary take-offs and landings. On each lap of the flight we gained altitude quickly and generally flew high above the clouds until a swift descent was made to the landing field, so that I saw almost nothing of the countryside.

To while away the time, I collected my notes on the recent celebration of the Thirty-sixth Anniversary of the Revolution, which I had witnessed in Moscow. This had three major events: a gala performance the first evening at the Bolshoi Theater, the great opera house, which traditionally is attended by the ranking personnel of the Government and by foreign ambassadors; next, the Red Square parade of the military and citizenry; and finally, Molotov's reception for foreign diplomats.

I believe that Ambassador Bohlen and I were the only Americans who were admitted to the Bolshoi Theater to see the celebration. When I entered, there were two or more uniformed members of the MVD elite guards checking papers at each of the numerous entrances. I had to present both my ticket, which bore my name, and my passport, and my interpreter had to present her ticket and her identity papers. Right behind us came a general and an admiral, and their documents got the same detailed scrutiny. (Literature reveals that Russians have been historically document-happy. Today Moscow students even have to present personal passes to get into their own university.)

We had box number eleven in the third tier of six tiers, about middle distance and height from the stage. Though we were very early, a citizen was sitting in the first seat on the left of our box. He never left his seat, even during the intermission. Box twelve to our right was occupied when we arrived only by a civilian, also sitting in the first seat on the left. I never saw him leave his seat, either, until the whole show was over. His box was later filled by four generals of the Red Army, two with three stars, two with two stars, and each had from five to seven rows of medals.

It is my best guess that the civilians in the front rows in each of those boxes were members of the MVD. Twice in 1946 I had attended sessions of the Supreme Soviet; our mission had occupied a little box which jutted out by itself over the middle of the assemblage below. Directly below us were many marshals and generals of the Red Army. The entire audience, like little schoolboys with hands folded on desks, was silently attentive while Zhdanov of the Politburo spoke—except Marshal Zhukov, who made a point of leaning over and talking to his neighbors. I have come to the conclusion that one of the marks of rank in the Soviet Union is daring to do this at a ceremony. On those 1946 occasions we were accompanied to our box by another "civilian," and the gun he carried was clearly discernible.

The ceremony at the Bolshoi opened with some forty-seven persons filing onto the stage to occupy three rows of chairs, while the "President," Voroshilov, delivered the address of the evening, complaining as usual about the West. In the group of leaders, for they were the most prominent people in the Soviet Union, were five women, two naval officers and four Army men. Just one military man sat in the front row—Marshal

Ceremony in Red Square

Zhukov, who was on the far right. The left side of the front row was occupied by the Presidium (the old Politburo), including Molotov, Khrushchev, and Malenkov. These three, incidentally, displayed their rank by being the only ones to converse while the talk was going on. When Voroshilov, once a famous general and now a shriveled old man in civilian dress with a quavering voice—the diplomatic circle reports that he is an alcoholic—finished his droning speech, the officials filed off the stage and Act I was over. I noticed that all of the Presidium were short in stature, being between five-four and five-six in height, and that all were in their late fifties or early sixties except Malenkov, who is fifty-two. The nation is one of aging political leaders and young business executives, for everywhere I went in factories and on farms, the top executive was usually in his forties or early fifties, and his chief assistants in their thirties, all born or educated under Communism.

The rest of the evening produced one of the finest theatrical displays I have ever seen. The leading singers, musicians, and dancers from each of the republics appeared in a variety of performances. There is much that I deplore in that State-run land, but their musical tradition and talents are of the highest. It was a memorable evening.

On the day of the great parade, the police and military of Moscow establish extraordinary police regulations, for this is the day that the top leaders stand on the tomb of Lenin, and now of Stalin too, while selected military divisions and then millions of people march past them. On that day the center core of the city is closed at 7:00 A.M.; a slightly wider ring is shut off at seven-thirty, and a still wider ring at eight. The only Americans who had passes for the stands on Red Square were the ambassador, his personal house guests, the military attachés, and myself.

That day I was particularly impressed by the remarkable security precautions which prevailed in the center of the city. My interpreter and I walked the less-than-a-quarter-mile distance to the grandstand on Red Square and we were stopped by (*a*) police, (*b*) soldiers, and (*c*) MVD elite guards, three times within one block, and our tickets and passports were thoroughly scrutinized at each check point.

Standing on the benches on Red Square, I began to snap photos of the waiting ranks of soldiers across the square. Though no guard was visible in the stands when I began, within a few seconds a soldier appeared, saluted, and asked for the tickets and passports of myself and my interpreter. I can only guess that an informer reached the guard. No soldier was in sight of the place from which I snapped. He told me I could not take photos but did not ask for my film. Thereupon, as the jets flew overhead and the military marched by, I began to take notes openly, just for narrative purposes. In a few seconds a soldier again appeared, saluted, and again asked for our documents. He gave me no orders after perusing them, but, since what I was noting was not important to me, I chose not to take any more notes. After the military had passed the reviewing stand and only civilians were milling by in thousands, I went personally to the officer of the section in which I sat and asked if I could take pictures, only to be refused.

Later the crowds began to thin out. It interested me that while millions of citizens were parading by and while the top Presidium dutifully reviewed them, the privileged Russian guests in the limited grandstand were rapidly thinning out. They were clearly bored with this "historic" Soviet ceremony. I saw some of the parading multitude carrying a photo of Harry Pollitt, the British Communist, so I stepped over a small two-foot barrier to enter the next section, which, like my own, was now three-quarters empty, in order to tease some fellow-traveling English ladies by pointing out their "representative." Immediately a Russian officer accompanied by several soldiers closed in on me and sternly rebuked me for jumping the little fence to the next section of the stands.

I noticed there was a line of armed MVD soldiers (identifiable by their military garb and blue tops to their peaked caps) the length of the Kremlin and in front of the tomb of Lenin and Stalin on which the leaders of the Government were

Ceremony in Red Square

grouped. While the military paraded, this elite guard was spaced out, about one officer every five feet. But when the populace went by, the MVD guards were reinforced and stood shoulder to shoulder the length of the square, taking no chances with the loyal civilians.

After a couple of hours my interpreter and I left the boring parade—now just millions of citizens stumbling along, pushing their way past the great moguls. It was like twenty subway crowds in New York, with no more zest or color, except that one in a thousand would carry a little banner or picture on a stick, a banner which the onlooker had already seen hundreds of times. This is supposed to be a "stirring, cheering demonstration." All I can say is that a big Red Square parade is just as dull as similar ceremonies in other lands.

We had to circle the center of the city for about an hour to get back to our hotel, meanwhile having our tickets and passports checked closely at least six times. Several times I pulled out my camera and each time I was stopped by a soldier or a policeman.

When I reached my hotel, a Western diplomat informed me that a number of people had been taking pictures in front of it. This was on the square next to Red Square. Here three great lines of civilians were converging, each of them herded in by parallel lines of soldiers. In the center of the square was a policeman's booth. While we were talking, a cop came up and spoke to me about my camera, telling me to not take pictures. A little later, by myself, I suddenly walked rapidly out into the square to the traffic policeman's booth. Then, with the booth between me and the sidewalk—where many cops were—I started taking pictures. The paraders and soldiers, seeing me alone by the police booth, apparently concluded I was an official photographer. I got bolder, motioned to soldiers to step aside, and cut through their lines still closer to Red Square. All went well till I went to snap some young girls in red sweaters who were waiting to finish out the parade. They were restive and, seeing my camera, broke ranks and rushed at me. I finally got them to step back so

I could take their pictures. One of the civilian officials herding them in came up to me and motioned for me to stop photographing and to go back to the hotel. I offered to show him my little Russian paper, concocted by myself, telling "my story" that I had permission, but he would have none of it. His gestures were unmistakable. I was content. It was a sunny day, and I had already shot about twenty pictures.

That evening Molotov gave a reception for the diplomatic corps. During the party Molotov and his wife invited some key ambassadors and their wives to a corner table; eventually everybody in the room herded about this table to listen to the impromptu speeches. Malenkov, Khrushchev, and Voroshilov were not there. But the next most important Russian rulers were present; Bulganin, Kaganovich, Mikoyan, and Saburov were the principal ones. Sitting with them were the American, British, French, Argentine, Chinese, and Burmese ambassadors, and Ulbricht of East Germany. The Russians had a lot to drink and started bouncing up with toasts. America is fortunate that its ambassador, Charles Bohlen, the Yalta interpreter, understands Russian well. The French and British ambassadors understood scarcely a word and presumably lost all the nuances of this exceptional experience. Many toasts were made to peace by the Russians. Early in the proceedings Bohlen proposed in Russian a toast "to justice."

A little later, Marshal Zhukov, who had taken Marshal Bulganin's place at the table, rose and proposed as his toast: "I wish to support the American ambassador's toast to justice."

One of the Russian civilian rulers cracked, "Haven't you a toast of your own?" and Zhukov replied firmly, "I said, I wish to support the toast to justice."

A little later the Soviet leaders needled the American representative, saying that he had not made a toast to peace, whereupon Bohlen, speaking in English for the benefit of the less qualified Western ambassadors, proposed a toast "against aggression" and defined aggression as the crossing of another's border. The Russians lamely acquiesced.

Ceremony in Red Square

There were some sharp thrusts at each other by the Soviet officials. Diplomatic circles say that Molotov's wife had been living in the country for several years, apart from him, until recently. So one Russian leader proposed a toast to her as "the long-time helpmeet who has aided Molotov so much."

Kaganovich, who was bubbling over, bounced up with a long outburst about the camaraderie of all nations of the Soviet Union. He enumerated them. "The Russians, the Ukrainians, the Kazaks, the Uzbeks, the Azerbaijanians . . ." and Mikoyan interrupted him in a stage whisper, "and the Georgians!"—no doubt meaning Beria who was about to die and possibly Stalin, also a Georgian.

At one time in the evening Molotov and Bulganin were conversing rapidly in Russian until Molotov remarked, "Be careful, Bohlen mustn't overhear our secrets—he understands Russian."

Marshal Bulganin answered, "I know how to solve that—let's make him our foreign minister." Then Mrs. Bohlen, on behalf of the housewives, proposed a toast to Mikoyan, who had recently made an important speech on the consumers' goods program. "You mean, you read my speech?" asked Mikoyan.

"Well, at least somebody's read your speech," cracked Molotov.

Most astonishing, however, was the moment when somebody asked why the Chinese ambassador had not proposed a toast, whereupon Kaganovich gibed, "Him? *He* hasn't got anything to say!"

Dulles and others have written of the grim solemnity of the Politburo men on the occasions when they have met Westerners. This banquet of toasts was certainly unprecedented and irregular. Next day censors passed all press stories describing the "Alice-in-Wonderland atmosphere." Only two sentences were deleted: that "Kaganovich's face was flushed" and that their private talk was more conciliatory than the official speeches of the holidays (Voroshilov's at the Bolshoi Theater, Bulganin's at Red Square). It was, at the least, a temporary crack in the Curtain.

CHAPTER 18

Over the Urals and Far Away

JUST AS I finished my notes on Moscow, after a couple of hours of flying, we came down to a landing in snow at the little airport of Penza. On the maps it appears just behind and at the foot of the Ural Mountains. In my memory nothing appears except two small white buildings nestled in a wasteland of snow. It was very cold, and none of us took off our coats while we waited. I noticed that Russians, however inured, make the same little satisfied gasps when they enter a room of even moderate warmth after stepping in from piercing frosty winds, and they rub their hands with satisfaction too. But they take other precautions: I watched two Russians order breakfast—a tumbler of vodka, followed by a chaser of beer, and then a meal of sausage, cabbage, mashed potatoes and gravy, all before eight o'clock in the morning. Lonya and I followed the adage, "When in Russia, do as the Russians do," and thereafter the trip seemed a little less boring.

On the second leg of the journey I got Lonya to while away the time telling me about his life. He was then twenty-four years of age, and he and I were to spend some three weeks together. He would be the first Russian born since the Revolution

—twelve years after that event—a complete product of Soviet Communism—whom I was to know well.

At the start I should like to say that he was clearly a loyal and patriotic Soviet citizen. He was proud of his country and genuinely happy in his own life. He was never belligerent about his views nor aggressively putting forward the Soviet cause, as do many older Russians, who seem to have an inferiority complex about their country. Leonide Hodorkov, or "Lonya" as his friends—and I—called him, accepted it as natural and right that he should think his country fine. He felt no insecure need to defend what was to him self-evident and accepted.

Lonya was a sweet person. His manner was mild, his wit gentle and dry, his spirit unflagging. I never knew him to be ruffled or irritable, nor did I ever see him despondent or indifferent. He was a perfect traveling companion. Frankly, I think he liked me too, so that we were able to have a great deal of fun out of what was many times hard work for both of us, especially for him, since he had to speak twice as much. This was his first trip to Central Asia also. Later I learned that he accompanied some young American student editors on a trip to the Crimea and the Ukraine. They christened him "Lennie," and they too fell in love with him. They told me they taught him poker on a train trip and thereafter he was ready to play at any hour of the day or night with anybody he could persuade to join him. And he threw them off by playing checkers with "Russian" rules, jumping his men in any direction.

Lonya was about five feet nine in height, of ordinary build—that is, not so stocky or dumpy as most Russians—and of very pale complexion. He had black hair, a tip-tilted nose, and a general expression which can be described as something between quizzical and quietly smiling. His eyes seemed ever to be laughing, but with you, not at you.

He took little baggage with him, a few shirts and a few knickknacks. Throughout the trip he wore a blue serge suit, a knitted sweater, a heavy blue overcoat, and an old gray fedora hat.

Lonya told me that at the time of the Revolution his father

was at medical college in Kiev and his mother was in school in Astrakhan. He knew little of that period, but he does remember one tale that for days his relatives had lived only on caviar taken from a local factory, eating soup plates of it. The first time I ever heard that the motto of the Revolution was, "Let them eat caviar."

Neither his father nor mother had ever gone to church. His father had been in some kind of trade union co-operative at the time of his death in 1924. Said Lonya blandly, "He died of drunkenness." His grandmother, who was also Russian, was "the happy mother of a happy daughter," and "she was very much the enemy of all priests; though she visited the church, she did not consider that it contributed to her development." He added, "She believed in the God, but not in the church." After the Revolution his father had become an Army doctor and his mother had worked as a nurse until the children were born.

Lonya was born in Kaminetz Podolsk in the southern Ukraine. In the first year of his life his father had gone to Smolensk to take care of an Army sanitarium. A few years later the family moved to Voronezh, where the father was director of an Army hospital. Here Lonya started school. Four years later they had been transferred to Moscow, where his father eventually became a major general in charge of administration of medical services. Lonya's older brother, aged twenty-nine, had been a first lieutenant in the Army in radio service, and was now in Riga, where he had married a nurse from Voronezh.

During the war Lonya had been in school in Moscow and in Kuibyshev. He graduated at twenty-two from the Moscow Institute of Foreign Languages and got a job as interpreter for Intourist at the Moscow airport. From this job he had moved on to the main Intourist office as interpreter. On graduation from college he had married a girl who was a building engineer, having studied at Moscow Building Engineers' Institute and Kuibyshev College. He told me, "We have a saying, 'Defend your diploma, and you can get married.'"

His wife had been born near Moscow. During the war she had

gone to school in Kuibyshev and Tashkent. Lonya didn't know much about his mother-in-law's past. "No specialty, I think." His father-in-law had been a State forester, but he had continued studying at night school until he became an X-ray technician. Now he is reputed one of the best in Moscow. His wife has a little brother still in school and a sister who was a typist before she became "simply a housewife" when she married an engineer and had a son. Years ago the Soviet Union organized special institutions to take care of the children of working women. But I found case after case among the more well-to-do where the wife stopped working after the first or second child. Or, if the wife continued to work, the child was taken care of by a grandmother or by some older woman hired for the job.

Lonya earns 1,100 rubles and his wife 1,050 rubles a month. They and their baby daughter live about thirty-five minutes by bus from his office in a flat which has two rooms plus kitchen, bath, and toilet. It had been his father's flat, which Lonya occupied when the general transferred temporarily out of Moscow. Lonya was not sure of the exact amounts he paid —since he just turned over the bills to his bank, which paid them out of his account—but he thought that monthly bills were: rent, 35 rubles; gas, 10; telephone, 29; television, 10; and radio, 3 (in the Soviet Union, in addition to a purchase price, you pay a use fee on a radio or television receiver). He said the building furnished steam heat. Lonya didn't know who owned his building—just "some division of the State." He transacts all his business with the manager of the building. He told me that it had 6 stories and 10 entries, with 120 flats, 20 to a floor, and that it had elevators. This means, I believe, an elevator operator for every 12 flats, and, if they go on the usual 3-shift basis, 30 elevator operators for 120 families—Soviet "full employment" again.

He told me that they had a gas stove and a gas heater for hot water in the bathroom, but there is no window in the toilet or bathroom. The walls of his apartment are painted, though some of his friends have wallpaper.

Out of the 2,150 rubles he and his wife earned, he said they could very easily save 500, even though they often went to the theater and frequently had visitors at home. When I asked him what he saved the money for, he replied, "We spend it first for clothes and then for vacations."

"Does your wife like clothes?"

"As all the women do."

I learned that he and his wife each got a month's vacation and that their next vacations were planned for the Caucasus, the Black Sea, and the Crimea. He had already spent two summers on the Baltic at Riga, and he had paid for his own vacations, having bought "general papers." Each industry and enterprise often has its own resthouses. When not filled to capacity, the vacancies are sold through special exchange offices in Moscow. He thought an average resthouse cost between 450 and 600 rubles a month, that a sanitarium ran between 700 and 1,200, and if you sought treatment by specialists, as high as 1,600 rubles a month for all expenses, except travel, which he estimated ran to another 400–500 rubles. Some people got free vacations from factories or trade unions; others had half their expenses paid by these organizations.

I asked what else he spent his money on. "Well," he said, "once my wife considered that the color of the walls was dull and did not correspond with the furniture. She had it all done over, and it cost me six hundred rubles. Those were awful days."

When I asked him what ambitions he had, he told me that after more experience as an interpreter, he hoped to teach English or to do some scientific work on the subject of the English language or in English history. This got us onto the subject of education. He insisted that anybody who wanted to go to college and could pass examinations had the opportunity, but that some people were good students and some good mechanics; some even said, "Why go to college when I can earn more money immediately?" He told me that students with passing grades received a small stipend while at college, enough to live on. In return for this education they were required to give three years' work—for pay—wherever the State sent them, but the State had to give them jobs in their specialties (confirmed in one of the court cases I witnessed).

Lonya said graduates were guaranteed a minimum pay of 880 rubles monthly. This must put quite a premium on seeking an education. He estimated the average pay for the country at 700 rubles monthly, and he thought some earned as low as 350—close to figures I obtained on the trip. Also, if students were sent out of town on graduation, they were compensated for travel expenses and were guaranteed living space. Lonya claimed that until a student found a job, the college had to go on paying him his stipend, and he told me of one student who lost his job when the organization he was working for was liquidated. Thereupon the student went back on the college pay roll until it found him a new place in his specialty.

Of a dozen fellow graduates he knew of, half were around Moscow, making about 1,000 rubles a month. Letters from the rest who had gone to the country indicated that they were quite satisfied, and some were earning as high as 1,800 rubles because there was a shortage of foreign-language experts in some areas.

I asked him about private enterprise and the right to leave a job. Could a maid in the hotel, for example, quit? "Certainly." Lonya stated that students were free to go where they chose after the three years' required work, and that others could quit at any time, though specialists might have to wait until a replacement was found. He thought there were some remnants of private enterprise, probably less than 1 per cent. "There are shoemakers, tailors, and some peasants who sell, and some dentists and doctors and lawyers. Also some country taxi drivers. But most individuals who are on their own pay rather high taxes."

How much sharing of apartments still went on? The answer was that there was none at all in the new buildings, except that students occasionally shared rooms. But in the big cities like Moscow and Leningrad where there are many old buildings with very large apartments, ten- and twelve-room apartments have been cut up into smaller flats. Today, he said, all new flats are for only one family, and he thought the maximum rooms to a flat were five, plus kitchen, toilet, and bath.

Later, in Tashkent, when I was jotting down some details about another English-speaking Russian, Lonya interrupted to tell me that if I wrote about himself to say he "played tennis and hockey very well."

He had been exempted from the compulsory military service for two years by reason of his studies, and said, "If we have peace, I'll never feel what the Army is."

He told me he could leave property by will to anybody, but that the law protected first the children, then the wife, and then the parents of the deceased.

I learned that he could drive an automobile, and when I asked if his wife could, he replied after reflection, "It's better to say No."

He finished this history just as we approached Aktyubinsk. We had flown the first leg of the trip at about 12,000 feet. This time we went along at 9,000 feet, still too high to see much of the terrain. The flight from Penza to Aktyubinsk took a little under three hours for the 580 miles, averaging 200 miles per hour. We landed in a mixture of snow and mud on an unpaved field at a little before noon Moscow time and about 2:00 P.M. local time. Here they asked us to take our bags out of the plane and then we were told that we were to spend the night at a little hostel attached to the airport.

The hostel consisted of a few dormitory rooms and a small restaurant. Lonya and I shared one room in which three cots were jammed together. Down the hall was a bedraggled toilet and one cold-water spigot over a sink. I didn't even think of asking about a tub. The day was misty and raw, the skies lowering. Here we were, over 1,000 miles from Moscow, with nothing to do but wait. At length we wangled a car and drove into town along a thick muddy road. To me it was just a dreary, battered, dismal weather-beaten country town; its proudest

Over the Urals and Far Away

building a three-story "new flats" whose length and depth I measured as eight windows by six windows. There was only one paved street. The shops reminded me of native huts I had seen in Java, dark little clapboard caves, often below street level, and using no electricity, though the day was dark and it was late in the afternoon. Lonya saw it differently. He was impressed, he said, by the neatness of the buildings, by their blue and green colors, and he was intrigued by the little burros pulling carts or being ridden by men bigger than themselves. These burros are the same as those one sees all over the Middle East and as those I was to see throughout Soviet Asia.

The materials in the stores were similar in quality and price to those I had looked at in the Ukraine; even women's hats were the same in style and material, and their price range was identical with what I had noted in Kiev's best department store. Food prices varied a bit, and butter was cheaper by a few rubles than anywhere else I had been ($2.41 a pound; in Alma-Ata it was to cost $5.11). The food stores had the same display windows, the same canned goods for sale. And on the wall of the store were the customary percentages for the workers for the previous day. Down the main street were familiar billboards, one urging, as in Moscow, that people try to win 100,000 rubles in State-loan lotteries, and another warning about children crossing streets, though here there was hardly any traffic. The designs were the same, the slogans identical, with but one exception—a painting showed chairs, clocks, a piano, a woman's wide flowered hat, a radio, a vacuum cleaner, and a suitcase—but no television set or refrigerator—and the sign announced, "Within five years . . . the quantity of goods will be increased 70%." One other sign drew my attention. It advertised the movie *Silver Dust* (about germ warfare) and showed an evil-looking man carrying a test tube. Behind him was a painted representation of American skyscrapers at night, and on them an electric sign beaming the unmistakable words "Coca-Cola."

The people here were different, for at least half of them looked and were Asiatic. There were, however, a great number of Ukrainians and Russians, and I noticed many western Russian women who were quite pretty.

In the evening we went to a local clubhouse near the airport to see a film called *Country Schoolteacher*, depicting in heroic style the brave life of a little girl who leaves a pre-Revolutionary finishing school to teach at a small grade school in the untutored wilds of Siberia. She survives Siberian hardships, the Revolution, attempts by the rich kulak farmers to kill her, World War II, and many other tribulations. It was patriotic and sentimental, and would win most any onlooker's sympathy, for it had none of the customary Communist diatribes against the West. It might have been the life of a country schoolteacher who went to California in the Gold Rush.

I do not recall seeing any soldiers in this town, but at the airport restaurant that night there were four officers, fourteen men, and one woman. I did a little second-hand eavesdropping through Lonya. Three pilots were drinking vodka. Another joined them—and this I never expected to hear in Russia—when they offered him vodka, the pilot replied, "If it were milk, I would accept it."

Over at the next table a lively conversation was going on, and I remember these snatches. Said one, "There's an old Russian saying, 'There is no smoke without a fire.'"

Then two of them discussed an absent friend, and one remarked, "He's not shy. He just comes from a polite town. He comes from Leningrad."

The restaurant itself was like every other airport restaurant I was to see at each stop. Always there were five or six tables, generally square tables seating four, and always the tablecloth was somewhat dirty, and never was it changed, but just brushed off for any new guest. There was always a potted rubber plant or two, and always a little buffet in the corner where liquor, cookies, candy, and cigarettes were sold. Always the chairs were wooden, stiff straight-backs. I have seen chairs like these in every restaurant, farm, and office in the land, so that I began

Over the Urals and Far Away

to believe that one factory and one designer supplied the entire country. Always in these restaurants the menu was bound in imitation red leather, usually labeled, "Ministry of Internal Trade—Road Restaurants."

These restaurants sold their food, however, in a new way. Next to each item was the total weight, in grams, of the full dish and of the particular item. For example, "Roast mutton with rice, 3.85 rubles (the average worker earns 3.5 rubles an hour), 100 grams mutton, 270 grams entire dish." Caviar was listed at "3.35 rubles—total dish, 60 grams; caviar, 20 grams (about two-thirds of an ounce for $.84; caviar was probably the item which by our standards was the cheapest in the country)." Beefsteak—they call it "bifstek"—with potatoes sold for 5.20 rubles for 100 grams of meat in a dish of 330 grams. This would constitute an hour and a half's work of the average Russian worker for a dish which weighed about two-thirds of a pound and for beef (quality dubious) which weighed a little over three ounces. If you put sugar in your tea, the sugar cost twice what the tea did (in fairness, they put in about four lumps); and if you put milk in your coffee, the price was increased one-third. Bread ranged from four-fifths ruble to one and a fifth rubles a pound, or twenty to thirty cents.

The next day we flew for seven and a half hours to Alma-Ata, stopping briefly at Kustanai and Karaganda. All three cities had been covered by an early snow which was melting into seas of mud. Each landing and take-off that day and on the following legs of my journey through the East was a harrowing experience. There were no real runways, just worn paths of dirt now turned to mud. At each airport we would motor between the plane and the airport shacks in a worn old bus, pushing through the quagmire in low gear. The mud was so oozy-deep that we tried to move directly between the step of the bus and the plane ladder without setting foot on the muddy quicksand. Coming down the runway, I have seen my plane hit such a puddle that the mud and water splashed over my window and over the top of the plane. Yet there was never a mishap. The whole business seemed to me to be like when young Lindbergh was flying the mails: the tiny, worn green two-engined planes, the cowfield runways, the dreary airport shacks, and the empty wild terrain —for usually no city or other buildings were visible near the airports. I began to keep a little count of the number of landings and take-offs behind me and ahead while in the Soviet Union. I now had ten of each behind me and twelve more take-offs and landings ahead, enough to breed forty ulcers.

One more word about the pilots: "In my country," I told a Russian, "the pilots have a reputation for high-flying, even when they're not in an airplane."

He grinned. "In that respect," he said, "our pilots and yours are brothers."

CHAPTER 19

Scratch a Tatar
and You'll Find a Russian

THE KAZAK Republic of the Soviet Union is the second largest republic in area, covering over one million square miles, which are thinly occupied by about six million people. The Ukraine, in which over forty million people live, is only about one-fifth the size of Kazakstan. Kazakstan's area is four times the state of Texas, over which seven million people roam. This Asiatic republic is best known for its extensive and varied mineral deposits and for being a wartime seat of heavy industry. It is supposed to have 50 per cent of the Soviet zinc, about 60 per cent of its lead and copper, the world's largest chromium deposits, and a great deal of coal and oil. In addition, about one-fifth of the Soviet's sheep and cattle live on its steppes. Many people believe the Soviet Union's atomic work is carried on amidst its vast spaces.

Its capital and cultural center is a city of 500,000 called Alma-Ata, which means "Father of Apples," where I ate the best apples in my life. They are considered by some Western experts to be the finest agricultural product in the Soviet Union. Most of the city's buildings are quite low, for around the turn of the century the city was twice destroyed by earthquakes within thirty years.

Alma-Ata is at the very edge of the Altai Mountains, great peaks forming a remote part of the mountain chain of which Mount Everest is a part. Lonya had never seen mountains and naturally gasped at their awesome snow-capped beauty. I was ignorantly casual. "Those aren't anything," said I, "you ought to see real high mountains like the Alps or our Rockies." I later found out that in this area the peaks run as high as twenty four thousand feet, averaging six to ten thousand feet higher than the Alps!

The first impression is one of primitiveness, emphasized by the barren airport in a sea of mud. We drove over a mud road which later turned into a cobblestone street to the city. There was almost no motor traffic, and aside from the main road, nearly every other street was unpaved and full of mud ruts. Except for the faces of many of the people—looking like Chinese or American Indians or even Eskimos—all seemed the same as in the cities of European Russia. A young Western diplomat had warned me, "Every city out there is just another Soviet town; if there is any basically native life, it must be off in the distant plains." I think he was right.

Under the czars this land was backward and neglected. The Soviet Government established the first higher schools and universities, and it sent in Russians and Ukrainians to run the newly developing industries. Today in these eastern Soviet territories, there are many Russians and Ukrainians everywhere, but the native stock is taking a larger share of responsible positions, though control is still largely in the hands of the westerners.

In the few days I was there, I went to see two factories, a huge collective farm, a mosque and an Orthodox church, the university, and a number of local prides such as a mountain skating-rink, the opera house, and a concert of "native talent." The top men in the factories, the farm, the church, and in the hotel where I resided were all Russians or Ukrainians. My

Scratch a Tatar and You'll Find a Russian

local guide and interpreter, however, was a Kazak, as were the rector of the university and the Moslem imam.

But the decoration in the hotels, the contents of the menus—except for an increased amount of mutton and spices—the billboards on the streets, the displays in the food and department stores, and the architecture of such stores, even the green-painted boards of the free-market stalls, were all the same as I had seen elsewhere in the Soviet Union. The padded coats and the boots worn by the peasants seemed identical, and the woman going down the street with a pig on a rope was a sight I had seen often in Kiev.

I tried to make a list of what was different: the great mountains in the background; the Mongol cast of feature of many people; the Eastern music and the Oriental voices of the singers; the brown mud huts of the countryside looking like villages in Egypt; the little burros; the more easy willingness to pose for my camera; the presence of mosques; the heavy and frequent fogs because of the altitude; the greater number of pictures of Mao Tse-tung; the women traffic cops (who had been all over the country in 1946); the Turkish-style toilets (you stand on two foot treads over a hole in the floor); and some slight variations in the questions raised by those to whom I talked. At nearly every meeting somebody was bound to ask me about discrimination against Negroes in America, and the questioner would be a yellow-skinned man or woman. The war in Korea too came up again and again, and now and then a question arose about Indo-China, which I had not heard in western Russia.

Here I had one lengthy free-for-all conversation with some young strangers which could not have been planned, and I was an unexpected guest at a local wedding. One Sunday our trip to the countryside had been postponed because of fog and rain. The city that day could have been London wrapped in a cotton fog. We explored a church in the morning and returned to the hotel for lunch. In the Soviet Union it is a custom that a person may occupy any empty seat at any table in a dining room. There was one large table with about ten seats, two of which were unoccupied. I, not Lonya, selected the table. A Russian girl, a Kazak girl, three Russian men, and three Kazak men were seated there. We began talking to one of them and pretty soon got into a general conversation with everybody at the table, most of them aiming their remarks at me. We sat there for several hours. Some persons went away to keep appointments and were immediately replaced by others. Still more people came up and stood around us and joined in.

A number of students were in the original group. The Russian girl was majoring in German, the Kazak lass in chemistry; one Kazak man was at law school, the other two at a teachers' college; one of the Russian men called himself "a dynamiter" and his two Russian companions worked on the railroad. Later four Kazak men replaced the Russians; two were from an agricultural-research station and two were medical students. As the afternoon passed on, other people came up and tried their French, German, and English on me. During the afternoon the talk went on in Russian, Kazak, English, French, and German.

First, after the ice was broken, they asked me questions about America. "Do you have teachers' colleges? . . . Do you have law schools? . . . Tell us about your skyscrapers. Are they like Moscow's? . . ." Then the subjects turned political: "What do the American people think of the Soviet people?"

When I told them how worried we were that the Soviet Union might make war on us, again there was incredulity and laughter. "But what do you personally think?" Once more I replied that their people were O.K., but I wasn't sure about their government.

I got the standard answer, "Our people and our government think the same." Then they belabored me; being young, they pushed their questions harder than others, it seemed to me. Certainly they spoke at times with unusual animation. "Why don't you admit China to the United Nations? . . . What about the Ku Klux Klan in the United States? . . . Is it a serious organization? . . . Why did you delay the armistice in Korea?

Scratch a Tatar and You'll Find a Russian

... Why doesn't your government abolish the atomic bomb? ... Why did England and the United States go into Korea so far from their homes? Why don't they stay out of Korea? ..."

For the first time germ warfare was mentioned: "Why has America failed to ratify the Geneva convention against bacteriological warfare? ... What do you have to say about the use of bacteriological warfare by your troops?" When I denied the charge, they went on: "But there was a lawyer's commission which reported on it, and the war prisoners themselves admitted that it was so, and there was proof." I retorted that our soldiers had been tortured into fake confessions, whereupon one Kazak said, "How do you know they were tortured? Did you talk to any of them? Don't you think they possibly changed their evidence because of pressure when they returned to the United States?"

I felt annoyed with frustration and sick with hopelessness and bafflement. How will we ever get to understand or trust one another with such completely different beliefs and information? I might as well have been talking to Martians.

Lonya laughed. He said to me, "This young lawyer is acting like a teacher with a schoolboy, very pompously. He says he is not satisfied with your answers; you seem to be afraid to criticize your own government."

"All right," I said, "watch." I took a piece of paper and wrote on it: "I think Eisenhower is stupid!" Then I signed my name and flung the paper on the table. "I don't really think President Eisenhower is stupid," I said, "but I'm not afraid to criticize him or anybody else in America. You can send that note to the White House, to Senator McCarthy, or do whatever you please with it." That shook them; they looked at me as if I were crazy.

"Now," I continued, pointing to each one of them in turn, "let me see one of you say something equally critical about any one of your top rulers in the Presidium."

There was a long silence. They looked at one another and squirmed. Not one of them took me up on my challenge. After a moment, one man at the table ostentatiously palmed the note and slipped it into his pocket, watching me closely. I ignored him. For the next two hours he sat staring at me, never taking his eyes off my face. I suppose he thinks he holds my death warrant in his pocket.

Finally one stirred. "Ours is a collective government; we are satisfied with our government. Why do you change your government every four years?"

Another picked up the theme. "We consider the fact that we have one and the same leaders for so many years a strong point. This indicates that they have the trust of the people. When you change your government every four years, we believe that this is a failure to keep the trust of the people!"

But much of their talk was what I had heard in the Ukraine. Once more they asked me why we surrounded them with bases, what about the chess players, what about Paul Robeson. The only variation was that one asked me where Robeson lived. Also a slight variation on the discrimination theme—"Can Negroes get a higher education?"

I asked, as I had before, what the average Soviet citizen thought about the average American, and I got this reply. "You can ask everybody in the room, and you will have the answer that the Soviet people do not want war." A reassuring if not responsive answer.

The reluctance of the young Kazaks to criticize any leading personality in the Soviet Government was not exceptional. I have never heard a Russian publicly say a word against any top personality until he, like Beria, has been charged by the Government with some crimes. Once such a man has been accused by the Government, I have never heard a Russian say that there was anything good about the man in his whole life. To me the proof of police-state control is this reluctance to voice such criticism. Russians have argued with me that criticism of the functions of a Governmental department amounts to criticism of the minister, but they were not convincing. In this entire trip I encountered complaints only from the old workers in Zaporozhe's steel mill, from a man who insinuated his gibes in Latin—

Cicero's "How Long, oh Catiline, will you abuse our patience?" —(I think he referred to his rulers), and lastly, from one other person who talked quite bluntly in German. He said when we were alone, "I make the equivalent of three hundred and seventy-five dollars a month. I'd willingly swap it for twenty-five dollars a week in America." He blasted the Government as a dictatorship, complained about the cost of living, and said most Russians were abysmally ignorant of conditions outside the country. I don't know whether he was a genuine griper, or—as Western sources say sometimes happens—a plant sent my way by the Government. But the conversation was so exceptional, I'm almost positive the man was an *agent provocateur*.

During our talk in the hotel dining room one young Kazak from the Ministry of Agriculture told me a story which has frequently had its parallel in the U.S.A. He said that while he was at the university, a professor's wife had become enthusiastic about the English language, and she had organized a study group. Everybody joined enthusiastically and enjoyed themselves, but after a month they gave up the project because it was too difficult.

Here we also observed an exchange between a Russian customer and a pretty mascaraed Kazak waitress, who sat at one of her tables, smoking a cigarette and exhibiting her well-painted fingernails. The Russian asked her for something and she replied in Russian, "In a moment," using the standard Russian phrase which literally translates, "This hour."

The Russian said, "In Russian that means 'in sixty minutes,'" and she blithely replied, "Yes, and in Kazak it may mean seventy minutes." The East again.

The same morning that I talked to the group at the hotel, I had one other unusual experience—a country wedding in which the bride carried on a running argument with bystanders.

I had asked to see an Orthodox church. The one I went to on the edge of the city was a small wooden building where about seventy people were attending a service. There I counted six men, one woman about thirty, two or three children, and three babies; the rest of the worshipers were old and poor women. A few beggars, including a cripple and a blind man, stood at the door of the church. (All the beggars I saw in the East were Russians.) After the main service, seven old women busily scrubbed the floor of one alcove, where a party of five were waiting for a wedding ceremony. This consisted of the bride and groom, the best man and bridesmaid, and the mother of the groom. The bride, in a pink dress, carried pink paper flowers and wore a white paper flower over her heart. The groom, looking like a classic country bumpkin—rumpled wild hair, ill-fitting blue suit with a shirt too tight for his farmer's neck—also carried paper flowers. The best man had on a blue cotton shirt and a sweater, but no tie. The bridesmaid wore her rubbers throughout the ceremony. At the open side of the alcove a number of peasants lined up with us a few feet from the couple and the little altar.

An old Tolstoyan character, complete with beard, long jacket, and high boots, came out, opened a Bible on the altar, and then addressed the heavy-set, stern-faced mother. "Have you paid?"

"No, not yet."

"All right. You must pay."

"We will. We will."

"But first of all, you must pay."

Eventually he got his money and retired behind the altar. Only after the payment did the handsome bearded priest appear in his gorgeous yellow robes. He was assured and polished, handling the couple like small children on their first day at school.

The ceremony was lengthy, with much recitation, chanting, and crossing. The peasants began to murmur. Apparently the bride was crossing her chest in the wrong direction, from left to right instead of from right to left. Finally the bride could stand it no longer; she snapped at the audience, "I will cross in my own manner. I will do as I please." When the heckling went on, during another part of the ceremonial crossing, she retorted to the bystanders, "I am not a Russian." I found out her mother was Polish and she was Catholic.

But the heckling had its effect. The poor bride began to cross first one way, then the other. Right in the middle of one of the priest's solemn intonations, she interrupted him: "They are quarreling with me. They say I don't cross in the right way."

He replied, "You may cross as you choose. In this church it is possible to have a marriage if only one is a believer. The other person can be anything. She can be a Moslem or an atheist."

"But the people are quarreling with me."

"Nobody has a right to quarrel with you; you may cross as you like." And he blandly whisked through the ceremony.

While this was going on, the bridesmaid, holding a crown on a stick over the head of the bride, got tired. So she let her hand rest on the back of the bride's neck, causing the poor girl to push her head forward like an ostrich. At one point the couple had to drink wine three times. When the bride sipped timidly, I heard the priest whisper, "Bravely, drink bravely," and she took such a gulp that she choked.

At the end he prayed for God's blessing upon them and then gave them a little homily. "Be kind, love each other, stay close, and overcome difficulties together. Bring your children up in the right way and remember your parents."

Civil marriages are much simpler. The couple simply sign statements at the marriage registry giving a few facts about their lives including a list of "significant scars" and the declaration: "We enter this marriage willingly and know that we will be prosecuted if we lie." Thereupon they receive their marriage card. Official registration creates the state of wedlock. The major problem is the choice of marital name, for the couple may adopt either the man's family name or the woman's. Until a few years ago they could combine the two. Most now pick the man's.

After these impromptu adventures on Sunday, we set about more formal inspections; to a candy factory which was running on three shifts, to one of the big collective farms, and to a heavy-machinery plant where they admitted they still were using a great deal of lend-lease equipment. All three of these organizations were being run by Russians or Ukrainians. I had my first formal introduction to Kazaks in authority when I was taken late one evening to a rather dark and worn building that looked like some of the Moscow grammar schools I had seen. This was the Kazakstan State University, where I visited the rector, Zacharin, and his assistant, Besembiev, both of whom looked like American Indians.

The office of the rector resembled any factory or farm office in the Ukraine, with the same paintings of Stalin and Lenin on the wall, the same rubber plant in the corner, the same double inkwell stand, the same furniture. The only difference was the physical appearance and color of the men to whom I was talking. As usual, both were members of the Communist Party.

From them I learned that the republic had had no higher schools of education before the Revolution. This university had been established twenty years before and was still, the rector apologized, using many of its original buildings. It had 3,000 students, 70 graduate students, and some 325 teachers and professors, with faculty and students both about equally divided between the sexes. There were nine main departments, or "faculties"—mathematics, chemistry, biology, arts, geography, geology, economics, philology, and history, and they intended soon to open a school of journalism. The Russian language was compulsory for all Kazaks, and the Kazak language for all Russians. Students had their choice, for a third language, of either English, French, or German. In the philological and historical departments they also had a choice of Chinese, Arabic, or Latin. In addition to foreign languages, other compulsory subjects were philosophy, political economy, and a two years' study of Marxism and Leninism. Classes ran forty-five to fifty minutes, and most students went to classes thirty-six "hours" per week.

As elsewhere in the country, students were admitted to the five-year college course after ten years' preliminary schooling.

Scratch a Tatar and You'll Find a Russian

The college year ran from September 1 to July 1, with students using January and June to study for exams without having classes, and with mid-term vacations running through the last week in January and the first week in February. Courses taper off as the years go by. In the fourth year students are excused from classes one day a week, and in the last year they have a few classes only during the first half-year, eventually spending all their time on final papers.

The tuition fee was 200 rubles a year, but only about one-fifth of the students had to pay. Orphans, children of invalid parents, children of teachers, and "original nationalities" (Kazaks, Tatars, Uzbeks, Bashkirs, Kirghiz, Uigurs) were among those who did not have to pay. About 90 per cent of the students who had passing grades received monthly stipends from 250–300 rubles (at Moscow University the stipend was a little higher), and those with high grades received 25 per cent more. Also there were certain special scholarship awards available of 500 to 800 rubles a month.

Instructors got 1,500 to 1,800 rubles a month, assistant professors, from 4,000 to 5,000 (same as the head of a big farm or factory), and full professors received 6,000 to 8,000, depending on length of service. The rector himself received 8,000 and his assistant, 7,500 monthly.

These figures were confirmed in several other universities I visited. It may be of tremendous significance in any long-range rivalry with the Soviet Union. There they are combing the land to find talent worthy of a higher education—and they pay students who maintain passing grades. Furthermore, the professors are among the highest paid men in the land (about 50 per cent above the directors of fairly large farms and factories) as inducement to put the best brains into education which stresses scientific studies. Now it is reported that the Soviet Union is graduating 43,000 engineers a year, more than twice the number in the United States!

When I invited the professors to question me, bango—the first mention of Indo-China. "What is your attitude toward

Korea and Indo-China?" This was followed by: "Why did you use bacteriological warfare in Korea?" Then they discussed the Chinese. "You need not be afraid of the Chinese Communists. Only a small part of the Chinese are Communists, and they helped the people to secure their independence. It is wrong for you to blame the Chinese people. The Chinese people would never attack anybody. They are one of the most peaceful people in the world." When I retorted that they had nevertheless come across the Yalu River, the rector quickly said, "Let's change the subject!"

Thereupon the rector started on the Negro question, Were there separate schools for Negroes in America. My answer led him to say, "So it is fair to say that in some states of the United States there are not equal rights among people. Why?" I explained how much improvement had gone on in this field.

They took a third line of attack. These two solemn yellow men sitting there in the middle of Asia in what had been one of the primitive areas of the world addressed themselves to the protection of Western culture. "Now we see a growth of McCarthyism. Books have been put in the fire, Chaucer, Shakespeare, Byron, and many other books of historical culture. You try to ruin them. How do you explain this?"

I just gaped at them. Their concern for our culture was startling, their misconceptions appalling.

After I tried to enlighten them, they challenged me once more by saying that heads of their colleges and universities were appointed by the Ministry of Culture from among their most famous scientists, and that there was a project to elect them. They asked me whether we had a similar procedure. Like all true professors, they then asked me to explain how Eisenhower, with only military experience, was ever made president of a university.

Then they asked, "What is your job? . . . What is your party? . . . Do you study religion in the universities in America? . . . Do you believe in God?" The rector, who was a mathematician, asked me how we reconciled science and reli-

Scratch a Tatar and You'll Find a Russian

gion. He claimed he had read of an American mathematician who had tried to prove by mathematics "that God exists and that it is necessary to have a race of armaments."

After dealing with those thrusts, we called it an evening, first making a short tour of the few classes then in session, where I noticed one class being taught by a dark-skinned young Kazak girl in which more than half the students were Russian.

CHAPTER 20

Home of the Uzbeks

I PLANNED to fly from Alma-Ata over the mountains to Frunze, the capital of the Kirghiz Republic. But delays by weather made us cancel this visit. I did not regret this omission, for it is a small republic with a population of about a million and a half, chiefly nomads, and of the same racial stock and mixtures as the neighboring republics. Most experts agree that the present division of central Asiatic republics is highly arbitrary so far as ethnic or racial origins are involved, or, for that matter, natural boundaries. Many believe that the Government gerrymandered Central Asia so that its basically Asiatic groups could be more easily "Russianized."

Also, I was not too eager to go tilting in fog and clouds over those rugged-looking mountains in an old Soviet plane. I had run up the white flag when the Kazaks suggested that we motor through the mountains to Frunze. They said it would be an arduous journey, but we could make it. My experience with Russian drivers and the brief glimpse I had had of mountain roads around Alma-Ata made me turn down this three-day trip forcefully. It would be memorable to look back upon, only I wasn't sure I would be around to look back. I think this is the only Soviet invitation or travel plan I have ever turned down. Anyone who condemns me must first see those mountains, a

Home of the Uzbeks

wintry Russian road, a Russian car, a bold Russian driver in action.

We were delayed in Alma-Ata several days, waiting for the fog to clear and for the weather to freeze or firm the mud on the airfields so that we could take off from a "solid" base. Finally we embarked for Tashkent, flying at a height of 6,000 feet, where all that was visible was that stupendous mountain range we were paralleling and vast stretches of barren, burnt-out wastelands. We descended for a brief stop at the town of Chimkent.

From here it was a short run to Tashkent, capital of the Uzbek Republic, the cotton center of the Soviet Union. Uzbekistan, as it is often called, is one of the bigger Soviet republics. In millions of people the Soviet republics rank as follows: Russian, 110; Ukrainian, 40; Byelorussian, 10.4; Uzbek, 6.3; and Kazak, 6.2; all others have less than 4 each. In terms of percentage of total Soviet population, Uzbekistan's people rank still higher. The figures are: Russians, 58.4 per cent; Ukrainians, 16.6 per cent; Byelorussians, 3.1 per cent; Uzbeks, 2.9 per cent; Tatars, 2.5 per cent; and Azerbaijanians, Georgians, Kazaks, and Armenians, between 1 and 2 per cent. The country is also reputed to have considerable mineral wealth and exports some fine quality caracul fur.

What surprised me on arrival was the heavy snow on the ground and the icy white lacing on all the trees. Here, far to the south, was more snow than I had seen anywhere in the Soviet Union. It was like leaving a sunny Minnesota to find snow in Atlanta. As we descended, I got quick glimpses of the city, revealing a considerable size—750,000 they told me—and the fact that one giant factory seemed to dominate the area. Later I visited this plant, which was a famous textile combine, a combination of many factories.

Again the landing field was a quagmire of mud and melting snow, and again an ancient, bedraggled bus, like a tugboat, slowly chugged us ashore.

We were met by two young Intourist officials in one of those big black seven-passenger Zims such as I had seen at Minsk. Both young men were under thirty; one, an Uzbek, spoke excellent English; the other, a Russian, spoke only that language, but was apparently the local "boss." He would appear to discuss all arrangements, and then leave me in the hands of Gofar, the Uzbek, and Lonya, who both escorted me about the city.

The Russian boss and the Uzbek assistant who met me typified the relationship of the nationalities in that area. In Tashkent I met Russians running the giant textile combine, the machine-tractor station, the Cotton Research Institute, the local orphanage, and the Intourist Bureau; also, three doctors who came to see me were all Russians. I met only two Uzbek executives, the rector of the university and the chairman of a collective farm. Even the entertainment I got was "Russianized." The star at the circus was Berman, a Moscow clown. The main film in town was *Silver Dust*, featuring an all-Russian cast, and the leading play was a current hit from Moscow, though its setting was in the Ukraine. When I asked to meet some local literary people, the result was the same. Two men came to see me, one an Uzbek poet, the other a Russian correspondent of a Moscow paper. At the university where the rector was an Uzbek, half of the deans, with whom I talked at length, were of Russian nationality.

On the trip to town from the airport I noticed the same shop windows, the same signs, the same busses. This again might have been any city in western Russia, except for the Eastern faces of many inhabitants and the new sight of some women wearing trousers—as in China. Occasionally the new style Soviet architecture, flats with ceramic or stucco facings and heavy stone first-floor shops (bank-rock pediments, I call them), would make a concession to the East by adopting a sort of Oriental archway.

When we reached the hotel I took to my bed and we sent for a doctor. I had a bad cold and a raging fever which gave me a hopeless, exhausted feeling. My little bedroom was dimly lit by a weak bulb high in the center of the ceiling, and my antique bed had a sag which almost touched the floor. The only window right overhead would open sideways to admit all the blasts of Russia, or not at all. And I had to totter in my bathrobe down a long hallway, at least fifty yards long, to a set of public toilets, which necessitated my always wearing shoes and rolling up my trousers as I waded through the human muck which lay about. As I have told the Russians often, the thing I liked least about their country was their toilets. They are incredibly filthy all over the country—in office buildings, museums, schools, theaters. I began to think I must surely die, and that with great good luck I had chosen one of the most Godforsaken places in the world.

But Lonya was busy, encouraging, and most considerate. I think he intended to bring every specialist in town. A handsome old man—one of the few gray-haired men I was to meet—wearing a white surgeon's coat, soon turned up to examine my throat and thump my chest. He gave me pills and a gargle, and prescribed penicillin lozenges, which are now manufactured there. His stethoscope consisted of a little rubber tube which he plugged in one ear. He asked me if I had any shaving lotion. Lonya gave him some eau de cologne, and he rubbed this on the nozzle to sterilize it before placing it on my bare chest.

Next day another specialist arrived—a Russian woman doctor, again in a white coat, accompanied by a young woman who carried a metal box. The specialist fished out a metal tongue depressor, looked down my throat with it, then threw it back into the box with all the other implements. She changed all the prescriptions and went away. Lonya cheered me up by announcing that the doctors thought I had flu or grippe. Despite all these forebodings, the realization of the expense of my trip and the tight schedule I was on quickly pulled me out of bed. Lonya insisted on my being examined once more. A third doctor, again a Russian woman, showed up from the clinic. Once again she changed all the prescriptions, but she did encourage me to live, and soon, against her orders, I tottered out to my interviews. I was too feeble to remember the medicines except one, valerian—"for the heart"—which American doctors tell me is an ancient and harmless remedy, seldom prescribed here. I did get well quickly, however, and there had been no charge for the doctors, in accordance with Soviet custom. I had had, under "socialized medicine" the advantage of three doctors, but really no choice as to doctor and no consistency. In fairness I should say that I liked all three as persons; they had at least the comforting air of a solid doctor, which sometimes is a quarter of the battle for the patient.

This was the only occasion I had for the services of Soviet medicine, though on both trips I visited a number of hospitals and clinics. In 1946 the situation in the hospitals had been heartrending. I had seen hospitals washing children's diapers with clay, operating tables consisting of a plank and a piece of linoleum, wards crowded bed against bed, patients without bedding or bedclothes, and I had had to shake hands and smile at little war-wounded children who smiled back because hopeful Russian doctors sought to make new noses for them from the skins of their own bodies. Now the hospitals, while still far behind American standards, seemed well furnished and sanitary. There was adequate equipment and enough space, and doctors were once more looking into broader fields, experimenting with new remedies, and not just desperately catching up. One famous Moscow cancer expert anticipated the present controversy in the West when asked whether he thought smoking caused cancer. "Well, not the cause, but smoking can speed development of it." And one doctor even startled my Russian guides. He was using mineral mud for feminine hygienic treatment.

Ordinary Soviet doctors earn about 1,200 rubles monthly; consultants at clinics, 3,000; doctors with professorial functions, 6,000 and above. Nurses I met were only earning 600.

Doctors to whom I talked never failed to bring out the high cost of medical care and hospitalization in the United States contrasted with their free care. Their manner on this subject was a bit like a Victorian lady looking at a savage from deepest Africa.

I went off to my first interview, at the local university, in

Home of the Uzbeks

rather a shaky state, so much so, that after my talk with the officials of the university had ended, I did not bother to tour the colleges but retreated to my bed. At the office of the rector of the university, the rector and seven others were waiting for Lonya, Gofar, and myself. The others were the assistant rector, the chairman of the student trade union, a leading zoology professor, and the deans of the Oriental, geology, biology, and history "faculties," one of whom was an Uzbek woman. One dean, a Russian named Bondarevsky, an aggressive man of about thirty-eight years of age, spoke excellent English. All were members of the Communist Party except the student and the professor and my two interpreters.

First the rector described his university in a story very much like the one I had heard at the university in Alma-Ata. Now there were thirty-six institutes of higher education in Uzbekistan, where there had been none before the Revolution. They specialized in such things as medicine, agriculture, polytechnics, textiles, traffic, and irrigation. His own university had eight "faculties": physics and mathematics, chemistry, geology, geography, biology, history, philology, and Oriental studies. The university had about 3,300 students, half of whom were women, 60 per cent of whom were Uzbeks. The faculty was 400 in number; almost half were Uzbeks or other local nationalities; about one-third were women. The students received stipends and scholarships and paid tuition on the same scale as in Alma-Ata.

After the preliminary information was unreeled, we moved rapidly to the usual discussion, whose pace was enlivened a bit by the sharp remarks of the English-speaking dean. I noted that three of the men in addition to the rector were Orientals.

They asked me whether our states paid students to go to college, how many nationalities we had (they claimed over twenty at that university), whether there were any Uzbeks studying in America, what the rights of American Negroes were, what the positions of our political parties on the rights of Negroes were, whether we had women professors in America, whether we had Negro professors, did we have women Negro professors, did we have postgraduates, did we have Negro postgraduates (a number of these questions came from the dark-skinned lady dean), who could become a postgraduate student, was there any difference in payment to men and women, and was there any difference in pay for whites and Negroes.

Some of these questions were not easy to answer with pride. When one of my answers led one of them to remark that they were not accustomed to discrimination, that there everybody worked together, I asked them to explain the violent attacks on "cosmopolitans" in the Soviet Union, who, I had noticed, had almost always been Jews. The history dean claimed that attacks on cosmopolitans had also been aimed at Kazaks, Uzbeks, Ukrainians, and others (which I thought quite revealing), and he blamed the American press for singling out Jewish names on purpose.

The questioning went on about American education: how did students win their doctor's degrees, how did people become professors, how many people could go to college, could people with high grades obtain employment easily, could graduates in the arts schools easily get employment, and to what extent was Russian studied in the States.

When I admitted that the majority of American students had to pay for their higher education, they remarked, "Then it is true in America that money decides everything. Money is everything."

And when I said we had nearly full employment and that the pages of our papers were full of ads for engineers, one dean cracked, "No doubt you want all these engineers for military purposes (a feeling I had gotten about the Russians after reading some of their ads)." One of my interrogators then asked about the opportunities for arts-graduates, for they too have a few arts-graduates.

The young student changed the subject and asked me how it happened Americans talked a master-race theory. I was angry and snapped back that this was a Hitler doctrine which we had fought, that not we but the Russians had been sworn allies of the master-race Hitlerites.

(One of the irritating things about arguing with Russians is their self-righteousness. I do not recall, in all my extensive contacts, any Russian ever conceding that he was wrong. This all Communists seem to have in common with the Nazis and with Joe McCarthy. The closest I ever came to getting a Soviet admission of error was from Bruslov. He needled me about the "dishonesty" of the American press. This was a couple of days after Molotov's diplomatic party, where the Red leaders had engaged in extraordinary convivial toasts with Western diplomats. Of course none of this appeared in the Soviet press. I started to relate the details to Bruslov, emphasizing as I quoted each toast that it had been cabled to the United States and was no doubt in all our papers. As I cited incident after incident, his eyes bugged, and each time I would repeat—"And that happened in the Soviet Union and is now in our papers, but not in yours!"

Finally he could stand it no longer; he made a pushing away gesture with his hand and boomed, "Quit kidding!"")

Another professor shifted the talk to world politics. "How do you explain the present state of unfriendly relations? . . . Do you think the presence of so many American bases will increase friendship and trust between us? . . . How do you explain the American attitude toward China ("And don't give us any propaganda for children," snapped the belligerent English-speaking dean)? . . . Why did the U.S. send troops to Korea? . . . Why did the U.S. drop bombs on China?"

I had one argument which used to be fairly effective concerning China and the UN. I would say, "When a man holds you up in the street with a gun at your stomach, you don't invite him to dinner." It usually silenced a Russki.

I denied we had bombed China and said that any stray bomb had been accidental, whereupon I got the inevitable reply, "Then there must have been a lot of accidents."

The conversation shifted to the American Constitution. They

told me we had a good document, but it was not enforced very well; for example, the trial of the Communists in New York. After I said the American Communist Party was the tail of the Soviet dog, the English-speaking professor responded, "And in America the Republican Party is the tail of the monopolist dog too."

And another chimed in, "If the Communist Party is so bad, why didn't Roosevelt denounce it in the war against Hitler?" He added, "Now they are attacking Roosevelt for his friendship with the Soviet Union."

I explained that the Republicans were seeking any stick to beat the Democrats with, and one laughingly remarked, "So the whole blame for everything in the United States is the Republican Party, because you are a Democrat?" He had me there.

This led to the Harry Dexter White case, which was then in the American headlines. They asked me what about it, and I gave them an answer which always left every Russian speechless: "I don't know all the facts, but I gather Mr. Truman got some reports of our secret police which he thought were unverified or exaggerated. Haven't *you* ever known a situation where *your secret police* were overzealous?"

The conversation ranged rapidly over a number of topics. The rector suddenly said, "We fight for real facts in science," and he blamed the American press for not giving Soviet scientists credit for many first inventions. Truth was truth, he asserted.

I told him about *The New Yorker* cartoon in which one Soviet marshal asks another, "When will we be the first to discover the atom bomb?"

The rector ignored this, saying, "In our country, we also respect foreigners. We consider Darwin and Newton and Leonardo to be highly esteemed, and today the writings of Dreiser and Mark Twain are very popular here."

When we got into an argument about the free press, and I complained about their misrepresentation when General Marshall was awarded the Nobel Peace Prize, he retorted that

The New York Times had forty pages and could print a lot of unimportant details, but as for themselves, such prizes were "not so famous or important." He continued, "We are not interested in printing the opinions of Morgan or Rockefeller." *Non sequiturs* like this are par for the Soviet course of discussion.

In these varied arguments I did get one new answer. Often in the U.S.S.R. I took up the point that Communists seemed to be running everything (the Party is reported to have a Soviet membership of about 7,000,000), and invariably I got a strenuous denial—even from Khrushchev—of what seemed apparent. But the little aggressive dean made no bones about it. "So the best people in the Soviet Union are the members of the Communist Party. They are the heads of everything, not because they are Communists, but because they are the best people."

The dean of history observed that from his studies he noticed that Americans were not using current Russian historical works, that we seemed to be following only nineteenth century textbooks (even as I had said they were reading out-of-date books about our economy). I sailed into him and said that was because every time their party line changed, they rewrote their textbooks. I cited Trotsky, who had been a key figure in the Revolution and a great organizer of the Red Army, saying they never gave him any credit, whereas we gave Benedict Arnold credit for his merits as well as his treachery. I got the standard line—this from a dean of history—that Trotsky had been (as Beria is now portrayed) "a traitor all the way." To my charge that Lenin had praised Trotsky highly and made him co-editor of the Party paper, the dean lamely replied, "Lenin's liking of Trotsky only showed the democracy of our party, but not the attitude of the Communist Party." How silly can a Russian dean get? He went on: "Trotsky simply was a spy. You will find that Lenin wrote, 'There was a flush of shame on Judas Trotsky's face.'"

"But," said I, "what about Lenin's writing that Stalin was too rude? You don't tell the people much about that."

The dean gave me a fancy answer. "In Lenin's statement about Stalin's rudeness, this was a statement about Stalin, not as a political character, but as a human character, and this depicted Stalin's attitude, not toward his friends or employees, but toward enemies of the State and the Communist Party. The State felt only Stalin's strength."

I said, "I do not mean to be rude, but I must be honest with you. I consider your statement not a historical statement or the statement of a historian. It appears to me to be a religious statement."

To which he replied, "Stalin was against religious statements about anybody in the state. Communists are atheists. We have nothing in common with religion."

I retorted that they treated Stalin as a god, as the purveyor of eternal truth, almost a supernatural deity. And I concluded that a vice president of the Ukraine had agreed that the cult of Stalin was exaggerated.

I put my head down and doodled on my pad, after delivering this declaration by a high Soviet official. There was an absolute silence, for nobody offered to speak or contradict the Government official.

One finally changed the subject. "You mentioned 'Russian' people. Why don't you say 'Soviet' people?" (To them "Russian" usually means one who stems by birth or blood from the Greater Russian Republic, which is only a part of the Soviet Union.)

From that we shifted to a few amenities, and I departed under the usual Soviet umbrella of words. "We hope there will be understanding as soon as possible."

From Soviet production of ideas, we turned to Soviet production of textiles.

The Tashkent Textile Combine—the big cluster of buildings I had remarked from the air—was a combination of many textile factories, called "a combine" and named, miraculously, "after Stalin." In most other factories I met a number of top executives, and then as we inspected the plants, the foreman of each section

Home of the Uzbeks

escorted us through his department. Here I met nobody but the boss, a Russian, and one English-speaking forewoman, also a Russian.

This combine was one of the three or four largest textile outfits in the country, employing more than twenty thousand workers and producing over two hundred million yards of cloth a year. Some of the factories spun yarn or made thread, and others produced a variety of materials. They had their own power station and foundry, a four hundred-bed hospital, a clinic and a maternity home, several grammar and middle schools and one trade school, and even their own farm. The combine maintained day nurseries, summer camps, a local "Pioneer Palace" for children, and a number of resthouses and sanitariums for its adult workers. They also had their own candy factory, made their own soft drinks, ran their own public restaurant and their own stores for workers who lived in the surrounding community, comprising some sixty thousand people. The combine employed shoemakers, tailors, and tobacconists. It even built and operated most of the flats in which the workers lived. The director claimed, too, that the combine acted as banker for any workers who needed to borrow in order to build their own homes, loaning them ten thousand rubles at 2 per cent for seven years.

We went through a few buildings which had the clacking looms one might see in any textile plant, only here the noise and size was many times greater. The factory was like any other Russian factory. It was a little bedraggled, but the lighting conditions were good and the workers did not seem tired or harried. The place was cluttered with slogans on red banners; every room had its bulletin board with statistics galore as to percentages of fulfillment; and, like all the other Soviet plants, here and there were boards with photographs of a handful of excellent workers (Stakhanovites). This country uses statistics, competition, and prestige to the limit.

That night in our hotel Lonya and I resumed the arguments we had encountered during the day. Often he would translate faithfully, helping others reply to me, as was his job, but he could not resist asking me if he too might dispute some of my remarks later. This time he said, "You know, I can't agree at all with the way you constantly say the Russians built up a North Korean Army and then helped the North Koreans so much. What about the British in your Civil War?"

My attention was distracted by my attempts to compile my notes, and, without thinking, I answered, "What do you mean, the British in our Civil War? I think they had hardly anything to do with it."

"That's my point." Lonya smiled quietly.

CHAPTER 21

Silver Dust and Golden Samarkand

IN EVERY city I had visited I had seen advertisements for the Russian film *Silver Dust*. I caught up to it in Tashkent. After all the peace talk and peace signs I had encountered, this was a shocker. Here is the plot:

An American scientist named Steel has acquired riches and the formula for making a product called Silver Dust (*no connection with any detergent of similar trade name!*) by marrying the widow of the inventor. She has a boy and girl by the first marriage who are "progressives." They show this chiefly by the companionable way they greet the old Negro family servitor, an ample-bosomed, charcoal-coated Russian actress who calls to mind the Mammy pancake ads. Their own son, a little rat, all but puts his boots to the Negro servant.

Steel is subsidized by Southern Trust, in which he owns stock. Silver Dust is a preparation of deadly bacteria which will kill all people within an area of two acres and leave no traces.

The plot unrolls at the Pentagon where Mac Kennedy, a lieutenant general, and his military buddies decide over a couple of bottles of whisky to purchase the formula for the Army (I call this scene "High Noon in the Pentagon"), but they intend to divert the formula's control first to Eastern Trust, which is owned by their relatives. To help them in their plot, they enlist a former Nazi colonel who works for Steel ("we military men understand each other and know who our enemy is"), an Elmer Gantry itinerant preacher to prey upon the religious credulity of Mrs. Steel, and a gangster, apparently as a reserve threat.

Nothing seems to be left out. The minister tells Mrs. Steel he has been at a séance with the local sheriff at which Christ appeared. Asked, "When will the war of justice begin?" Christ replied, "You had better hurry." Also, when asked about the danger of Russian troops, Christ said, "But I have blessed my troops." The minister claimed, of course, that her deceased husband had joined Christ at the séance and advised that the formula be given to Eastern Trust.

The progressives in town, including the young Negro son of the Steels' maid, hold a parade for peace. But the evil minister drowns out the speeches by leading in a blaring Salvation Army Band. He adjourns to a local bar, pinches a floozy named Flossie, and gets tossed out. After the ensuing row, Flossie and six Negro "progressives," including the maid's son, are hauled off to jail.

By now Steel needs live human beings for experimentation in his laboratory, which looks like something out of "Captain Midnight" or "Space Ship to Mars." So he calls up the governor of the state (who has a resemblance to Tom Dewey) to find some human guinea pigs. Steel explains that Korean war prisoners are too far away and use of them might entail foreign entanglements and too many speeches at the UN. The governor therefore gets the sheriff to set about framing the Negroes. This is accomplished by bribing Flossie to accuse them of rape. Naturally, this being a Soviet film, they are convicted.

The country is stirred by "The Case of the Six." The Ku Klux Klan kidnaps them and is about to burn them at the stake when Steel gets the chief of police to save the Negroes for his experiments. The six are secretly transported to his laboratories.

About this time Steel's bad son sneaks into the lab, touches

Silver Dust and Golden Samarkand

some active germs, and dies horribly while the German colonel coldly notes all details of the death process so that he can report accurately, as he does, to Steel, the imperturbable father. A progressive assistant learns about Steel's purposes and tips off the local doctor and town progressives, who break in on General Mac Kennedy and the gangsters as they are torturing Steel for the formula. The mob carries off the Negroes to safety, just before the police arrive to stop them. When the general tells the progressive leader, "The electric chair awaits you," the leader, before fleeing into the night, replies, "Come on, let's get out of here. We don't want to be under the wheels of American justice."

When I got outside, I was boiling. Lonya tried to console me. "It doesn't show all Americans as bad," said he. "At least the good Americans won out." Even in the U.S.S.R. all's well that ends with Hollywood happiness.

After I thought about it for a while, I realized that the Russians had used a clever device to lend authenticity to their theme: they showed conditions of life materially better than in the Soviet Union. The men and women wore better clothing than that usually seen in their country; the home of the scientist was "Hollywood-modern"—even the painting on the wall was in modern style, and not bad in design by non-Russian standards—and the automobiles were among America's best. After the war Russian soldiers brought home tales of the wealth of the West which most citizens must have gossiped about; the truthfulness of the background of this picture might lull suspicious minds into accepting the rest of the story, with all its evil mayhem. Their sheriff nearly persuaded me, too. He had on a cowboy hat, went around in his shirt sleeves which were rolled just below the elbow, and, most convincing of all, walked with a limp!

The next afternoon we drove through a drizzle to a Moslem mosque. This took us through the old quarter of the city, which could have been an exact replica of the back streets of Cairo, with its narrow streets, its high walls of clay, the mud huts, and, above the cold of Russia, the pervading smell of the East.

Just outside the mosque, a flock of Moslem dignitaries were hovering around the ninety-five-year-old leader of the Moslem Church in Central Asia as he was trundled from his big 42,000-ruble seven-passenger Zim automobile. I was introduced to him, and he showed as much recognition of what was happening as a one-month-old baby.

One of his assistants questioned me briefly. "Are there any mosques in the United States? Does the pope have a representative in the United States? We have heard that the pope has been discussing the possibilities of war." Then he too got in his propaganda for peace. "Do you know that the customary Moslem greeting for centuries expresses our concern for peace? The words are, 'Peace be with you.' "

There were about five hundred turbanned Moslem men out in the rain worshiping on their prayer rugs. On high ground behind and to one side were about twenty veiled women in black dress watching the ceremony. They looked exactly like the women of Egypt in dress, manner, and figure.

I wanted to photograph the Moslems worshiping, but desisted because Lonya and Gofar were too nervous.

On our way back from the mosque, I began to question Gofar, our Uzbek interpreter, about his life. He was a bit of a tease. He kept telling me he had no other names except Gofar, but one day he confessed to a string of Uzbek names, none of which I could pronounce or remember.

Gofar was an orphan who had been born and raised in Tashkent. He had lived in four or five orphanages with boys of all nationalities, and then went on to a local pedagogical school where he majored in English. He was particularly proud that two of his fellow orphans had become famous composers.

During the war Gofar worked on a collective farm with other children and women and old folks, since he was too young to fight. His wife had studied for three years at the local university, and they had met at some athletic events. She was a

Silver Dust and Golden Samarkand

sprinter; he was a boxer. When I asked about her family, he replied that he had never heard anything about them.

He and his wife had married when they were students and had been able to live on their university stipends because each got 25 per cent extra for high marks, and his wife got an additional prize scholarship of 500 rubles monthly for unusual excellence in Oriental studies. She had dropped out to bring up their two daughters, Jenat and Dinnara ("I chose international names—Jane and Dinah"), but continued with correspondence courses. Now she was to return to college, and "that extra five hundred rubles monthly will mean a lot to us." His salary from Intourist was 1,050 rubles, and he managed to pick up another 900 by giving lectures on the English language in the local university.

Gofar lived in a three-room flat in an old one-story building; there was a wall stove for heating and a wood stove for cooking, but no hot water. "We had an argument about the toilet," said he. "My wife wanted it inside because she didn't like to take the children out in the cold; but I wanted it outside because most of the year it is pretty warm here. Fortunately, I won."

They did not have a telephone (according to the last official figures—1936—the Soviet Union had only 860,000 telephones. The United States has over 45,600,000), but they did own a radio, a Philips (Dutch) radio.

"Do you hear the Voice of America?"

"Yes."

"What do you think of it?"

"It's very good—wait a minute, I mean the radio set, not the Voice." But Gofar did acknowledge hearing some excellent concerts on the BBC. He said he also owned a painting of a beautiful dancer. "Her name is Mucharoma Turgumbaieva. She is a lovely dancer and I respect her, and my wife, without too much argument, lets me keep her picture in my bedroom." Gofar summed up many problems of life there, showing its backwardness and its hopefulness: "In two years we will have central heating; in three years on our street, a trolley bus; and in a few years, according to the plan, we will have an underground sewer."

I asked him how much rent he paid, but he didn't know. He said he earned the money and his wife paid it out. "It is not my business—in general, scientific workers don't bother with such things."

"Does your wife control all the money?"

Gofar: "Of course."

I asked him what he wanted for the future. His personal ambition is to write a textbook which teaches English directly to Uzbeks, for at present they must go through Russian texts first. He went on: "We want to live more comfortably—we want more space for our children and a room to receive guests. My wife particularly wants a cow; and I want an automobile." He smiled. "We have had much discussion about this. Maybe we will get a little Pobeda car in a couple of years, and maybe a cow in three years." His smile broadened. "And maybe we will buy both in one day to keep peace in the family."

I said, "You are talking like a bourgeois capitalist, yet everybody in America thinks you are slaves."

Lonya interrupted. "In truth, we are slaves to our wives only; that's all."

Lonya and Gofar had got so in the habit of using English at all times in my presence that after Lonya asked his fellow citizen what the Uzbek word *hop* meant, he received the reply, "O.K."

But once Gofar, who was an excellent interpreter, became so absorbed in a play that he forgot himself. "What did the actor say?" I asked, and received this translation, "He makes joke and she laughs."

Still, this was clearer than one local interpreter's remark: "The occupancy of this automobile is insufficient."

But an interpreter's life has its difficulties, too. Victor Ionkin, my Ukrainian companion, who was very well read, asked me if we still used expressions such as "drat it" and "egad." Since I barely recognized these words, he pointed out that they came

Silver Dust and Golden Samarkand

respectively from Mark Twain and William Makepeace Thackeray.

Later, when I asked Gofar what he had not liked in his life, he told me of his unhappiness at not being able to afford a celebration at his wedding and at not having any family. "I thought to myself, 'Who am I? Who were my parents? Who are my relatives?' But I have been happy since. I have been educated; I have a family. I will be happy if there is no war."

Then I asked Gofar's boss in the local Intourist office, Vladimir Yaroslavetz, a few questions about his life. He told me he was twenty-eight years of age, born in Tashkent of Russian parents—a schoolteacher and a housewife who were still alive. Vladimir had majored in German at a pedagogical college and then had fought "at the front," as a second lieutenant, in the Ukraine, Austria, Hungary, Czechoslovakia, and Rumania.

When I asked him about his grandparents, he knew nothing about them. He said he didn't know whether they had been for or against the Revolution and he wasn't interested in anything about them.

He and his twenty-five-year-old wife, who is a kindergarten teacher and was about to have her first baby, live with his parents in a three-room flat in a three-story building. They have a radio, a telephone, and steam heat. He didn't know how much rent was paid and he wasn't sure about his taxes, but he thought they might be about eighty rubles monthly.

When I asked him what he wanted, he replied quickly, "An automobile."

This led me to inquire who in that area had been able to purchase the most expensive cars for sale, Zims at 42,000 rubles each, a sum equal to almost five years' pay of the average citizen. They told me these cars had been purchased by a professor of mathematics, a professor of chemistry, a miner, a farm Heroine of Soviet Labor, and the chauffeur for an archaeological expedition!

Following my tour of Tashkent, I had intended to go to Samarkand for an extended stay in this legendary city. I had read that from 1403—when González de Clavijo journeyed there from the court of Spain—until Khanikov reached it in 1841, no Europeans had ever touched Samarkand, and only two Russians. Since that time, only a handful of Westerners had seen this city of glamorous history. Naturally I was determined at the least to touch base there and catch a glimpse of its historic relics. But delay by weather in Alma-Ata and Tashkent almost made any trip there impossible. The plane to Baku from Tashkent flew only at odd intervals. If we missed it, we would be stranded in the East interminably. The morning before our plane was scheduled to leave Tashkent for Baku, the skies cleared and the ground hardened enough to permit a precarious take-off. So I flew over to Samarkand one morning, wandered about the city for a few hours taking pictures, and ricocheted back to Tashkent in the evening.

The two take-offs and landings that day were the most shuddering of my trip, rolling across gigantic muddy ruts over great frozen patches of mud and water, breaking the puddles as we taxied to the runway. Lonya and I were the only two passengers, all the other seats being loosely covered with miscellaneous freight, none of which was tied down. Any accident would have buried us under the debris inside the crowded cabin. What looked like bales of cotton occupied many of the seats, and the only job of the stewardess seemed to be to hold back these bales on take-offs so they did not tumble on us.

At Samarkand we were met by one Hamdomov, an amiable little fellow who was Chairman of the City Soviet, or mayor. We learned that his father was an Uzbek and his mother a Tajik. This poor man had been apprised of our arrival just ten minutes earlier, and had bustled out to the airport in the first car he could find. He led us agreeably about the city to the five or six most famous and ancient monuments. Tamerlane had once started out from here, beginning as the ruler of this city, and one of the ancient monuments is over his grave. Genghis Khan had been here, too, and had laid the city flat.

We were shown some bare and uninhabited mounds, full of

Silver Dust and Golden Samarkand

caves, the seat of the original city before Genghis Khan destroyed it. Next we visited the monument of a fourteenth-century astronomer, and then various palaces and tombs. All were built in the fourteenth and fifteenth centuries and were now in partial decay, though the Soviet Government is slowly restoring them, or at least propping them up. All were identical in their white and blue shiny tile color, but greatly varied in their Eastern designs, in the Asiatic multiplicity of patterns and carvings within their walls.

We went to the tomb of Tamerlane and tried, in the cavernous darkness, to take some color-flash photos, though the two main graves, of Tamerlane and his teacher, were only flat stone slabs of no particular distinction. Outside the tomb I met three tattered children who wandered out of a near-by mud shack. It was all a great disappointment. The whole thing could have been in any Arabic country of the Middle East. The Oriental-Moslem architecture, the Eastern faces, the brown huts, and above all, everywhere, the mud of the East, so thick that as we walked down the main street, we often formed a human grapevine from tree to tree to pick our way through the slippery stuff.

Once I had visited Baghdad during the war, to experience the same disappointment. Now the sites of ancient Baghdad and Samarkand, story-book seats of power and romance, are sprawling cities of mud, decay, and stench. The splendor of their palaces now sinks in a sea of mud, and their fabled towers are replaced by the smoking chimneys of the twentieth century. The castles of an Asiatic Richard the Lion-Hearted have been superseded by the sooty furnaces of an Eastern Birmingham.

Hamdomov, the mayor, provided the only color. I had heard of golden Samarkand, but its brilliance appeared only in Hamdomov's smile. The whole visible upper part of his mouth was a ribbon of gold. But even he would not support the legends. I said, "You know, Tamerlane was the ruler of this city, and you are the hereditary successor."

He answered, "But he was an aggressor, and I am not." And he let his upper teeth shine upon us.

I didn't ask Hamdomov any questions. He was his own chamber of commerce, and volunteered some miscellaneous information. The city now has about 200,000 inhabitants compared with 85,000 before the war. Now the city has a university and sixty-nine institutes of higher learning, he claimed, where there had been none before the Revolution. Hamdomov pointed out what an active community it was, having factories which produced bread, wine, clothing, cinema equipment, and machine tools. "And many, many pretty girls," he interjected. I was told Samarkand's grapes were world famous, and that the area produced a large amount of cotton and citrus fruits. He even boasted that they "were in close connection with Chinese scientists and exchanged many scientists and scientific products."

From that our voluntary lecturer switched to the historical as we waited for our return plane. He claimed that Tamerlane spoke the Tajik language, still used in the town, though Uzbek was spoken in the countryside. He went on to tell us a long story about the palace of Bibihanum, Tamerlane's beautiful queen (her well-preserved body has been excavated recently, minus one finger, which Russians believe was chipped off at the time of her burial for the sake of some rings on it), how the architect stalled completion of her palace because of infatuation for the queen, how he implored the queen for affection, and how she put him off, showing him several eggs from different hens and telling him he could not tell one from another, thereby suggesting he take any other woman. How the architect kissed her cheek so passionately that it scarred her, and when Tamerlane thus learned of all this, he sought out the architect, who went to the highest part of the palace and then flew off into the heavens.

"That is the end of my legend," said the Chairman of the City Soviet.

CHAPTER 22

Oil City

We tend to forget how many countries border on the Soviet Union. In Tashkent we were about three hundred miles from the point where China, India, Pakistan, and Afghanistan almost converge on the Soviet mountain border. From Tashkent Lonya and I flew southwest, paralleling the Afghanistan border, across the great Kara Kum desert to Chardzhou in the Turkmen Republic, one of the smaller Soviet states, having about a million and a quarter population. After stopping briefly for some food, we flew on for another three hours, still going south and west, to Ashkhabad right on the border of Iran. The airports at both Chardzhou and Ashkhabad were like all the other smaller airports at which we had landed—little flat dirt fields with no hard runways, nothing in sight except one or two airport buildings and a few old-fashioned biplanes, which were lined up on all these remote fields. But southern sun had baked these fields hard, and we no longer staggered through melting snow ruts. As we swooped down to land at each of these places, I glimpsed a few flat-roofed Eastern mud huts of the peasants. We continued the same day for the third leg of our journey, which again lasted about three hours, flying high above the clouds, due west, across the Caspian Sea, which has an area more than five times that of Lake Superior.

It was almost dusk when our plane landed on the broad concrete runways of Baku. In a sense I was now "back in civilization." Many have called this city the real heart of the Soviet Union. It is exceeded in size only by Moscow and Leningrad, and in importance possibly only by the home of the Kremlin, for from the Baku area comes almost all of the oil of the Soviet Union. I was not surprised to see a modern airport, a great concrete runway, and three lines of polished new jet fighters. I saw thirty of them at one spot on the edge of the landing field. All over the area were many two-engined transport planes.

What did surprise me was the multitudinous number of oil derricks, all looking like Don Quixote windmills, or Martian storks. We were twenty-five miles from the city. As we drove through the twilight, I started to count or estimate the derricks, only to give up in a few minutes, for they seemed as thick and numerous as grains of sand. Not tens and twenties or even hundreds, but thousands. The next day, as I stood upon a hillside overlooking the port, I saw lines of these same derricks extending far out into the Caspian Sea. Later, coming into Baku by train from Tiflis, this same growth of derricks began when the train was about two hours away from our destination. The actual sight, in contrast to what my imagination had expected, seemed to me like the difference between atom bombs and previous bombs.

The Republic of Azerbaijan is dominated by Baku, which has almost one third of its three million population, most of whom are of Turkish or Persian origin. Once again it was necessary frequently to have a second interpreter, in this case one who could speak Azerbaijani, and Kamil Tariverdiev, the local music critic, served as both guide and interpreter. He was a tall, dark, mustachioed man of thirty who looked something like a Spaniard, and who had some of the same verve.

In every city I made a tour such as any traveler might make to all the main sights and monuments. I always tried to cover the colorful free markets and the food and department stores,

Oil City

and in the evenings I went to as many shows, movies, operas, ballets as possible. In each city I would suggest an inspection of at least one factory and one farm. To these sights I sought to add whatever unique things might be feasible, whatever I had not yet experienced.

Tariverdiev, or "Tary" as we called him, worked hard to produce.

We started out with some local bankers. Hitherto my only Soviet banking experiences had been at the Foreign Exchange Bank in Moscow, where cabled transfers of dollars to my Moscow account and, later, back to New York, were handled expeditiously. There I had seen only women acting as cashiers and clerks, and only abacuses being used for calculations. What surprised me more was that inside the bank, customers on their way to the tellers' windows had to pass a barber's open shop and an open rest room for the help, where several were playing chess, at ten in the morning, with many kibitzers, and where others lay sprawled on old couches, their feet jutting out toward the customers. This was like a cartoon I saw of two men playing chess, their office equipment pushed on the floor. One says to the other, "Hurry up, Comrade—only ten minutes more working time, and we still have twenty moves to fulfill our plan."

At the State Bank of the U.S.S.R.—Azerbaijan Office, there was no such disarray. There I met the three local chiefs, Krupkov, the director, and Suchnev and Hassanov, the assistant directors. All three were members of the Communist Party and two were Russian. Only Hassanov was an Azerbaijanian. Later we were joined by the chief of the planning department, who was an Azerbaijanian and a Communist. The director wore a handsome dark blue uniform with brass buttons and pink piping, and on his lapel were three little brass emblems like crowns. When I remarked that all the bosses in the country seemed to be Communists, the director gave me the most straightforward answer yet. He said it was no wonder they were all Communists—"Paragraph one hundred and twenty-six of our Constitution says that the leading and organizing power of the Soviet Union is the Communist Party."

Krupkov delivered a short lecture on Soviet banking. There was no need for a gold backing for the ruble, he assured me, since the ruble was covered by the volume of all goods in circulation in the country. The State Bank, in addition to being a bank of issue, had three major tasks: (1) to promote monetary circulation and to guarantee the stability of the ruble; (2) to establish short-term credit for enterprises and to calculate the basis of the credit; and (3) to function as cashiers, managing the accounts of the various enterprises.

They told me long-term loans were made by special agricultural and industrial banks. This bank made three types of short-term loans: loans for periods of 8, 11, or 12 months at 4 per cent per annum; "demand loans" at 2 per cent per annum for shorter periods; and emergency loans for 45-day periods at 6 per cent per annum in cases where plants had an emergency shortage of raw materials or accidents or similar unusual occurrences. In case of a default in payment of the regular loans, interest was raised automatically to 6 per cent. In the Western world when a borrower gets in trouble, he sometimes gets a readjustment, but apparently the Communist leaders tighten the vise.

I asked him how they handled a defaulting factory. He took a lumber plant as an example and divided its assets into four categories: its equipment, its finished goods, its raw materials coming in, and its wood which might be drying for three years. The bank cannot touch the equipment, nor the drying lumber, which he called "the concrete value of the enterprise," but the bank can force the plant to sell its raw materials and its finished goods to pay the bank; in effect, the bank can levy on these. Also, the plant cannot dispose of the drying lumber—the unfinished material—without permission of the bank.

I asked him what power or influence the bank had on the management of the borrowing factories. Krupkov replied that loan agreements are signed by the manager and chief accountant of the factories. If the loan agreement is violated, the bank

Oil City

checks up. "Rather often we demand that they change the manager." He explained this was done by the bank going to the Ministry of Finance and to the ministry in control of the factory. If the bank has no success with the ministries (according to this story), or if it is necessary for a quick change, they "apply to public opinion." Public opinion turned out to be the local Soviet government, the Communist Party, and the local trade union of the particular enterprise, with the banker claiming the trade union was "basic." So, as I understood this dizzying account, if the Communist banker can't get satisfaction from the borrowing factory, he complains to the federal ministries; if this doesn't work, he rushes to the local city government or the Communist Party or the trade union of the enterprise. In American terms, this would mean that if General Motors didn't pay the Chase National Bank, the bank would appeal to the U.S. Treasury and Commerce departments. Not getting satisfaction there, it would go to the mayor of Detroit, the Republican Party, and the United Automobile Workers—and the latter would be "basic"!

The granting of loans to enterprises was pretty automatic, for it was all determined by over-all budgets and credit plans approved by the Soviet Council of Ministers, although a reserve emergency fund was available for emergency loans in the discretion of the bank director.

I was told that in the Soviet Union loans to individuals were rare. Individuals may only borrow from banks for building construction or repairs or for the purchase of cattle, usually on a ten-year basis, the amount generally for 10,000 rubles, but sometimes as high as 25,000 rubles, at 3 per cent on construction loans and 2 per cent on cattle loans, with no interest the first couple of years.

In case of default by an individual borrower, the bank takes up the matter successively with the individual, his trade union, and his employer, and after that, if necessary, with the court. In no case can the court levy on the borrower's property, but it can garnish 25 per cent of his salary. If the man is not working, the director said, the debt in hardship cases can be abolished. A form of Soviet bankruptcy.

When we discussed earnings of bankers and bank employees, I learned that they were pretty well off. The top three men, for example, received 5,400, 4,000, and 4,000 rubles monthly, the highest set of executive wages I had encountered outside of the universities. The average wage was said to be 850 rubles, higher than any average wage given me in other enterprises, and the lowest pay, 550, was also higher than other reported "lows." Said the director, "In the Soviet Union we pay much attention to the prosperity of bank employees. We give them an extra percentage for long records; we give them uniforms, and we allow men to retire at fifty-five and women at fifty. If they have had twenty years in the banking system, we give them fifty per cent of their last salary as pension, and they can keep on working with salary and pension."

While we had tea and cakes, which were offered to me all over Baku, as Middle Easterners offer coffee, they began to question me. Right off came the old dig: "In America, can a Negro become the head of any state office? . . . What explanation do you have for the Negro's position in the South, and, as a lawyer, what can you say about lynching? . . . All of the republics and nationalities of the Soviet Union are represented at our sessions of the Supreme Soviet. What percentage of Negroes do you have in Congress? . . ."

I naturally sought to explain, and then I gibed at them about the fact that in the Soviet central government, all of the Presidium members except the Armenian, Mikoyan, were of Russian origin (that is, from the Russian Republic). I got some feeble answers: that the Presidium operated in Moscow, where there were more Russians; that there were only nine or ten men in that group and that the country had many more nationalities; that the leaders of the people prefer to be with their own people and in their own district; and—one better argument—that the larger Central Committee of the Communist Party had a more general representation.

When I reiterated that the powers-that-be in the Party, in the Army, and in the Government were by-and-large Russians or Ukrainians, they said this was not true and asserted that only Azerbaijanians were in the Central Committee of the Azerbaijan Communist Party. (I have not checked on Azerbaijan, but in recent months Russians or Ukrainians have been sent to the sticks to run several native Communist Parties.) The director answered that he himself was a Russian and he saw no difference in his attitude toward the people of Baku or in their attitude toward him, an argument any white politician might have used in the South.

The discussion was shifted by them to other subjects: "Why has the United States expelled over a hundred and fifty people for progressive ideas? . . . The main idea of Communism is to improve the prosperity of the working people. How can you call that a conspiracy? . . . Why don't you nationalize your banks? . . . How does the rate of progress under capitalism compare with our system? . . . Why did you elect Eisenhower if you do not approve of military control (I had been stressing the influence of their military)? . . . How do you explain the power of McCarthy? Attlee said McCarthy was more powerful than Eisenhower. . . . Why did the Republicans win the election? . . . Why did you go into Korea?"

Inevitably they mentioned Robeson, the chess players, the American military bases "surrounding them." Once more I was asked why we didn't let China into the UN, and I was told that there had been no Russians in Korea, that Russians had never attacked anybody, and that it was not true that they had attacked Finland. When I accused them of attacking Finland, they quickly changed the subject, after some flat "noes" and "not trues," but with no elaboration of their reasons for this position.

The respect of the bankers for the trade unions naturally sent me in quest of some trade-union men, and the indefatigable Tariverdiev brought me to the offices of the Trade Union of the Workers of the Oil Industry of Azerbaijan. Again the boss was a Russian, a big, handsome sturdy-faced Russian named Lunin, who was about fifty. His deputy was a slender dark Azerbaijanian named Abdulaev, who was in his thirties. The office was almost identical in size and decorations and furniture with the one at the bank, and again we were served tea and cakes.

There were two major differences from the bankers which puzzled me. Neither union man was a member of the Communist Party, and their salaries, though the trade union was so powerful, were much lower—2,500 and 1,800 rubles monthly, respectively.

Lunin gave me a short course in trade unionism, Russian style. All trade-union officials are "elected." There are shop stewards for each brigade in a factory, shop committees for each section which has a hundred workers, and a plant committee elected at a general meeting. This committee elects delegates to the District Trade Union of Oil Workers, which elects delegates to the National Trade Union Committee of Oil Workers, which elects delegates to the All-Union Conference of Trade Unions, which elects a central committee, all by secret ballot. I began to feel that in Russia they elect and elect and percentage and percentage. He denied there were any single-slate elections and said it was an exception when there were no extra nominees (not true of most Soviet political elections), citing that in a plant on a three-shift basis, each shift put up nominees and that, for example, if you were electing thirty-five people, you would have about fifty nominees. He even spoke of the victory of a write-in candidate; but, on cross-examination, this turned out to have occurred long before the war.

From his description, a Russian trade union is a combination of an American social-security bureau, an old time Tammany club, and a company union, with the brigade (group of workers, from twelve to thirty-five, depending on the section of the factory) trade-union organizer functioning something like a New York political district captain. He or his "insurance" associate organizes trade-union meetings; arranges for tickets to movies and theaters; organizes Sunday recreation; checks up when workers are sick and when they need help at times of funerals or weddings or other accidents; applies to the district committee to send workers to sanitariums; influences the decision as to which children are sent to pioneer camps; gets medical aid and medicines for laborers when they are ill; and, in general, deals with the problems of the workers in their day-to-day life. (Since the trade union represents the State, too, it no doubt also sees that workers punch the clock regularly and do a good day's work.) They asserted that most of this work by the trade-union men was done between shifts and in the evenings, and without pay, except for occasional yearly prize awards of not over five hundred rubles.

The union collects dues amounting to 1 per cent of a man's salary (but only half a ruble if he earns less than five hundred monthly) and also receives from the plant a percentage of the pay roll, from 9 to 11 per cent, depending upon the particular type of oil plant. (In a Moscow vaudeville skit a worker threatened to commit suicide. "Stop," said his girl, "you cannot do that. You are a member of a trade union." And he replied, "I guess you are right; besides, I haven't paid my dues.") This union fund, which is augmented by Government grants, is used to pay the trade union's central elected staff, to improve the standard of living of workers with special emergency grants, and to provide social insurance. In the case of a plant which is not earning much money, the Republic Trade Union Committee somehow can manage to get a contribution from other plants, which must be paid back eventually by the aided factory. Out of their funds the unions also build sanitariums and pioneer camps for children. Their funds are used to help women before the birth of a child, to aid a family in case of a sudden death, and to pay for permanent pensions. In the case of oil workers, these were unusually high, amounting to 80 per cent of the last salary.

Lunin claimed that a union had the power to get a manager of a factory removed for "violation of conditions of labor." He gave me only one example, a case where they got a deputy manager bounced for failure to observe regulations as to hospital housing.

When I put my finger on the central weakness, in my mind the completely nullifying aspect of Soviet unions—their lack of the right to strike—he attempted the following explanation: "Why should men strike for a higher wage here? They can, if successful, earn up to five thousand rubles monthly. In the United States, workers strike against the masters of the enterprise. They lose nothing if there is a stoppage of work. Here, workers are owners of the enterprise. They would be striking against themselves. They see prosperity everywhere. They have had seven reductions in prices since the end of the war. (Our statisticians calculate that average Soviet take-home pay is better than it has been for almost twenty years, but is still less than in 1928, when all individual income was drastically sacrificed to the long-term build-up of heavy industry.) They see a good future. They know only that the development of factories and the increase of output means their prosperity. Therefore, there is no one to strike against."

As was my habit, I encouraged them to ask questions of me. Among the queries were these: Is there a trade union of oil workers in the U.S.? . . . Why do you have two big unions in America? . . . How can the workers be protected if there are two unions in a plant? . . . What about conditions in non-union factories? . . . What help do unions give American workers? . . . Do unions have sanitariums and vacation camps? . . . Do American workers have paid vacations? (When I replied that most American workers have them, but that they prefer self-determination of their own vacations, the director replied, "It is better to organize the recreation of the worker.") . . . Can trade unions in America remove factory heads as in the U.S.S.R.? . . . Are American trade-union leaders elected or appointed? . . . Can they make collective-bargaining agreements? . . . Are American trade unions anxious for peace? . . . Why did the U.S. unions stay out of the world congress

Oil City

of unions? . . . Wasn't this a reflection on American unions?

Lunin concluded the interview with a lengthy, earnest dissertation, his clear brown eyes shining with seeming sincerity. He said he would appreciate my making the following statement to the people of the United States: "All the Soviet people have suffered war and have lost so many lives in war that they have seen the evil which war has, and that's why I hope that the American workers will realize that war is evil for the whole world. If the American people fight against war, I'm quite sure there will be no war and there will be no great suffering in the world."

We moved naturally from the oil trade union to an oil refinery, named this time after Andreev, and run by two Azerbaijanians, though the chief technologist was a Russian. This was the third office in a row which gave Malenkov a play. His picture was right there alongside Stalin and Lenin; but in the banker's office, Malenkov, instead of the semimilitary jacket, wore a pin-stripe suit, presumably from Brooks Brothers.

We were hopelessly lost. I had never seen an oil refinery, nor had my interpreters, one of whom had been a language student, the other a music critic. Soviet security certainly remained unbreached here, notably when the closest my interpreters could come, since they had forgotten their dictionaries, was to call various items a "tube stove" and a "warm exchange." What did strike me was that all the equipment looked so old and worn, and that the chief fire-prevention control device was a pile of sand and five red buckets outside each building. I saw no chemical equipment. Here I found in a control room the first man in the Soviet Union who operated with only one inkwell. They still don't understand why I congratulated him. In the same control room was a revealing poster, with four cartoons, showing an office manager failing to detect embezzlement, and bearing the legend, "There is no excuse for gapers. A gaper must answer for his faults."

This constant exhortation by poster and banner goes on all over every factory and farm. In this plant's club I saw a banner which solemnly intoned in Russian and Azerbaijani, "Workers, technicians of the oil industry, much more products and of good quality!"

Again I encountered high pay. They reported between 5,000 and 6,000 rubles monthly for the director, 3,000 for the chief technologist, an average pay for the 1,000 employees of between 1,200 and 2,000 rubles, a new record for me, and a low pay of 900, also a new record.

They opened up on me with stock questions on these subjects in this order: peace, American bases, American unemployment, status of American Negroes, the chess players, the Harry Dexter White case, and a request for an explanation of the Republican victory. Again they asked me, "When did the Soviet Union ever attack anybody?" and again they stated, "The Soviet people do not want war in the same way as the working people of the United States do not want war." Once more they seemed to be astonished when I enumerated activities of the Russian Government and of the Communist parties which had created world dissension.

The director was one of the few people I met who was uncomfortable about our discussion. He changed the subject to the history of the refinery, which had been there for eighty years, asserting that since the Revolution, all new equipment had been brought in and the production had been expanded from kerosene alone to gasoline and diesel fuels as well. He did not know the fate of the two original owners, a Russian nobleman and a Swiss capitalist, though he added, "One of the owners, Tadeev, died long after the Revolution, and died quietly." Except for Lonya, whose grandfather "died of drunkenness," most Soviet citizens seemed to be full of blank minds when you ask about their forebears or about people in pre-Revolutionary positions of power.

At the oil refinery's swimming pool, where I watched some boys and girls train for races, I found the quotation, "Soviet swimmers must break all world's records" in the never-failing white letters on red banners. The girls wore rubber caps and one-piece cotton suits; the boys wore tights and multi-colored, multi-patterned rubber hats which did not cover their ears. The pool was 25 by 10 meters, the practice similar to swimming practice in America, only it was very mild. Swimmers would kick the width of the pool and then rest (at Yale over twenty years ago we were often kicking many lengths of the pool at a burst). One strange exercise consisted of holding onto the side of the pool with one hand, and then submerging, possibly for breathing-control practice. It was at this pool that I saw the only special separate emphasis on Malenkov in my entire trip. Over the entrance lobby was a huge oil painting of Mr. Big.

This was the off-season for sports contests, but my guides tried hard. They took me to the local stadium to interview its director, Pivovarov, a Russian. The stadium's name was no surprise—Azerbaijan Republic Stalin Stadium. It could hold 70,000 people and could be emptied, they boasted, in seven minutes. At the entrance were bas-reliefs of Stalin and Lenin, and inside the stadium on one side were two great billboard paintings of Stalin and Lenin. In the offices underneath the stands were paintings of a girl's basketball game, of a men's volley ball contest, of Lenin—that great athlete—in his study, and of Stalin and Mao looking out from the Kremlin walls. There was also a flock of slogans.

Pivovarov, like so many Russians, gave me a long spiel, not on what they had, but on what they were going to have in about five years—a sports community costing about thirty-eight million rubles, or almost ten million dollars. Everywhere I encountered that kind of talk: "This is the plan, the blueprints are ready, the money has been appropriated, and then, construction has begun." Some students argue that Soviet citizens, by the nature of their philosophy, always consider the future more important than the present.

People "win their letters" in Russian sports, too. They have Honorable Masters of Sport of the Soviet Union, Masters of Sport, and Sportsmen, first, second, and third class. My host wore his "letter"—a silver-plated pin with the letters U.S.S.R., a picture, and the title, "Master of Sport." He got his award for excellence in basketball, playing on the Republic team, which in a five-year period finished not less than third in the country championships. He and one other on the team got the award for "technical achievements in the game; that is, speed, scoring, passing ability." The Ministry of Health has a special committee on these awards, which must be rather hard to win. For example, to get an award like Pivovarov's in sprinting, a man would have to run 100 meters in 10.5 seconds, which is about 100 yards in 9.6 seconds. Men get the top title of Honorable Masters if they hold a world's record or if they play on a Soviet team in international contests.

There have been stories that the Government subsidizes its athletes and frees them from other work while in training. (Not unlike our well-known "tennis bums" and some of our companies who have amateur athletes on their pay roll.) Pivovarov denied this, though he had already cited a couple of champions who were "physical-culture teachers." When I pressed him, he named some local athletes who were teachers, doctors, and students, and he included among his "athletes" the Azerbaijanian chess champion, who taught math. Just as revealing were his questions. He asked me how we rewarded our athletes, and I enumerated badges, medals, cups, and letters, omitting, for clarity of course, the subsidized tours and "football scholarships." Then he asked why we paid our athletes. After I explained the difference between amateurs and pros, he asked how amateurs made a living and what the standard of living was of the amateur sportsman. I still think Soviet amateur athletics somewhat suspect, too, when I recall he named Dadashov proudly as the Soviet free-wrestling champion, and then, before we discussed amateurism, said Dadashov earned his living as a physical-culture teacher, namely, as a trainer of wrestlers.

"That was a crazy idea of yours," said Lonya later when we finally could mention our trip to the Baku Meat Combine of the Azerbaijan Republic, and it was. The man in charge, the

Oil City

chief engineer, who was a Ukrainian named Simvol, one of the few men I met who was over sixty and still holding a responsible position, put me through the toughest moments of my trip. This combine was the only one for the city, and it produced lamb, beef, pork, and some poultry meats, also making cutlets, sausages, gelatin, and some oils and medicines. The old man said they did not produce horsemeat, that this was eaten only in a couple of republics which I had just visited.

As he talked about all the medicines they made, I got the wrong impression and said sharply under my breath to Lonya, "Listen, I wanted to see a slaughterhouse, and you've got me in a damn drugstore." I was to eat those words, but little else.

My experience in meat factories had been on those streamlined tours through the stockyard companies of Chicago, which is a bit like witnessing it all on television, as you stand on special ramps and platforms and observe the panorama of death and slicing below. It had not occurred to me how different such inspection might be in other countries.

We donned white cotton coats, like surgeons; the old man took us across a yard, opened an iron door, and there we were on the floor of the abattoir. The only way I can describe it is to say that I have read of many nightmares in novels, I've read Dante's *Inferno*, I have seen weird modern paintings of ruin and destruction, of blood and death, and I have seen macabre photographs, and now and then a gruesome accident. In my youth I read fairy tales of horror and monstrous witchery. At this moment all the images I knew of torture, nightmare, and horror seemed combined. Added to all these images was the awful stench of the slaughterhouse.

I won't go through all its gory details. I found myself standing right behind a man sawing cows in half with an electric saw, the bone splintering over us. Everything was at a fearful pace, and all seemed bedlam and confusion. The old man took us across the center of the floor—on the edges of which carcasses of cows and sheep were circling on pulleys—toward the killing spot. At this point I noticed that I alone did not have on rubbers as we slithered across the crimson floor, where blood and guts ran into open sewers. (I had noticed before that Russians riding or pushing anything on wheels seem to drive pell-mell through anything. More than once we were inspecting factories, and, as we started through doorways, were almost bowled over by a flying Russian rolling something smack at us.) As I trod gingerly across this floor, a man came roaring at me pushing a wheelbarrow full of liquid yellow ooziness. I stepped aside, narrowly missing a sewer, directly into the path of a man pushing a cart at me which held trays of bloody sheep heads. To get to the sanctuary of the platform where the killer of cows stood, and off the bloody turmoiling floor, I had to pass within two feet of stunned cows just strung up to bleed to death.

I remember vividly the pathetic struggle of the cows to get into the runway which took them, not to safety, but to oblivion, at the hands of a man who stunned them with an electric rod. (I understand we still slug the animals with a hammer.) I remember, too, the claimed speed record in pulling off a cow's skin in twenty seconds by attaching pulleys, the skinning which went askew, and the big cow which bounced back, bowling over a stripper, and, above all, my own thoughts that if I slipped and fell, I wouldn't be able to eat for months.

But my torture was not over. When we returned to the head office, a spread was laid out, consisting only of a variety of meats and tea. The State inspector was there, showing more pride than the managers in the output, and under his prodding I "sampled" seven kinds of meat. Tariverdiev had been unable to touch a piece and later remarked, "You are a very brave man." After that, however, Lonya and I could not touch any meat for about three days. As we lifted it to our mouths, the smell and memory of the slaughterhouse would come back to us.

They told me there were fifteen veterinarians in the plant and five check-points in that hellish room, but I hadn't noted them. I did call to the attention of the engineer that truckers were walking in dirty boots all over their loading trucks and then throwing the meat where they had trod. He excused the plant for this unsanitariness by pointing out that the truckers belonged to another part of the Government.

CHAPTER 23

Inside Russian Homes

ALL TRAVELERS who finally penetrate the Iron Curtain to the Soviet Union admit that a still more impenetrable barrier is the door to a Soviet home, particularly an urban flat. In the past on rare occasions a few Americans and other Westerners visited some Moscow flats. Now and then on infrequent trips to the countryside they managed to see one or two peasant homes. In 1946 I had been inside a few peasant homes, and some of my associates visited one city flat and one *dacha* belonging to Ukrainian officials, making the record for the entire fifteen-man mission one urban residence visited during a period of sixteen months.

On this trip I went much beyond that. First, I saw a number of rural residences: several on a State farm in Moscow; another on a collective farm outside Minsk; a couple on a farm near Kiev; one in a rest home on the outskirts of Kiev; and several more in the mountains of the Caucasus. I also got some idea about the inside of a city flat by visiting buildings ready for occupancy in Minsk and Zaporozhe. Finally, in Baku, I went into four different flats in which families were living, which is four times the previous record, and I made another new record by taking photographs within them. Experts who have analyzed my experience believe that the people I visited were not warned,

Inside Russian Homes

but that the guides who escorted me had general permission to take me into some flats and knew perfectly well that those they were showing me were in an acceptable "show-place area." If this speculation is true, the show places I saw reflect badly upon what was unrevealed.

At the Moscow State Farm I inspected some newly erected farm homes. Some of the group were unfinished, and while construction of these was going on, families were doubling up. The farm chairman took me into these homes without giving any visible warning to the occupants. These were all one-story brick affairs, with two apartments to a house, and each, in addition to a glassed-in sun porch used for storage in winter, had three small rooms plus a kitchen. Near each dwelling was a tiny barn. In one flat, two couples lived, a chauffeur and his wife who tended cows, a carpenter and his wife who worked in the fields. In a second one, I met an elderly-seeming grandmother, all of forty-five years of age, and two other older women who shared one very small iron bed. All flats were steam-heated, the radiators being connected with a wood stove, reportedly a local invention, and all were spotless. There was a great deal of crochetwork on tablecloths and curtains, a number of rubber plants, one icon, pictures of one or two relatives, and one or two books. In another building, whose occupants were absent, I saw a living room containing a little table, a sofa, three straight-backed chairs, and one small clothes chest. There was one narrow cotlike bed in the bedroom. The living room was about fifteen by twelve feet, the bedroom even smaller. While all was cramped and somewhat bare, all was spotless and rather cheerful. There was no slovenly filth.

At the Minsk collective farm I had stopped on my own to talk to a group of workers including the woman in charge of pigs. She invited us to her home, and we walked across the fields to it together. She lived on a little street which had about a dozen small wooden cabins, each fencing in its own yard. Her yard included a small orchard and a little barn with two pigs, all zealously guarded by a fierce mongrel dog. She and her husband had three rooms—a living room and two bedrooms, all a little larger than in the Moscow farm flats. Again the furniture was sparse and simple. Again there were only one or two pictures, apparently of relatives. Again the rubber plants. Again there was a religious icon. Again all was spotless, including the eighty-eight-year-old grandmother.

At the First of May Farm outside Kiev I saw the homes of the chairman of the farm and of one of the workers. We were walking along a street when I asked if I could go into a private home. The farmers turned toward the gate of the nearest one, but a dog kept us off, and nobody answered our call. So we went into the one next to it, again, I believe, without any preparation. The woman of the house was there with her mother and her two small girls. We took pictures of the exterior of the dwelling and of the family inside the little house. This place had two small rooms plus a kitchen; its outer wooden walls were painted white, and it had a tin roof. The interior rooms were all neatly painted in solid blue and green, and once more it was spotless, though very meager, livened a bit by the painted walls, the orange lampshade, and the crocheted Ukrainian curtains and bedspreads. When I saw the icon on the wall and remarked, "I see you are religious," the housewife replied, "I believe in it. There is a church in the village which all are free to attend and I take my children." I asked whether her husband went to church, too, and she replied, "He believes in more essential things."

The home of the farm chairman differed from the peasant woman's only in that the two rooms were much larger, almost double the size of hers, and all were whitewashed inside and out. The furnishings were equally simple.

In the mountains of Georgia I saw the finest Soviet peasant homes ever—comparatively large two-story affairs made of stone. They used the lower floors for a combination cellar and barn. The upper floors had wide glassed-in terraces, and usually three large rooms. Once more they were sparse in furniture, but extremely neat in upkeep. Still the potted rubber plant was the main decoration, with now and then a Government poster or a map.

I got my first glimpse of city flats in Minsk. These were empty ones in buildings which had been recently remodeled. Later I was to see the exact replicas of these flats in the museum in Moscow, and after that, occupied flats of similar design in Baku a thousand miles south of Moscow. The ones I saw first were three- and four-room flats, two to a floor in a four-story building which had massive stone steps and no elevator. All over the country there are many buildings no higher than this, thereby eliminating the need for elevators. In these flats the measurements were as follows: corridor, 76 square feet; kitchen, 86 square feet; bathroom, 43 square feet; toilet, 20 square feet (kitchen, toilet, and bathroom were about this size throughout the country); living space in three-room apartments, 600 square feet, and in four-room apartments, 800 square feet. This means the kitchen was about 9 feet by 9; the bathroom, about 9 feet by 5; the toilet, about 4 feet by 5; the rooms, about 18 feet by 11.

In each room the only light came from the center of the ceiling, and almost all electric connections were by exposed wiring. In kitchens and toilets the drainpipes were uncovered; that is, the sewage and drainage from the apartment above passed by uncovered pipe through the rooms below. Hot water was provided only if tenants installed gas heaters; the toilets were of the chain-flush type; the sinks were without stoppers (I thought this was primitive until I heard of a Russian lady who had traveled abroad. She was shocked by our sinks with stoppers. Said she, "Why they wash their hands in their own dirty water!"); the bathroom and toilet cabinet, without windows; the kitchens had wood-burning stoves (though I did see gas stoves in Baku); the only clothes space consisted of a bedroom closet 4 feet wide by about 2 feet deep, and one half-closet over the kitchen doorway; the windows were usually double windows, badly puttied; and the walls were painted pink or green or gray. To their credit, there was good light, occasional cross-ventilation, steam heat, and quite a bit of hall space.

At Zaporozhe I went through some smaller unoccupied flats of almost identical design. The two-room flats had 340 to 400 square feet of living space, the four-room flats, 760 square feet, and the rooms were respectively 200, 200, 180, and 180 square feet. When I asked why the pipes were exposed, the Ukrainian accompanying me replied, "How would you fix them if there was trouble?" And when I asked why toilet and bathroom were separate, he replied, "What if you want to use the toilet while your wife is taking a bath?" I guess we are primitive after all.

In Kiev we visited the series of buildings which constituted the trade-union "resthouse," and the director kindly invited us to his home for tea. My notes again list "meagerness . . . neatness . . . crowded sleeping arrangements." They had two small rooms. In the living room were two couches and in the bedroom another couch and a single iron cot. Here, in 320 square feet of living space, dwelt the director and his wife, his mother, and sister. Once again the saving grace was that he only paid 45 rubles monthly rent out of a salary of 880. (Having married a divorcée, he asked me this question [Victor's translation]: "In America would a man take a woman who has been divorced and has a kid?")

This was all I had seen of Soviet homes until one day as we walked down a street in Baku, I asked Tary to take me into a new building we were passing. He selected the name of a professor, and we mounted three flights and rang the bell. Professor Gadjiev, a short, dark-eyed man in brown trousers and smoking jacket, opened the door. The Gadjiev family was truly surprised at our incursion: the wife went off to change her shoes, reappearing in fancy red leather half-boots with fur tops, the kids changed some of their clothes, the professor his coat. My guide seemed startled, too, for Gadjiev turned out to be the president of the university and one of the highest paid men in the land, living in a lovely six-room flat with a small terrace and a view overlooking the harbor.

A corridor ran through the center of the apartment. From

Inside Russian Homes

the entrance going down the corridor on the right were the professor's study, a living room, a room for the two smaller children, and the bedroom of the couple. On the left were the bedroom of the teen-age boy, the dining room, and then an area which we did not see, which I took to be the kitchen, bathroom, and toilet. From all statistics, and in view of their income, this must have been one of the most spacious apartments in the Soviet Union.

The furnishings were in proportion. In the professor's study was a backgammon table with a game half-played. He said he and his brother had been playing when we arrived. I recall his mahogany desk with a small bust of Lenin on it, and a glassed-in five-shelf bookcase. There were thirteen volumes of de Maupassant, nine volumes of Theodore Dreiser, sets of Hugo and Balzac and of the two Tolstoys, and many other Russian works, including an *Encyclopedia of the Works of Lenin and Stalin*. There was also a couch and settee in the study.

The older boy's room was much like any older boy's room in America. An iron bed, a few books, a desk, a couple of chairs, and some impedimenta which could belong to any boy. The room belonging to the two younger sons had neat cots and two trim little desks. The professor's bedroom had a large double bed, a chest for clothing and a dressing table (one of the few I ever saw in the land) on which were a couple of bottles of perfume. The living room and dining room astonished me. I remember seeing tapestries on the wall (one of a hunting scene in which the men wore red coats, either from England or pre-czarist times), oriental rugs, a Bechstein grand piano, a collection of cut glass, a silver samovar, and some lovely vases. There were also groups of wax flowers and the inevitable rubber trees. It was far more luxurious than anything I had ever seen in the Soviet Union; yet its like might be found in thousands of bourgeois homes in Europe.

I learned that Gadjiev earned 11,000 rubles a month as a professor and rector of the university and that his wife earned an additional 1,000 as a grade-school teacher. Out of this they paid

200 rubles for rent, 100 for water, electricity, and gas, 20 for telephone, and 3 for their two radios. The total space of the apartment was 2,400 square feet, of which 1,700 square feet comprised living space, making the rooms about 50 per cent larger on the average than the largest I had seen up till then.

The rector and his brother, a professor of nuclear physics, talked to me over cognac, tea, and cakes while the wife bustled about waiting on us.

Right away Gadjiev told me about his university, and the story was like the ones I had heard in Alma-Ata and Tashkent all over again. How they had no higher institutions before the Revolution; but now there were twenty institutes of higher learning in the Republic of Azerbaijan, and 5,000 students in the university, which had over 400 Azerbaijanians as teachers and professors.

Gadjiev took up familiar questions, beginning with Robeson first, and the friendly attitude of all Russians toward the world as the second topic. He and his brother toasted the progressive people of America, saying the Russian people wanted to be closer to them, and they asserted that understanding would come "despite all attempts to prolong the misunderstanding." Next they asked me with pride what I thought about Moscow University and about their movies.

This discussion led me to say that they saw few of our movies and knew little of our literature. The rector said I was wrong. "We translate many of your books and papers." Thereupon I told him how shocking it seemed that their customs inspectors had to ask what literature I carried. Here is the answer I got from the rector of one of the largest universities in the Soviet Union: "Maybe customs wanted to know what was interesting."

The wife came in at this point to ask me about the literacy of women in America, how much education they had, and whether they could become professors. Then the brother asked me if a woman could be President of the U.S. He started to talk about Dreiser's *Sister Carrie*—"Her life had been broken by the bad conditions in America for women." When I said this book was ancient, he retorted, "Perhaps the *American Tragedy* is closer to more recent times." They moved on from this to ask me about the number of unemployed at home, whether we had pensions, whether we had free medical care, and what was the average pay of American workers and professors.

They brought up the life of professors in Russia as a comparison. "Take my brother. He works five hundred and fifty hours a year, including about a hundred hours of lectures, and he receives a salary of sixty-five hundred rubles monthly. He is mainly a leader of postgraduate students. So he has about two hours a day as a lecturer and professor and sometimes a little more. And sometimes he's entirely free. The maximum hours for even the lowest assistant in the university are not more than six hours a day, and for the technical staff, not more than eight hours." Then he told me about two of the highest-paid men in the land, the president of the local Academy of Sciences at 20,000 rubles monthly and the president of the same Federal Academy at 25,000. The only higher-paid couple I met than Gadjiev and his wife were a man and woman in Tiflis who each made 8,000 rubles monthly and who had also been awarded a 100,000-ruble Stalin prize for their work as co-managers of the Georgian folk-dance ensemble.

Aside from the talk about income, it was much like visiting a home in other lands. The wife made us try some jam she had put up. The host asked us to sample his favorite cognac. The fourteen-year-old boy played Grieg and an Azerbaijanian piece on the piano, and the four-year-old was introduced to us as a chess prodigy. Then the family smilingly posed for pictures. They could not have been more open and gracious. Gadjiev even insisted on taking me upstairs to visit the architect of the building. The architect was away, but his wife willingly showed us through her apartment, identical in size and format with the one below. The main differences were that it had quite a bit of classical statuary and some paintings, including one of the architect. The family had only three people dwelling in six rooms, proving what the Kiev architect had declared, that some creative people got more space than the average worker. This tenant was also the architect of that very building, which made me reflect a bit about Soviet politics.

It made me think too of a skit I saw in Moscow in which a house is built so transparently that the neighbors talk to each other through walls and ceiling, criticizing the building. One said, "These are not the mistakes of the architect. These are the remnants of capitalism that he built so badly." Then a voice from below moaned, "When I built this house, I never thought I would be given a flat in it." And as they all filed off the stage, one reached into his icebox and pulled out his brief case!

These visits to occupied flats were pleasant and revealing, but hardly typical. I pressed Tary to take me to something less elaborate. One evening on our way to dinner he stopped at a more modest building and began his unexpected knocking. The first flat we entered belonged to an oil-refinery technician named Mamadov.

The apartment consisted of three tiny rooms—living room, bedroom, and a nine-by-nine-foot kitchen—plus a small bathroom and toilet. Mamadov lived there with his wife and three children. There were cheap cotton rugs on the floor, a small rubber plant in the corner of the living room, and a couple of photographs of relatives on the wall. There also was a color portrait of Stalin torn from a magazine, a man's watch and a woman's handbag (relics of departed parents) hanging on the wall. I saw no books. The wiring and the plumbing were exposed—running down the inside of the room—and though there was steam heat in the apartment, Mamadov had to pay extra for hot water, which was provided by a gas-fired heater in the bathroom (but then, his rent was only forty-four rubles a month).

A dining-room table, four or five stiff-backed chairs, a corner table with a radio on it, and a sleeping sofa took up most of the living room. The bedroom was crammed with a narrow cot-size iron bed, in which both the husband and wife slept, and two iron cribs. There were no closets—just one large clothes cabinet; Mamadov's suits hung from the hooks on the wall.

I asked Mamadov how much money he made, and he said, "Eighteen hundred rubles a month—and twenty-five days' vacation a year." I was surprised when I learned his salary. It was equivalent to $450 a month—nearly two and a half times as much as the average Russian worker makes. Yet his standard of living could be compared only to what you would find in a tenement flat in America. I would guess offhand that an American oil-refinery technician of the same skill would own his own home, live in three times the amount of space, and have an automobile, a television set, and other luxurious consumer items. The only luxury I noticed in Mamadov's apartment was a little bottle of perfume belonging to his wife.

The apartment below also belonged to an oil operator who earned a bit less than Mamadov—1,500 rubles monthly. The apartment was identical in size and similar in its limited furnishings. This family had no rugs, but a much larger rubber plant. In the bedroom was a single iron cot for the husband and wife, another for the two girls of six and eight, and a crib for the boy of two.

I went away pitying the meagerness of their possessions—and they were earning at least double the average wage, but I was also impressed that they were happy, that life was looking up for them. To me they were most courteous and hospitable, and Mrs. Mamadov, despite the suddenness of our arrival and our own haste, insisted that we join them in a cup of tea. I will never forget the eager, curious dark eyes of the children, the pleasant friendly smiles of my Azerbaijanian hosts.

CHAPTER 24

Mustaches and Toasts

TIFLIS, or Tbilisi in the native Georgian language, is one of the showplaces of the country. If foreigners are permitted to tour outside Moscow, they are most frequently sent to Kiev and Tiflis, the capital of the Republic of Georgia and one of the ten largest cities in the U.S.S.R., with a population of over 500,000. I had read the literature of Russia emphasizing the vast extent of the great Russian plains and the flatness of the terrain, only to find myself, first in Alma-Ata and now in the Caucasus, in cities surrounded by mountains higher than the Alps or the American Rockies. Not far from Tiflis is Mt. Elbrus, the highest peak in Europe.

This little republic of about three and a half million people is famous in the Soviet Union for its resorts and its wines, for its manganese mines, which are the largest in the world, and for two individual products—Stalin and Beria, its native sons. The experts tell me that Stalin was so much a Georgian that he could only speak Russian with a dreadful accent. Even his fierce mustache was strictly a Georgian product. There, almost every man wore one. I counted forty-three out of the first fifty men I saw one night at the theater, and eight out of ten on two college basketball teams—three of whom were wearing hairnets! All the men were very dark, and seemingly all bore a resem-

Mustaches and Toasts

blance to Uncle Joe. I used to walk about pointing out people, "There's his brother; that's only a cousin; Stalin must be still alive; and that's his old man for sure." The Georgians have a great reputation for vigor, bravery, and outspokenness, and a capacity for long lives. Their women seemed to me, and to other travelers I know, to be the loveliest in the Soviet Union. They tend to jet-black hair, dark flashing eyes, straight Roman noses, and good figures compared with the general short, dumpy builds of many Russian females. There's a Latin grace to their carriage, and they seem to resemble Italian women, who have always been famed for their beauty.

We made the journey from sunny Baku on a train which took most of a day and night to make its slow ascent, for some 350 miles, to the Georgian capital. At each stop I tried to take pictures, hunting desperately for some color. It was a bleak, bare, hilly countryside, a bit like the poorer terrain of Montana or Utah. But the city of Tiflis itself, snug against a mountainside, basking in an Indian summer sunshine, was one of the handsomest cities I had seen in that land. This Russia I had not encountered in any story books, though I had thrilled to some of its strange beauty in a Russian "wild West" film about their border guards, which had the enchantment of new scenes substituted for the too-familiar California and Colorado backgrounds of our Westerns.

Throughout my stay here I was accompanied by Lonya, my Russian traveling companion, and by a young mustachioed Georgian, named Colbalitsa, for most conversations had to go from Georgian to Russian to English. This would be the fifth Soviet Republic in which a language other than Russian was frequently used by the natives in our conversations. The other languages I heard were Ukrainian, Kazak, Uzbek, and Azerbaijani.

In the city I first paced through the tourist routine: to the theater to see a Georgian ballet entitled uniquely, *For Peace;* around the town for hours and up the near-by mountain; into the major stores and markets; through one factory; and to one show place, the local Palace of Young Pioneers. For entertainment I went to a basketball game and saw a special showing of a documentary film about the Georgian vacation land and a historical film about an ancient poet, their great literary idol.

Then I managed to get out of the city and take a fifty-mile journey by auto to the little town of Gori, high in the mountains, where Stalin was born, and then on a bit farther to a mountain collective farm.

The town of Gori is a pleasant little mountain town, consisting of a few one-story buildings and one or two main streets. You come up the country road, suddenly swing around a curve, and you are in the middle of the town, and in about two blocks you are at Stalin's birthplace near the center of Gori. Stalin's father, a cobbler named Djugashvili, rented a room in a two-room, one-story frame house, the whole of which is now encased in a covering stone edifice with handsome columns. Next door is a museum devoted to the story of Stalin's life, with many original memorabilia. The tiny room—about 13 feet by 10 feet —in which Mr. and Mrs. Djugashvili and little Joe lived has been refurnished, supervised as to accuracy by the old lady. The furnishings are poor and scanty—a little slat bed with a straw mattress and quilt cover, a small table and old tablecloth, a chest with an oil-cloth on top, three wooden chairs, an oil lamp, a beer glass, an earthen jug, and a samovar are all that are visible.

In the museum I was struck by the record of the years in prison and exile which the young Stalin endured. I also made notes on a couple of documents translated to me from Georgian. One, undated, written by the inspector at the seminary in Tiflis, where Joe studied from about age fourteen to nineteen, said, "Djugashvili 31. I found he has a paper from a cheap library, and according to this, he is using books from this library, and today I found in his chest the work of Victor Hugo, *Toilers of the Sea*, and in his book this paper from the cheap library."

The other was a poem, published when Stalin was fifteen:

"A rosebush opened and met with the flowers;
The narcissus awakened and bowed its head to the wind.

Mustaches and Toasts

High in the sky the lark is singing
And the glad nightingale repeats the song in sweet voice.
Be beautiful, O wonderful land, and be glad, country of Georgia;
And you, Georgian, with your education,
Assist the development of your country."

From Gori we drove further on into the mountains to the village of Mejvriskhevi, where we met a collective-farm chairman, two brigade leaders (farm foremen), a schoolteacher, and the leader of the collective-farm ensemble. They bore typical Georgian names: Tomashvili, Rtvalliashvili, Chelibdza, Homasdurigdze, and Huzishvili. Not a one spoke any Russian, so that all afternoon the talk moved along in double translations. All the men had mustaches, all were dark and Stalinesque. This was the usual large collective farm, with about 12,000 acres and about 1,200 families, different from others that I had seen only in that it was a couple of thousand feet above sea level, that its mountain cows naturally gave less milk, and that it had more orchards than other farms I had seen. This latter fact led to trouble.

After we trudged through the snow inspecting fields, barns, village clubs, and schools, they finally headed for the winery. Having almost disastrously surveyed one winery in Kazakstan, I approached this one gingerly. On a collective farm near Alma-Ata we had been led to the winery, where a spread had been "laid on." This consisted of bread and cheese and sausage—and a variety of wines. Altogether, and in a row, the Kazak farmers and I had downed successively, and in goblets, a dry white Riesling, a white "dinner wine," a red "dinner wine," a muscat, a repetition of the dry white Riesling, a red "dessert wine," and we concluded with a heavy red wine called "a church wine." Having weathered that, I was under the mistaken impression I could face anything in Russia. At the Georgian winery I was relieved to find no meal awaiting us. We started sampling a couple of their best wines, which I guardedly sipped. Following that, we stopped at the homes of a couple of peasants and then progressed to the homes of the men who were accompanying me, eventually winding up at the residence of the chief brigadier, where a banquet awaited us. At each place we stopped, the wine of the house was produced, and everybody drank one glass. Fortunately these were often small glasses. But still there were quite a number, and the assortment was varied. As we approached the brigadier's home, all language difficulties, speaking doubly as it were, seemed no problem to anyone, and everyone was in relaxed spirits.

When we entered this home, it became obvious to me that once more I was about to face one of those special dinners in which Russians of all republics delight, for the table was covered with a huge variety of foods, and I could see a number of glasses and bottles on the table.

Inadvertently, as a gesture on behalf of American-Soviet good will, I claim to have eaten and drunk my way through more Russian banquets and farm feasts than probably any American alive.

In 1946 I tried to inspect as much of the Ukraine as I could, going to every principal city and to many small towns, and also to farms around those urban areas. In addition, I met Russian hospitality, official and unofficial, in Moscow, Minsk, and other cities outside the Ukraine. At that time several causes contributed to my "ordeal." We were members of an accredited diplomatic United Nations mission. Possibly they thought they had to entertain us. Secondly, there was a shortage of food. So, in a curious way, the giving of a formal dinner or putting on a spread assumed a special significance, as a gesture. Third, I often suspected that our visit was an excuse for local officials to throw one of their rare parties on the old expense account and get a little rich food otherwise unobtainable. Lastly, it has been long a Russian custom to entertain foreign visitors in such fashion.

Wherever our mission went, we encountered these relatively elaborate meals with the inevitable succession of numerous toasts. Often I would say as we made our plans, "Now try and get us out of any of these dinners—we have a lot of work to do." And I would receive assurances from the local Kiev officials that they would follow our wishes, only to run into the usual ceremony. Once a group of us arrived at Dniepropetrovsk at about eight at night and were met by the mayor and other officials. When asked if we wanted to "discuss our agenda" that evening or the next morning, we requested that it be done as soon as possible. We waited in our rooms until about nine, when we were led into a room, where a long table was decorated with the familiar viands, and until after midnight we "discussed the agenda" over a score of toasts and courses.

On another occasion at the little town of Zhitomir, as they started to pour out great gulps of vodka, I quickly suggested that we all state our toasts at once and cover them all with one drink, for, I rather foolishly explained, I had a fiancée who was a teetotaler and did not want me to drink too much. The Russians took care of that. "Oh," they said, "you have a fiancée! That calls for a special toast to the absent love, which you must drink alone." That's all the heed my proposition got that day.

Of course you don't really have to drink anything. But it is a custom of the land, and refusal certainly does not gain face for the visiting foreigner. Further, the Russians propose these toasts with a resourcefulness and persistence matching Molotov at his adroitest, and they add on these occasions the leavening quality of great good spirit and high humor. The round of toasts there is like bull-fighting in Spain, which has been called variously a national custom, a religion, their favorite game, and an art.

There are many tricks to the "game." Before our mission left for the Ukraine, some Russians in Washington, at a formal dinner, taught us the elementary rules—probably one of the best things any Russians ever did for Americans. They also taught us some "old Russian proverbs" to assist the drinks, such as "Either a full kiss or none" and "It goes down like a lie in the village." There we learned the two basic rules—*one*, that with vodka you always gulp the entire drink and never sip at the colorless stuff; and *two*, that you always eat steadily as you drink it, preferably oily foods.

Working our way through the Ukraine, we perfected our technique. *Rule number three:* As soon as you sit down, maneuver by changing seats or just grabbing a miscellaneous glass to get the smallest glass you can find and put it in the middle of the collection in front of you. For they play a bottom's up game with wild abandon, in which the size of your glass never counts. Many a Russian no doubt wondered why as we entered any room where there was food, we became only vaguely attentive to the conversation going on, our eyes "casing the joint" in search of tiny crystalware.

Rule number four: Line up a lot of oily food in a hurry. At every banquet, my first words to Mary, my American interpreter on my first trip, would never be about what the Russian near me was saying but merely urgent implorings. "Mary, get that caviar. Mary, grab some bread and butter—and quick, that little glass over there."

Rule number five:—this is the kingmaker! Duck any toast you can by any means you can, for it's a long, long trail, of uncertain variety and with an indefinite and dangerous ending. It's infra dig, and you may lose the contest and your reputation if you get caught slipping water into your glass—though it's usually impossible to find any water anyway—so this is inadvisable. But trying to put a light wine in your glass is fair play, if you can prevent your opponents, by strenuous talk or some other diversion, from then taking the glass away and filling another glass three times larger brimmingly with vodka.

Now and then as the evening moves on, you can improve on this. Variation A is to try and get away with only a sip on each toast. Late in the dinner and far from the center of the toast, you may accomplish this, especially if there is a veteran near you who wants to coast. But if the guy next to you has just swallowed water or wine, count on him to call everybody's attention to the fact that you are soldiering on your vodka. Variation B is to cup your hand around your empty glass, which first requires an ability to avoid the pourer. Variation C, which has several subclassifications as to style and timing, is to spill your drink. When the toasts are rapid, nobody cares about one spilled drink. When the bottle or bottles are at some distance, they may not get back to a noticed spill. The semi-unnoticed spill is one where you pour it down your own shirt. (It only gets noticed later.) An unnoticed spill occurs as you swing the glass down in front of you or to your side on standing for the toast. When the pace is fast, a better variation is to throw it over your shoulder behind you in protesting exuberation. One American I know was heavily penalized; instead of the roundhouse overhead play, he made the short Jack Dempsey jab, a quick low thrust just clearing his shoulder—only his unnoticed maneuver hit the waiter behind him dead center.

Failure to observe rule five quickly reveals an amateur. Amateurs first show their inexperience by eagerly joining in any toast to people sitting far from them. Experienced in-fighters always escape a full drink with one of the above-established procedures whenever toasts are being concentrated on people far from them or when the toast-giver and center of attention is a distance away. After you know this rule, you shrivel up and go as thin as possible when somebody rises to toast your lifelong friend.

Rule number six: If it's a hard game, don't go volunteering toasts. Before you know whether it's going to be a fast tough game, don't be an early pacemaker with toasts unless protocol demands. I used to work under quite a handicap. The first toast would be to the President of the United States. Sitting next to the chief Russian, I would have to take that toast bottoms-up openly and then respond with a similar full one to their leader. Toast number three from them was to our mission. So there was a running start of three unduckables for me, but my associates at the far end of the table finally learned to "sleep" on these when they could manage it. Above all, don't leave your place to accost some selected guests with a special private toast; they are bound to return the hospitality. Once in my inexperienced days I observed a general and an admiral far out of the show. Since they had just fought a war on our side, my interpreter and I marched down to them and drank a toast to the armed forces of our countries. Whereupon, individually, the two Russians marched up and separately proposed toasts to me, putting me three up—or rather down—on many of my neighbors.

Rule number seven: This should be called the power play. Now and then a tough and persistent Russki will pull a real low blow. Occasionally if you yell foul loud enough, the surrounding referees may save you. He will come up to you with his small glass filled, fill for you a very large glass in front of you, and propose a bottoms-up. He will give you a lot of talk that difference in size doesn't matter, that a man is honor-bound to drink a full glass on each toast. Here's your play. Get your opponent to put his glass alongside yours as you argue how much larger his is. As it sits there, he will mock you that it doesn't make any difference. So you quickly grab his little glass and gulp it, and then you ride him hard. I thought this up in a hurry one night, but on one or two succeeding occasions it knocked an importunate Russian just about out of the ring.

Such is the game in the cities and at formal dinners. Farmers are more direct and simple. They merely fill up a water tumbler of vodka, and everybody starts the meal with a bottoms-up of the full glass. After that they pour at random and drink at random. In fact, everything quickly seems "at random." The first drink is customarily followed by quick devouring of chunks of black bread, great hunks of meat, or a bowl of cabbage soup, and now and then I have seen farmers put a fork in slabs of butter and eat the butter like cheese.

Despite all my claimed experience in these "wars," this Georgian farm had a new wrinkle. There was course after course, including five different meat dishes consisting of chicken, ham, lamb-shashlik, beef, and then a mutton course, plus an assortment of sharp cheeses and many vegetables and fruits—for food was more abundant in Georgia than anywhere else I had ever been in the U.S.S.R. For once there was no

Mustaches and Toasts

vodka, but throughout the dinner wine flowed in a river. I was appalled to find that I was expected to join the others in drinking bottoms-up toasts out of a huge oxhorn filled with wine. I don't think I've ever been pumped so full of wine in my life.

The brigade leader's pretty daughter was at the table, and when the Georgians urged me to make one last toast, I said I would do it on one condition—if I could kiss the hostess goodby. Everybody laughed and we drained the oxhorn—and then, to the merriment of the entire assemblage, they brought out an elderly woman and presented her to me. "This is the hostess," they roared. They thought it was a wonderful joke, and I did too. I kissed the old lady. Then the brigadier's pretty daughter stepped up and kissed me. So did all the other ladies in the room, and I departed in high spirits.

It wasn't until later that an American diplomatic official told me how only a few years ago men were found still wearing medieval coats of mail in that area, and how to this day they are reputed to kill strangers for even looking at their women. Later, too, I read about a married man who went up into these same Georgia hills to visit an old girl friend. The next day his body was delivered to his wife's doorstep—chopped up in little pieces. Since reading that, I go a bit weak-kneed whenever I think of my own little episode at Mejvriskhevi.

CHAPTER 25

Homeward Bound

FROM THE high altitudes of Gori and the mountain farm I began the toboggan run homeward—down from the mountains by train to Baku again, northward by plane to fabled Stalingrad for a short survey, then back to Moscow to clean up a few details, and out hurriedly by way of Leningrad to Helsinki and the Western world. I did not dare to pause at Leningrad lest I lose my precious notes and photos, which, after many worried moments and a number of discussions with Russian officials, I had been allowed to take out of Moscow uncensored. After we touched ground in Finland, as I started from the Russian plane to the Helsinki terminal, I turned for a last look and swung my handbag in a parting gesture. The Russian pilot waved good-by —and I was once more safe in the West.

In those last hectic days my most vivid memory is of the thrilling sight of Stalingrad—a Soviet hero city—whose defense had loomed so importantly for all of us in World War II. Here the Germans were first repulsed and then overwhelmed, and at this point the tide of war changed. The city of Stalingrad, almost alone of Russian cities today, still brings back grim memories of that struggle. Except for a little uncleared rubble in Kharkov and Poltava, the Russian towns and countryside seemed fully restored from the ravages of the war until I came to Stalingrad. This city had been almost completely destroyed. It was still in process of reconstruction almost eleven years after the battle. I carried away with me a picture of a city which seemed to sprawl at great length like Los Angeles; a city of thousands of small homes, hurriedly thrown together—little jerry-built one-story shacks of the returning refugees; a city of board fences surrounding many great new buildings still only partly finished. But the famous tractor factory is thriving, the giant steel mill smokes at full blast, and there are a few lovely new public buildings: a great stucco opera house, its interior combining the best features of the two other finest Russian opera houses I have ever seen—the Bolshoi in Moscow and the opera house in Kiev: a handsome new railroad station very similar to the ceramic-shiny new one I had seen in Minsk a thousand-odd miles away; and a great planetarium which was not quite finished. Yet for all its amazing recovery, it is still a battered, tattered city, showing the deep scars of devastation. Everywhere are battle monuments, usually immobilized tanks, marking the flow of battle, revealing how perilously close to the banks of the Volga the Germans came. In the rubble were labor gangs of women sturdily wielding pick and shovel at the unending debris, just as I had once seen similar women work gangs fretting away at the crumbled bricks of Germany.

There were unreal aspects too. The Russians pointed out, across the street from my hotel, a busy department store and proudly said, "Paulus, the German commander, was captured in the cellars of that building." It was a little like pointing to Macy's in New York in the midst of the shopping rush and saying, "Hitler was captured there"—it seemed so improbable in that normal city scene.

As in Moscow, again I had the sense that I had known all this before. As I looked across the frozen Volga from Stalingrad's banks, the view from the city was totally familiar, no doubt because I had read, and forgotten I had read, many vivid descriptions of the city and the river at the time of its heroic struggles.

Despite its painful wounds, the city is bustling and hopeful, its atmosphere charged with energy. Because of its history, Stalingrad has become the Grant's Tomb of Russia, a place to show all sightseers, and a visit to its Volga–Don Canal sites is its "Radio City Tour." I avoided the journey to the canal and instead asked to talk to people who worked on the Volga River and to some editors.

The two river boat captains to whom I talked looked like all the grizzled sea captains I have met or read about. They had a certain healthy rugged aspect and also an air of quiet assurance. Life on the river, monetarily, was about the same as in a factory. Sailors who studied at school received stipends, a little less than those granted students at universities. Seamen received about 650 rubles monthly, the pay of unskilled labor generally, though the seamen also got room and board. The pilots were paid like shore engineers, and the captains about the same as factory managers. The only surprising information was that the crews were composed indiscriminately of men and women, and that seamen could take their families with them, so they claimed.

They asked me questions about the way of life in America —the conditions of labor on American boats, how a captain kept one ship, what the captain's privileges were. Like everybody else I had talked to, of their own volition (possibly prompted before the meeting) they spoke of war and peace, asking me for the umpteenth time why the U.S. built bases around the Soviet Union, why the U.S. built atom and hydrogen bombs, why the Soviet Union was left out of the Bermuda Conference, why the U.S. was "taking all sorts of measures to increase German militarism," and, of course, why we didn't let the Koreans settle their own affairs, and why we didn't recognize Communist China. They concluded, "River sailors, as well as the Soviet people, do not want war. You can be sure the Soviet people never attacked anybody."

I repeat these by now monotonous questions and statements to emphasize what happens to a foreigner from the West as he goes through the Soviet Union. The sentiment may often be

Homeward Bound

admirable, but the remarkable uniformity raises many doubts. I can hear some Soviet citizen telling me this proves the urgency of the issues and the identity of their beliefs. The reiteration of certain themes anywhere is understandable. Much more significant are the questions that were *not* asked, the astounding lack of variety of thought or query, considering the many people talked to. This is apparent a thousand times more clearly when one discusses the same subjects in other lands in the West.

I remarked upon this unusual conformity to the five editors of the Stalingrad *Pravda*, whom I interviewed that same day. The secretary of the paper quoted Abraham Lincoln, "You can't fool all of the people all the time," and argued that their unanimity was because the Soviet people were so well informed.

But the reply of Saprikin, the editor-in-chief of this paper which had a circulation of a half-million, revealed the conscious control exercised by the Soviet press. "Oh, we know exactly the questions our citizens have been asking you," he said. "They've been asking about American bases surrounding the Soviet Union, and why not abolish the atom bomb, and why militarize West Germany, and why didn't the United States allow our chess players to enter America without restriction to play in a tournament."

He was almost precisely right. All over the U.S.S.R., I was pounded by the same three questions: bases, the chess team, and one the editor omitted: "Why do the Americans persecute Paul Robeson?"

By the time I left the Soviet Union, I was pretty tired of answering the three inevitable questions. Surely there must be somebody in this country, I thought, who has been struck, as I have, by the constant repetition: bases, Robeson, chess; bases, Robeson, chess . . .

At the airport in Moscow, just before I boarded the plane that carried me on the first leg of my trip back to the States, I stood talking to one of my Russian interpreters. Lonya, who had shared my experiences halfway around Russia, now said he wanted to ask me something. His face was serious.

"Sure," I said. "What is it?"

"I have three questions for you, Mr. MacDuffie," he said. Suddenly it seemed to me his eyes twinkled. "What about the bases? How about Paul Robeson? And when are you Americans going to let in those chess players . . . ?" They arrived in New York the following June, and defeated the American team 20 to 12.

CHAPTER 26

"I Said I Wouldn't Generalize, but . . ."

EVER SINCE my return to America, I have been asked again and again what the Russian *people* think about war and peace. It's a difficult question to answer.

There are two tremendous conflicting currents running through the U.S.S.R. The first is a propaganda-stimulated but unquestionably sincere desire for peace on the part of virtually all Soviet citizens. Wherever I went in the Soviet Union, the word "peace" continually assailed my eye and ear.

In Moscow's one synagogue, there were "peace" prayers displayed on both sides of the pulpit, one in Hebrew and one in Russian. In Baku, 1,000 miles away, a 70,000-seat stadium was decorated with two huge banners, one in Azerbaijani and one in Russian, reading, "Peace for the World." When I interviewed the famous Soviet biochemist, Alexander I. Oparin, I noticed that he wore two badges in his lapel—a Picasso "peace dove" and a tiny scroll inscribed, "Peace for the World."

In Kiev, an official of the Ministry of Culture told me, "My father and mother and two brothers were killed by the Germans. People in the United States have not fully felt the impact of war, but every Russian has been touched by death and injury. How can we desire anything but peace?"

In Baku, an intense young poet asked, "Do we have any bases

near American territory? We speak of peace, not of fear. We saw how awful war was. We want peace because we want to live happily."

I saw "Peace for the World" spelled out in white stones on a pile of coal in the wilderness of the Caucasus Mountains. The famous Moscow Circus is decorated with banners carrying the word "peace" in ten different languages.

I spoke to an old woman in Georgia. "Tell the mothers of America," she said intensely, "that I'm a mother and it's hard labor to bring up a child and see him killed in a war. You tell the mothers of America we want peace."

An Uzbek boy, when I said I might write something about him on my return to the U.S., said, "Say only that I wish to live in peace."

I took a picture of a judge. "Put on the picture our desire for peace," he said.

A Volga river-boat captain gave me this message: "Convey my greetings to the river-boat men of America and tell them we want peace."

In Stalingrad, a newspaper editor said to me, "This city knows war, yet you have not heard any air-raid sirens while you were here. I understand the sirens blow in air-raid drills in New York."

The principal of a school in Moscow baited me with, "I have read how pupils in the United States are being taught to lie on the floor in their classrooms to avoid injury in an atomic attack."

Whenever I tried to explain to ordinary Russian citizens that American war fears are prompted by Soviet actions abroad, they expressed astonishment; and I was constantly berated for U.S. defense preparations. A conversation I had with a group of court officials in Moscow was typical. One inspector said, "The United States has sent so many soldiers to foreign countries that if you had just one soldier at each base, you would still have a big army." He added, "We have no soldiers near the borders of your country."

"I Said I Wouldn't Generalize, but . . ."

I replied, "No, but there have been reports of Soviet planes over Western territory and reports of submarines in our waters."

To which the inspector snapped back, "The American newspapers have also said that the sky is full of Russian saucers—but we use them better in the kitchen."

It was then that an elderly court employee made a remark that summed up the response of most of the Russians I talked to. He said, "In the Soviet Union we have no time for war. We must build, not destroy."

The State prosecutor, who was standing near by, added that he had been a sailor in his youth and had eaten with men from many lands. Said he, "If the people of different countries can sit down and eat together, then there is hope that nations, too, can live peacefully together."

But, taken alone, Soviet "peace" talk is misleading—because it's only one of the two main undercurrents in Russian life today. The other flows directly counter to it. As I have related, the Soviet Union seemed to me to be an armed camp, teeming with soldiers. And I had seen flocks of jet fighter planes over Moscow and Tiflis, at Leningrad and Baku airports, and at great bases in the Caucasus. Coupled with this heavy militarization is a violent and crude anti-American propaganda campaign. The people live under a constant barrage of distortion about the "ruling classes" of the United States—in newspapers, magazines, radio, in the theater, even in textbooks.

I went to the circus in Kharkov. Two clowns came out with a long rubber cow labeled, "U.S.A." "This is the longest cow in the world," they explained. "It feeds in Western Europe and gives milk in the United States." (U.S. Ambassador Bohlen pointed out to me later that the cow gag originated in the West as a crack about Russia. In the Western version, the cow feeds in Czechoslovakia and gives milk in the U.S.S.R. Since then, I learned the joke was even older. Bryan Democrats used it to accuse the Republican cow of feeding on the American Midwest and being milked in Wall Street.)

A typical "factual" story in *Trud* said American food growers are having trouble selling their products because "the impoverishment of the working class and the ruining of the toiling peasants are narrowing down the internal market." Another "news" story accused the U.S. Army in Korea of "burning prisoners of war alive, using them as live targets, burying them alive, tearing out their hearts, and gassing them. The Americans hung up prisoners by their feet, broke arms and legs of prisoners with wooden cudgels, stabbed them with bayonets, cut away pieces of their flesh, forced nails under their fingernails, tortured them with electrical current, poured hot water into their stomachs, put prisoners in cells flooded with water, and shut them in cages with sharp nails."

Children studying English were using textbooks which contain reading exercises like this: "John Smith is an American. John's elder brother is an engineer. He is not married because he cannot afford to keep a family. He is out of work now."

A Moscow newspaper carried a story November 29 that not only did colonial countries have "forced labor and actual slavery. . . . In the Southern states of the U.S.A., for example, more than five million Negroes are kept in slavery."

The Soviet propaganda machine constantly identifies Americans as the enemy. I have already described in detail the vicious movie, *Silver Dust*, displayed throughout the country, depicting Americans as guilty of everything from superstition and corruption to rape—frame-ups, ruthless experimentation on unwilling human guinea pigs, and germ warfare.

I saw another movie in which villainous-looking spies shed unmistakable U.S. Army uniforms and then infiltrated across the border into Soviet Central Asia, presumably from Afghanistan. They were tracked down by "heroic" Soviet border guards—in the approved fashion of our own western movies.

In their finest art gallery there were savage cartoons depicting Uncle Sam as a snake and American soldiers as despoilers, and these "works of art" were on the wall right alongside of similar wartime attacks upon the Nazis.

Of the two contradictory points of view—on the one hand,

the expressed desire for peace; on the other, the grim readiness for war and the vicious anti-American propaganda—which represents the true feeling of the Russian people?

There's no question that the common people of the U.S.S.R. are sincere in their desire for peace—as are the common people of every nation in the world. But in the Soviet Union this normal hatred of war has been pumped up by the unrelenting propaganda campaign into something close to fanaticism. Peace is an obsession with the Russians. I believe the Kremlin leaders may be counting on their ability to switch this obsessive desire for peace into a feeling of righteous rage in the future emergency, by charging that some nation has broken the peace every Russian holds dear. The groundwork has already been laid by the concurrent propaganda drive depicting American leaders as warmongers and criminals.

If the Russian rulers did want to prepare their people for war, they might, ironically, choose that very method. The Soviet people, incessantly indoctrinated over the years, seem to believe their government is incapable of starting a war; from the discussions I had, if they were told the United States was the aggressor in any future struggle, most of them would accept the statement without question. Time after time Russians said to me, "The Soviet Union has never attacked any other nation."

When I asked, "How about Finland?" they replied, "Finland was encouraged by France and England to attack the Soviet Union." They seemed to find nothing illogical in the picture of a nation of 4,000,000 people attacking a nation of over 200,000,000.

In the light of the double-barreled propaganda campaign, one of the most thought-provoking sights I saw in the Soviet Union was a poster on the wall of a clubhouse in Aktyubinsk in Central Asia. It read: *"We are not afraid of any threats of aggression—and we will return double blows against any blow that unleashes a new war."*

Americans also constantly ask me one other question. "Well, all right, you don't want to make any ponderous earth-shaking generalizations, but tell me, at least, what's your *general* impression of the country?"

It's a land of startling contrasts: efficiency mixed with inefficiency; the old entangled with the new; brilliance and mediocrity; logic and illogic, side by side.

Perhaps the explanation for the contrasts is that the U.S.S.R. is a country in transition. Because it has a long way to go before its standard of living matches that of the West—and particularly that of the United States—and because it is trying hard to do so, it gives the impression of being a boom country.

The people are proud of the nation's reconstruction and development; they feel they're going somewhere—like Americans in the nineteenth and early twentieth centuries.

I saw no signs of unrest among the Soviet people—but then I saw chiefly the surface of life in Russia. I'm not kidding myself. If there had been rebellion brewing all around me, I doubt that I could have seen it. I was denied a chance to visit Soviet prisons and slave-labor camps. But I didn't have to see oppression to know it was there; the testimony of those who have suffered from it is indisputable.

Still, I got the impression that the average Russian is fairly happy with his lot. The people seemed cheerful and full of bounce, despite the restrictions to which they're subjected—restrictions no American would stand for.

Their views about life in America are best summed up in the remarks of the director of the Tashkent Cotton Research Institute. "In the United States some people have millions and others have none. Too many people have too much and too many people have too little." He did not say so, but his second sentence aptly fits his own country.

The apparent contentment of the Russian man-in-the-street is not hard to understand. In his daily life he's not directly involved in Soviet oppression (unless he has displeased his rulers—in which case he's presumably no longer a man-in-the-street, but probably is someplace where I couldn't see him). All his life he has known rigid governmental control—as his forebears did under the czars—so he doesn't seem to chafe under it. Finally, he *is* living a better life than he has in many years, even if it isn't much by our standards.

Many a Soviet family has a room or two to itself now, instead of having to share a single room with six other people and perhaps a pig. Illiteracy has been stamped out and education is within everyone's reach. Consumer products are becoming more widely available; people talk of someday owning a television set and an automobile. The future looks good to them, and the present doesn't look bad.

They apparently *don't* expect war—but it's on their minds, as the present "peace" talk indicates.

For a final contrast, I'd like to quote a Briton whom I met in Moscow after he had seen quite a bit of the country. "What do you think about the Soviet Union now that you've been around it?" I asked him.

He pondered. "Better than most Englishmen think it is," he granted after a moment. Then he thought a bit longer, and concluded: "But not nearly so good as most Russians think it is. . . ."

Index

Abdulaev, trade union official, 278
Abdulaeva, jurywoman, 53
Advertising:
 characteristics of Soviet, 62–73
 Russian reaction to, 79
"Aeroport," 18–19
Airplanes, 12, 15–17, 120, 217, 272
Airports, 17–20, 120, 224, 230, 233, 271, 272
Aktyubinsk, 230–233
Alma-Ata, 91, 215, 233, 235–247
Altai Mountains, 236
American Embassy, 26–28
Andreev oil refinery, 281–284
Apples, Kazak, 235
Architecture, 22–23, 127–128
Armenians, 249
Art:
 Minsk paintings, 95
 Soviet realism, 95
Asia, Central, 215–216
Asiatic Republics, artificial divisions, 248
Austrian film, 125
Automobiles, 267
 factory at Minsk, 108–116
 travel by, 23
 see also Transportation
Azerbaijan, 53, 216, 272–287
 billboards in, 73
 people of, 249
Azerbaijan Republic Stalin Stadium, 283

Baikov Cemetery, 152–153
Baku, 216, 272–287
 ballet in, 102–103
 court cases in, 53–61
 housing in, 292–297
Baku Meat Combine, 284–287
Ballet, 102–105
Banks, 273–278
Banquets, 301–307
Baptists, 33
BBC, 133–134, 152, 181
Beer ads, 69, 73
Beggars, 80, 124, 141
Beria, 3–4, 140, 151, 223, 298
Berman, clown, 250
Besembiev, assistant rector, 244
Betting, 90
Bicycles, 80
Billboards, 63, 67, 71–72
Bohlen, Ambassador, 104, 167, 222
Bohlen, Mrs., 223
Bolshoi Ballet, 94
Bolshoi Ballet School, 102–103
Bolshoi Theater, 166–167, 217–219

Book publishing, in Kharkov, 187–191
Books:
  Russian reading, 186
  sale of, in Kiev, 129
Boulder Dam, 163
Bread, 129–130
Bridges, photographing, 169
British, "standard approach to foreigners" incident, 33
British Broadcasting Co., 133–134, 152, 181
Bruslov, 28, 140
Budyenny, Marshal, 63
Bulganin, Marshal, 4, 151, 222–223
Burinsky, UNRRA official, 146–147
Busses, 80
Byelorus, book publisher, 187
Byelorussia, 79–80, 249
Byrnes, James, 166

Capitalism, under Communism, 92–93
Carmen, in Kazakstan, 98
Caspian Sea, 272
Cattle, 235
Cemeteries, 152–153, 191–193
Chabuckiani, benefit for, 104–105
Champagne, 69–70, 132
Chernova, juror, 43
Chess-players question, 142, 180, 209, 225, 240, 284, 311
Chewing gum, 82
Children, 180–181
  Soviet care of, 34
  TV programs for, 107
China question, 162, 238, 246, 255
Chinese, Russians and, 17, 24, 270
Churches, 152
  Kazak, 237, 241–243
  Kiev, 121–122
  mosque, 261–267
  number of, 123–124
  see also Religion
Churchill, Winston, 120
Circus, gypsies in, 132

Civil Aviation Department, Baku, 53
Clothing, 36–37, 117–118
Colbalitsa, interpreter, 299
Collective Farm Mutual Aid Fund, 93
Collective farms, 85–93, 133, 301–302, 306–307
Colleges, see Education
Collier's, xi, 119
Communism, 89, 92–93, 181–182
  current interpretations, 135–153
Communist Party, American, 256
Communist Party, Soviet, 3–4
  celebration of the Revolution by, 218–222
  graves of members, 152–153
  leadership position of members, 257, 273–274
  post-Stalin attitudes, 203–212
Competitions, job and study, 67–68
Complaint books, 130
Complaints, 156, 240–241
Concentration camps, xii, 138, 185, 318
Concerts, 94–97
Constitution, United States, 255–256
Construction, 83, 84
Consumer goods, 25, 68–69, 80
Corrective labor camps, xii, 138, 185, 318
Cosmopolitans, attacks on, 254
Costs, 26–27, 128–131, 203, 231
  automobile, 267
  clothing, 117–118
  household expenses, 227, 294
  rent, 110, 117, 118, 292
  taxi fares, 28
  tuition, 245, 253
Country Schoolteacher, 232
Courts, 38–60
  labor cases, 46–51, 53–60
"Cow" gag, 315
Cripples, 174–175
Crocodile, 84, 93
"Culture," use of word by Soviets, 63

Index

Dadashov, wrestler, 284
Dams, 154, 163
Dancing, 34, 94–96
Danilkin, 41–42
Darwin, Charles, 150
Death, newspaper notices of, 71
Dekunin, lathe operator, 183–184
Department (universal) stores, 69, 70
Divorce, 43–46, 65
Dniepropetrovsk, 303
Dnieper dam, 154, 163
Doctors, Soviet, 251–252
  see also Medicine
Dogs, 80, 132
Dorfman, jurywoman, 53
Dramatic arts:
  character and significance of Soviet, 94–107
  see also Theater
Drunks, 34
  court case involving, 39–43
Dulles, Allen, 143
Dulles, John Foster, 180

Education, 142, 182, 228
  factory workers', 114
  graduate theses advertised, 65–66
  Soviet attitude toward, 91
  university, 60, 244–247, 252–258
  see also Schools
Eisenhower note incident, 239–240
Engels, portraits of, 62, 150–151
Evening Moscow, advertising in, 65–66
Everest, Mount, 236

Factories:
  auto, 108–116, 267
  banks and, 274–275
  Kazak, 243–244
  management faults, 115
  oil refineries, 281–284
  steel, 154–165
  textile, 258–259
  tractor, 179–184

Farms, collective, 85–93, 133, 301–302, 306–307
Free-press questions, 255–257
Finance, Soviet methods, 273–278
Finland, 13, 277, 317
First of May Farm, 133, 290
Fischer, John, 203
Food:
  cost of, *see* Costs
  crops and farm statistics, 86, 88, 91–92
  hotel and restaurant, 121
  Kazakstan, 237
  meat, 284–287
  Russian breakfast, 224
  store, 115–116
  Ukrainian markets, 194–195
For Peace, ballet, 104
"Freedom of speech for foreigners," 33
Free markets, 130–131
Frunze, 248
Frunze Book Publishing Factory, 187–191

Gadjiev family, 292–296
Generals, MacDuffie and the, 79
Genghis Khan, 268
Georgia, 216, 249, 290–291, 298–307
Germ-warfare question, 239, 246
  church accusation, 122
Gofar, escort, 250
  life of, 264–267
Golden Lake, 101–102
Gori, 300–301
Gorki Drama Theater, Tashkent, 98
Gorki Street, 25
Gortova, Maria, 131
Gostello farm, 88
Grand Coulee Dam, 163
Graves, 152–153, 191–193
Grechko, General, 79, 135
Grechnikoff, Ivan, 39–43
Greek Orthodox Church, 152
  wedding in, 241–243
Gypsies, 131–132

Hamdomov, mayor, 268–270
Hassanov, assistant director, 273
Help-wanted ads, 66–68
Helsinki, 12, 13, 15
Highways, *see* Transportation
Hodorkov, Leonide (Lonya), 215, 251, 266, 284, 286, 311–312
  life of, 224–230
Horses, race, 89
Hospitals, 252
Hotels, 81–82, 120–121, 148, 237–241, 250–251
Housing:
  apartment-sharing, 229–230
  Asiatic, 237
  city flats, 291–294, 296–297
  contrasts in, 194
  farm, 288–290
  homes, 80, 288–297
  living space as job compensation, 68
  see also Soviet people
Hydrogen bomb, 141–142

Ilchenko, chief engineer, 109
Indo-China question, 237, 245
Industry:
  auto, 108–116, 267
  factories, *see* Factories
  in Kazakstan, 235, 236
  oil, 272–287
  steel, 154–165
  textile, 249, 258–259
  see also individual industries
Intourist Bureau, 29–37, 74, 176
Ionkin, Victor, 120, 171–172, 184–186, 266
Iskanderov, judge, 53
It's for You to Decide, 102
Ivanov, director, 163
Izvestia, 63

Jakovlev, chief engineer, 163
Judge, 38
Jurymen, 38

Kaganovich, 150, 222–223

Kambarian, teacher, 60
Karaganda, 233
Kazak Republic, 98, 215–216, 235–247
  collective farm in, 91–93
  population of, 249
Kazakstan State University, 244–247
Kennan, George, 10, 166–167
Kharkov, 72
  book-publishing house in, 187–191
  police incident in, 173–178
  tractor factory in, 179–184
Khomyak, Vassily V., 4, 127
  MacDuffie and, in Kiev, 135–147
Khrushchev, N. S., 82, 109, 135, 139, 167, 219
  background of, 197–200
  character and appearance, 198–200, 212
  interview with, 197–214
  MacDuffie's acquaintance with, 3–6, 8
  portraits and busts of, 126, 150–151, 197, 200–201
Kiev, 18, 117–134, 167
  advertising in, 71–72
  concert in, 96–97
  housing in, 292
  MacDuffie's reunion with old acquaintances in, 135–153
  police incidents in, 171–172
  rebuilding of, 84
Kiev Resthouse, 149–150
Kiev University, 33, 150–152
Kirghiz Republic, 248
Korea question, 90, 237, 238–239, 246, 255
Kremlin, the, 22–25, 32–33
  photographing the, 169–170
Kreshchatik (street), 126, 172
Krupkov, director, 273, 274
Krupkova, actress, 147–148
Kuibyshev, dam at, 163
Kuibyshev Publishing House, 86
Ku Klux Klan, 238
Kustanai, 233

Index

Labor:
  automobile factory, 108-116
  book publishing, 187-191
  characteristics of workers, 115
  compensation for accidents, 60-61
  farm, 86-93
  job competitions, 67-68
  job freedom, 229
  law and, 46-51, 53-60
  manpower shortage, 80-81
  piece-work, 89
  regulations concerning, 46-52
  speed-up, 190
  steel industry, 156-165
  textile combine, 258-259
  theater, 101-102
  tractor factory, 182-184
  trade unions, 277-281
  vacations, 149-150
  see also Soviet people
La Guardia, Fiorello, 203
Language, 270
  court, 53
  English use, 152, 228
  numbers used, 299
  similarities between Russian and English, 14
  study of, by dancers, 103
  uses of foreign, in Russia, 19
  word choice in slogans and advertising, 63-73
Legal procedures, 38-52
  use of attorneys, 53-54, 58-59
Lehman, Herbert H., 203
Lenin, portraits and busts of, 62, 109, 126, 150-151, 190, 244, 281, 283
Leningrad, 17, 19
Lenin Hills, 23
Lenin Library, 37
Lenin Teacher's College, 60
Libraries, 37, 150-151
Literature, 186-187
Lonya, *see* Hodorkov, Leonide
Lottery tickets, 70
Lubyanka, the, 138
Lunin, trade-union official, 278-281

Lvov, 122-123

McCarthy, Joseph, 31, 208
MacDuffie, Marshall, *passim*
  air trip to Moscow, 12-21
  arrangements leading to return to Russia, 3, 6-11
  banqueting experiences, 301-307
  conclusions on the U.S.S.R., 313-319
  first Russian trip, 3-6
  illness, 250-253
  journey to Minsk, 74-84
  MVD experiences, 75-78, 166-178
  reunion with old acquaintances in Kiev, 135-153
  slaughterhouse experience, 284-287
Machine tractor stations, 86
Maculova, Mrs., 39
Magazines, *see* Press
Maksienko, assistant director, 154, 156, 161-163
Malenkov, 3-4, 129, 201, 219
  portraits of, 63, 126, 190, 281, 283
Mamadov, technician, 296-297
Manuilsky, Dmitri, xii, 135, 145
Mao Tse-tung, portraits of, 63, 237, 283
Marriage, Soviet, 241-243
Marx, Karl:
  communist dogma, 93
  portraits of, 62, 150-151
Masters of Sports, 283-284
Matzkevich, architect, 83
Meat combine, 284-287
Medicine:
  MacDuffie's experience with Soviet, 250-252
  state control of work in, 53-59
Mejvriskhevi, 301
Mesta, Perle, 31
Metropole hotel, 24
Meyboroda, director, 109, 110-111
Michurin, 150
Micronov, judge, 43-46
Mikoyan, 150, 222-223
Military-bases question, 311-312

Mineral deposits, 235
Minsk, 71, 81-83, 171
  city flats in, 291-292
  concert in, 94-96
  soldiers in, 205
  stores in, 115-116
Minsk Automobile Plant, 108-116
Minsk Collective Farm, 88, 289-290
Molotov, 3, 166, 201, 219
  portraits of, 81, 150-151
  reception given by, 222-223
Moscow:
  advertising in, 63-71
  character of the new, 22-27, 34, 36-37
  churches in, 123-124
  district court in, 38-52
  old, 22-23
  parade and celebration in, 217-223
  sightseeing routine in, 32
  soldiers in, 205
  theater in, 105-106
Moscow State Farm, 289
Moscow State University, 23, 24
Moslems, 263-264
Mosque, in Tashkent, 263-264
Movies, 65, 69, 124-126
  anti-American, 261-263, 316
  Soviet three-dimensional, 33
  see also Theater
Murmansk, Allied graves near, 193
Museums, 84, 150
MVD, 8, 138, 214, 218
  MacDuffie's experiences with, 75-78, 166-178
  see also Security measures *and* Police
My Little Friend, film, 125

National Hotel, Moscow, 24-25
Negro question, 90, 157, 180, 237, 240, 246, 253-254, 276
Neon signs, 63, 64, 71-72
Newspapers, 85-86, 136-137, 144-145, 147, 208-209
  advertising in, 64-71
  see also Press

New Yorker, The, 145, 256
New York Times, The, 104, 143, 257
Not to Mention Any Names, 98-101
Novikova, Zorya, 31-32, 201-203, 213-214
Nudity, absence of, in art forms, 105

Oatis, William, 10, 177
Oil industry, in Azerbaijan, 272-287
Olifirenko, Mr., 6-8

Palaces (and Parks) of Culture and Rest, 63, 83
Pamphlets, political, 130
Parade, anniversary, 201, 219-222
Passport incident, 9-11
Patriarch of All Russia, 33-34
Pavlov, portrait of, 150
Peace, 189
  Khrushchev on, 207
  slogans for, 72-73
  Soviet people's attitude on, 181, 313-317
  see also War
Penza, airport at, 224
Petrov, Mr., 6-8
Picture-taking:
  in Kharkov, 173-178
  in Moscow, 31-32, 168-171
Piece-work, 110
Pivovarov, director, 283
Plays, *see* Theater
Poker, 225
Police, 168-178, 219-221
  see also MVD *and* Security measures
Politics, opinions of Russians about, 135-153
Pollitt, Harry, 220
Poltava, 191-196
Port Arthur, 97-98
Portraits and busts, 81, 150-153
  displaying of, 62-63
  see also Lenin, Stalin, *and* names of other Soviet leaders

Index

Posters, 190, 281–282
  see also Billboards *and* Portraits and busts
Pourabayev, factotum, 145–146
Power stations, 163, 164–165
Pravda, 85–86, 98, 136, 311
Press, 311
  magazines, 129
  Russian attitude toward American, 28–29, 31, 255
  see also Newspapers
Prices, *see* Costs
Priests, Soviet, 122–123
Prisons, xii, 138, 185, 318
Procurator, public, 38–39, 47
Propaganda, 108, 313–319
  as expressed through the dramatic arts, 94–107, 261–263
  see also Press
Proverbs, Russian, 209
Publishing, 129, 187–191

Queues, prevalence of, 133

Radio, 106–107, 133–134, 265
Railroads, characteristics of, 74–81
Rank, in USSR, 164
Rays of the East Collective Farm, 91–93
Reception, Molotov's, 222–223
Red Square, 23, 25
  parade in, 219–222
Religion, 121–124, 226
  Stalinism as, 257–258
  see also Churches
Rents, 110, 117, 118, 292
Resthouses, 149–150, 228
Riffing, 88
Roads, *see* Transportation
Robeson, Paul, 142, 180, 240, 277, 311
Rogoff, of Intourist, 29–33
Rosenbergs, the, 185–186
Rubber trees, 81, 244
Rudnitsky, MacDuffie and, in Kiev, 135
Russian Orthodox Church, 121–122

Russians:
  dominance in U.S.S.R., 236, 244, 250, 276–277
  see also Soviet people
Rykin, performance by, 105–106

Saburov, 222
Saint Basil's Cathedral, 23
Samarkand, 215, 216, 267–270
Sanitariums, 228
Saprikin, editor, 311
Satires, 96–97, 105–106
Schools, 36–37, 65–66, 150–151, 186–187, 252–253
  see also Education
Security measures:
  American Embassy, 27
  church-belfry, 33
  Russian attitude concerning, 137–138
  travel restrictions, 27–28
  see also MVD *and* Police
Senin, MacDuffie and, in Kiev, 135–143
Services, advertising of, 68–71
Seven Beauties, The, 103
Sex, in ballet, 105
Shavchenko, portrait of, 151
Sheep, 235
Shipley, Mrs., 9–10
Shortages, 80, 158
Shvernik, portrait of, 150
Silver Dust (movie), 231, 250, 316
  story of, 261–263
Simvol, engineer, 285
Sing Sing, 138
Slaughterhouse, visit to, 284–287
Slave labor, xii, 138, 185, 318
Slogans, 62–63, 72–73, 283
  factory use of, 112–113
Smirnova, Mrs., court case of, 47–52
Social security, farm conditions under, 93
Society for the Cultural Relations of the Ukraine, 135, 139–140
Sophie, interpreter, 146

Soviet people, 224–230
  attitudes and questions on America, 29, 90–91, 111–113, 134, 140–141, 147, 157, 162–163, 180–182, 187–189, 211–212, 238, 277, 282, 294–295, 310–311, 313–317
  basic concepts of, 135–153
  borrowing by, 275
  characteristics of, 13–14, 25–26, 35–36, 79
  concern for American culture, 246
  distribution of, 249
  foreigners and, 135–153
  friendship for Americans in Ukraine, 191–192
  home life of, 227, 288–297
  peace desire, 313–317
  private lives, 264–267
  reading habits, 129, 130
  reluctance to criticize leading officials, 240–241
  self-righteousness, 255
  sense of humor, 222–223
  standard of living, 297
  twin drives of, 24
  uniformity, 250, 311
  western leadership among Asiatics, 236, 244, 250
  women, see Women
"Soviet Specialists" farm, 88
Spanish dancing, Soviet, 95
Sports, in Baku, 282–284
Stalin, 3, 5, 129
  Georgian home of, 298–301
  portraits and busts of, 62, 72, 81, 109, 126, 150–151, 163, 190, 197, 244, 281, 283
  Russian attitude toward, 139–140, 257–258
Stalingrad, 102, 204, 308–311
Statistics:
  dam, 163
  population, 249
  steel production, 158–161
Steam bath, 155

Steel industry, in the Ukraine, 154–165
Stefanek, MacDuffie and, in Kiev, 135–142
Stockholm, 12–14
Stores, state, 69, 70, 115–116
Strikes, 280
Students, see Education and Schools
Suchnev, assistant director, 273
Suicides, 136–137
Sverdlov District Court, 43
Swimming, 282–283
Switzer, juror, 43
"Sword Dancer," 105

Tamerlane, 268–270
Tariverdiev, Kamil (Tary), 272, 277, 286, 292, 296
Tarzan craze, 99
Tashkent, 215, 249–267
  play presented in, 98–101
Tashkent Textile Combine, 258–259
Tatars, 249
Telephones, 109, 202, 265
Television, 70–71, 106–107, 164
Textile industry, 249, 258–259
Theater for Children, Moscow, 102
Theaters:
  design of new, 104
  Kiev, 124–126
  magnificence of, 94
  mechanical effects, 95–96
  Moscow, 65
  movie, see Movies
  radio and television, 106–107
  satire in, 105–106
  Stalingrad, 102
  Tashkent, 98–101
  Zaporozhe, 97–98
Theses, 65–66
Tiflis, 104, 216, 298–300
Tiflis . . . Theater of Opera and Ballet, 104
Titles, Russian love of, 169
Toilets, 14, 237, 251

Index

Tractors, 80
  factory in Kharkov, 179–184
Trade, 34–35, 210
Trade unions, 277–281
Traffic, 196
Transportation:
  air, 215–217, 224, 230–233
  Central Asian, 248
  costs, 117
  Moscow, 70
  motor, 94, 196, 236
  railroad, 74–81
  roads, 72–73, 194, 236, 248
  "thumbers," 193
Tretyakov Gallery, 208
Trotsky, 257
Trud, 111, 315–316

Ukraine, 120, 145
  billboards in, 72–73
  countryside and towns in, 191–196
  friendliness of people, 134
  population, 249
  steel industry in, 154–165
  UNRRA mission to, 4–5
Unemployment, 141
Uniforms, wide use of, 163–164
Union of Soviet Socialist Republics (USSR):
  anniversary celebration, 217–223
  Central Asian areas, 215–216
  conflicting currents in, 313–319
  countries bordering, 271
  population of, 87, 249
  power struggle after Stalin's death, 3–4
  Russian dominance in, 276–277
  twin drives of, 24
  uniformity of culture, 250, 311
  use of punitive example, 10–11
  war preparedness in, 82–83, 315, 317
  war ruins and reconstruction, 79–80, 82, 83
  see also Soviet people *and* separate Republics

United Nations, attitude of Russians toward, 137
United Nations Relief and Rehabilitation and Administration (UNRRA), 4–5, 135–136, 144, 147, 160, 161, 191–192, 203–204
  entertainment problems, 302–307
  Khrushchev and, 198–200
  MVD and, 166–168
United States:
  air base at Poltava, 191–192
  anti-Americanism in Russia, 315–317
  embassy, 26–28
  Russian ideas of, *see* Soviet people
Urals, the, 224
Uzbekistan State University, 252–258
Uzbek Republic, 215–216, 249–260

Vacations, 110, 149–150, 228
Valkovich, 88
Vekilova, Lena, 102–103
Vlasov, architect, 127
Voice of America, 133–134, 162, 181
Volga River, 310
von Paulus, General, 186, 204
Voroshilov, 218, 219

Wages, 179–180, 183
  bank employee's, 276
  book publishing, 187
  college graduate's, 229
  Communist Party members, 206
  factory, 110, 113
  farm, 89, 90, 93
  limiting factors, 110
  official's, 202–203
  oil worker's, 282, 297
  savings, 228
  seaman's, 310
  steel mill, 156–160
  student, 245, 253
  teacher's, 293
  theater, 97, 101–102
Waiting rooms, 19